Interpreting the New Testament

Interpreting the New Testament

AN INTRODUCTION

Sherri Brown & Francis J. Moloney, SDB

WILLIAM B. EERDMANS PUBLISHING COMPANY

GRAND RAPIDS, MICHIGAN

Wm. B. Eerdmans Publishing Co.
4035 Park East Court SE, Grand Rapids, Michigan 49546
www.eerdmans.com

25 24 23 22 21 20 19   1 2 3 4 5 6 7

ISBN 978-0-8028-7519-8

Library of Congress Cataloging-in-Publication Data

Names: Brown, Sherri, author. | Moloney, Francis J., author.
Title: Interpreting the New Testament : an introduction / Sherri Brown &
    Francis J. Moloney, SDB.
Description: Grand Rapids, Michigan : William B. Eerdmans Publishing Company,
    2019. | Includes bibliographical references and index.
Identifiers: LCCN 2019011766 | ISBN 9780802875198 (pbk. : alk. paper)
Subjects: LCSH: Bible. New Testament—Introductions. | Bible. New
    Testament—Criticism, interpretation, etc.
Classification: LCC BS2330.3 .B765 2019 | DDC 225.601—dc23
    LC record available at https://lccn.loc.gov/2019011766

In memory of Joseph A. Fitzmyer, SJ

Contents

Illustrations

Preface

Interpreting the New Testament: An Introduction is a project that both of the authors accepted as a necessary consequence of our successful publication of *Interpreting the Gospel and Letters of John: An Introduction*. First suggested by Michael Thomson, our ever-attentive editor at Eerdmans, it has been a joy and a challenge to bring it to fruition. We have decided once again that one of us would write the preface, and the other would write a conclusion. I (Sherri Brown) would like to start by sharing my experience that led to the writing of these books that interpret and introduce the Johannine writings and then the rest of the New Testament. In my years teaching undergraduates and early graduate students, I have been called upon to teach classes on specific books or traditions in the New Testament, or more general survey courses on the whole of the New Testament, each semester. Across this time, I have struggled to find a suitable textbook to guide the students through the material. Many fantastic commentaries and thematic volumes are available, of course, written by top-notch scholars. Many undergraduates, however, come to the course with little to no background in the Bible or organized biblical studies. A close analysis of the text alone or sometimes complicated discussions of the historical and theological themes can lie well above their level of preparation. They need the background unfolded and a systematic approach to the entirety of the task at hand in order to make any sort of sense of the text beyond basic Christian teaching. Lists of the required texts for class, then, began to get longer and longer, as I wanted to find something that responded to all the questions that an undergraduate class might ask. Therefore, I initially began to consider constructing a textbook of my own, dedicated to the Gospel and the Letters of John.

The task was daunting indeed, and I wondered whether I could manage it alone. Like any good student, therefore, I went to my own teachers for help and guidance. While enjoying the annual meeting of the Catholic Biblical Association at Gonzaga University in the summer of 2013 with my teacher and mentor Francis J. Moloney, I was struck with the notion that we should collaborate. His years of expertise with the literature alongside my recent experience in the undergraduate and early graduate classroom could make a winning combination, I thought. At the same time, we began to talk to Michael Thomson at Eerdmans about the project, and it did not take long for Frank to warm to the idea and then eventually to get on board with his customary enthusiasm and work ethic. It was again at a meeting of the Catholic Biblical Association, this time in 2015 at Xavier University in New Orleans, that the present book was conceived. As we discussed our almost completed Johannine study, Michael Thomson saw immediately that a more general introduction to the whole of the New Testament, along the same lines, was called for. He suggested that we might attempt such a project, and we both readily agreed, seeing it as a natural companion piece to our more detailed work on the Gospel and Letters of John. The first four chapters of this book closely follow and rely on the first chapters of our book on John.

As any scholar or teacher knows, pointing out the weaknesses in the book options we have before us is easy enough, but developing an alternative that meets all the perceived needs is another matter altogether. Over the years, therefore, this project has gone through several versions and subsequent iterations. That was already the case for our earlier book on the Gospel and Letters of John. It is even more the case for the book that follows, where so much more had to be considered. Every semester I teach, and every new student I encounter, gives me more food for thought. What I determined was that teaching a New Testament survey course in one semester is a heavy task for any instructor. Further, assigning readings that cover background material and each book of the New Testament *as well as* the primary texts themselves can be a recipe for *discouraging* the reading of the books of the actual New Testament. Therefore, we determined to compose a "full-service" textbook that attempts to provide all the steps needed for a beginning student to approach the biblical literature in general, followed by an overview of the books of the New Testament, grouped by genre and category. This would include discussions of the origins of the Bible, a sound methodology for biblical interpretation, some detail of the overarching biblical narrative, and the introduction of Jesus, his teachings, and his followers. Only when this is in place do we begin guiding students through interpreting the New Testament. This gives instructors a lot of room to work through the primary texts and set up the course content as they see fit.

The rest, as they say, is history. We have had a smoother ride this time, as we have sorted out our partnership and working arrangement, even through the challenge of working together across the thousands of miles that separate Omaha, Nebraska, from Melbourne, Australia. Now that we have seen it through to completion, we are pleased indeed. Frank joins me in thanking Michael Thomson for his original suggestion, and also for his trust in us and our vision as he encouraged and supported us along the way. We are also indebted to Trevor Thompson, who has seen both projects through to their completion. We would also like to thank all the teachers and students with whom we have shared our love of the Bible, and especially the New Testament, over the years. We have learned so much from all of them.

We dedicate this book to one of the greats of New Testament scholarship, in the USA and across the world. Joseph A. Fitzmyer, SJ, taught the books of the New Testament, the Dead Sea Scrolls, the larger early Christian tradition, and the methodology of biblical scholarship; he also directed major doctoral seminars and dissertations at the Catholic University of America for decades. The Anchor Bible series alone has his major commentaries on 1 Corinthians, Romans, the Gospel of Luke, the Acts of the Apostles, and the Letter to Philemon. He was a giant in biblical scholarship. Frank first met him during his doctoral studies at the University of Oxford in the early 1970s, when Professor Fitzmyer was in Oxford as the prestigious Speakers Lecturer. In 1999, Frank was honored to become his colleague in the Biblical Studies Department at the Catholic University of America. As I concluded my studies at CUA, I followed his work closely and had the good fortune to participate in his doctoral seminar on the Dead Sea Scrolls, as well as his final doctoral seminar ever, on 1 Corinthians, and never ceased to wonder at his knowledge and passion for the Word of God.

With this dedication, we recognize three generations: Joseph A. Fitzmyer taught Frank, Frank taught me, and I am privileged to continue that vocation into a further generation of students and scholars. Although Joseph A. Fitzmyer taught each of us many things about the Bible, he did more than that. He showed us what it means to be at the same time both a rigorous scholar and a good Christian. He passed away, at ninety-six years of age, while we were working on this book, and so we send it on its way in memory of all that he gave us and so many others who had the good fortune to meet and work with him.

SHERRI BROWN
Creighton University
Omaha, Nebraska, USA

FRANCIS J. MOLONEY, SDB
Catholic Theological College
University of Divinity
Melbourne, Victoria, Australia

The New Testament

PURPOSE The introduction discusses the New Testament in terms of the sacred text of Christianity and the literary approach that will be the foundation for analysis in this textbook.

The New Testament makes up the latter third of the Christian Scriptures. In order to begin our introduction to interpreting the New Testament, we must explore what these writings are and what it means to be both "testament" and "new." These are topics that will be discussed in more detail later in the course, but we will lay out some basic terms here to get us started.

Introduction to Studying the New Testament

The term **Scripture** comes from the Latin term *scripturae*, which literally means "writings." This Latin expression is a translation of the Greek word *graphē*, which also means "writing." Both the Jewish and Christian traditions use the term **sacred Scripture**, and, when used in the religious sense, especially with the adjective "sacred" attached to it, the term refers to those writings a community of faith has set apart as holy. Indeed, Christians understand their Scriptures to be inspired by God. In our contemporary multicultural world, with its diverse religious faiths and practices, we must be aware that there are other religious traditions that regard writings as sacred, or even written by God by means of a chosen prophet. This is especially true for Islam, as Muhammad is understood as the prophet who communicates the words of Allah; but Buddhists, Hindus, and other religious communities also regard certain writings as sacred, even though most would not regard them with the veneration that Christians have for the Bible or Muslims have for the Qur'an.

Scriptures arise in religious communities to serve their particular needs as they struggle to understand their experiences of God and define themselves in relationship to the rest of their society. This is an important idea to take

1

> **Calendar Designations and Abbreviations**
>
> The Gregorian calendar that is commonly used today divides history into two eras.
>
> Traditionally the eras have been marked as **BC** (Before Christ) and **AD** (Anno Domini [beginning with 1 as the "Year of the Lord"]).
>
> In academics, respect for religious diversity leads to the use of **BCE** (Before the Common Era) and **CE** (Common Era).
>
> The latter is used in this textbook. When exact dates are not available, the abbreviation **ca.** is used. It is derived from the Latin word *circa* meaning "about" or "approximate."

to heart in approaching the books that form Christianity's sacred Scripture. They express the experiences of real people in a very real world—however distant from ours in time, geography, and culture—in their struggle to tell one another and others what they believe, why they believe, and why they are prepared to live and die for that belief. The earliest Christian Scriptures were the letters of Paul. They were the first to be preserved as this early missionary sought to keep in touch with the churches he founded as he traveled through the eastern region of the Roman Empire. It is even possible that the last of his letters were written in the early 60s CE in the city of Rome, as he faced imprisonment and death. The Gospels began to be composed later as the first generation of disciples died out and the community faced the uncertainties of the future. Paul's letters take it for granted that the earliest Christians knew of Jesus, his life and teaching, and his death and resurrection, but this was not so for second and third generation Christians. With the Gospels and later writings, it had become necessary for early Christian authors to inform their contemporaries about the significance of the life, death, and resurrection of Jesus. The Gospels are narratives about Jesus and the good news he brings, and the later letters and Revelation depend upon the early oral traditions, all written by and for the burgeoning communities of belief in what eventually became Christianity.

Jesus had many **disciples**, a word that in both Greek and Latin means "learners." In the Gospel of Luke and the letters of Paul, some of those in his inner circle (known in all the Gospels and Paul as "the Twelve") are also called **apostles**. They were "sent" (the meaning of the Greek word behind "apostles") on missions to spread the good news about Jesus and the kingdom of God and thus eventually founded communities of faith. Some of these apostles eventually either wrote about the good news or had their experiences and teachings written on their behalf. In the end, what we now call the New Testament is but a fraction of the diverse thinking and massive literary output of early Christianity. That said, what eventually came to be called the New Testament is made up of three types, or "genres," of literature:

1. Narrative (four gospels and one book of acts)
2. Letter (twenty-one; fourteen originally attributed to the apostle Paul and seven with other apostolic authority)
3. Apocalypse (one example, known as the book of Revelation)

Christianity developed over the next several centuries with many writings deemed sacred Scripture by various communities around the Roman Empire. Once Christianity was accepted in the Roman Empire, and the need for a discrete, authoritative group of books arose, these twenty-seven were accepted by the church leaders on behalf of the community of believers.

The Sacred Text of Christianity:
The Bible and Covenant with God

The sacred text of Christianity is called the **Bible**, a term that comes from the Greek words *ta biblia*, which can be translated as "the books." Acknowledging this origin helps us recognize something important about the Bible: even though it may look like a regular book in its contemporary editions, it is more like a library of books than a single volume. Like a library, the Bible is a collection of books, written by different authors in several different genres or styles, over a long period of time. Nonetheless, all these different books reveal the interaction between God and humankind in creation, telling multilayered stories of this relationship that begins with the dawn of history and continues all the way through the first century CE. Therefore, also like a library, we should not expect all these books to tell an identical story or all to have the same perspective on the complex relationship between God and God's creation, with its highpoint in the relationship between God and human beings (see Gen 1:26–31). Consequently, the Bible gives us many voices through its books and shows the growth and development of this relationship over time.

The library of books in the Christian Bible is made up of two parts: the **Old Testament (OT)** and the **New Testament (NT)**. The use of the adjectives "old" and "new" can sometimes be taken as a suggestion that the "old" is now a thing of the past and is of lesser importance than the "new." To use the terms "old" and "new" in this sense when speaking about the Bible would be seriously mistaken. As we will see, both "testaments" are essential to the Christian Bible, and there would never have been a "new" testament if the earliest Christians had not been inspired by the Jewish sacred Scriptures that are now called the "old" testament. The expressions merely indicate that the former is "older," written roughly between 1000 BCE and 50 BCE, than the "new" Testament, written between ca. 50 CE and 110 CE. *Together* they form the one collection of sacred Scriptures for Christians: the Bible.

Citing the Books of the Bible

A list of all the books and their common abbreviations is found at the beginning of Bibles. The books of a modern Bible are divided into chapters and verses.

To cite the Bible, the abbreviated book name is followed by the chapter number (e.g., Gen 15). If a specific verse is indicated, the chapter and verse numbers are separated by a colon (e.g., Gen 15:10). If several verses are included, they are separated by a dash (e.g., Gen 15:1–10).

When a verse or verses of a given chapter are designated, the abbreviation **v.** for one verse or **vv.** for more than one verse is used (e.g., v. 15 or vv. 15–20).

The term **testament** means "will." The English word comes from the Latin *testamentum*, which was used in the first Latin translation of the Bible, known as the Vulgate and largely the work of Jerome (ca. 347–420 CE). This Latin term translates the Greek word *diathēkē* used in the earliest Christian writings, which itself is a translation of the Hebrew word *berit*, meaning **covenant**. In the Jewish Scriptures, the term "covenant" often refers to agreements initiated and spelled out by God, with mutual commitments of promises and obligations. This concept of covenant is the principal means by which the Jewish Scriptures describe the relationship between God and his people Israel. The earliest Christians seem to have understood the **Christ Event** to be the formation of a **new covenant** between God and all humankind. "The Christ Event" is a term that is used to point back to what God did for humankind in the life, teaching, death, and resurrection of Jesus. It is the foundation of everything in the New Testament. That said, it is still a long step from the establishment of a new covenant to calling a collection of writings the New Covenant, or New Testament. Christians eventually made this step, as we will discuss in chapter one. As we have seen already, we cannot refer to something as "new" without a concept of "old" or understanding another body of literature as the Old Testament. The early church incorporated Jewish Scriptures into the Bible as this Old Testament. This indicates that contemporary Christians understand God's activity recorded in the New Testament to be the fulfillment of God's activity in the previous covenants as recorded in the Old Testament. By including the Old and the New Testaments in their sacred collection, early Christian leaders indicate their conviction that God's new covenant with creation can be fully understood only by having the fullness of God's relationship with humankind though history. For this important reason, in chapter three we survey the Old Testament narratives, including key figures and events that appear both in that lengthy story and the New Testament.

The stories of Jesus Christ in the New Testament are called **gospels**, a term that means "good news." But what exactly is the news, and why is it good? This is the subject of chapter four, but for the moment we can say that for Christians the good news is that God has fulfilled all his prior covenantal promises in the incarnation, death, and resurrection of his Son and has put in place a new covenant relationship that completes and perfects what God has done in and for Israel, now available to all humankind. How that takes place is explained in different ways by the various authors whose books appear in the New Testament. In their diverse ways, this is the story all the gospel writers, whom we call "evangelists," share with their original listeners and all later communities and individuals who hear and read their works. These gospels also summon their communities to live in faith in a larger society and culture that was shaped by a very different understanding of the world, the gods, and how people should relate to one another. The early narration of this experience and resulting development is provided in the New Testament example of the genre of **acts**. This challenge proved to be difficult, and the New Testament also contains **letters**

Maiestas Domini by
Haregarius of Tours

that provide both encouragement and warnings for this community. The genre known as the **apocalypse** is a development of both these previous genres. An apocalypse almost always includes a revelation by a supernatural being to a human recipient concerning cosmic mysteries or the future. That faithful human is then charged to share this message in written form. The New Testament book of Revelation has the literary form of an apocalypse, even though its message is somewhat different from other apocalypses, because it is written in the light of the death and resurrection of Jesus. This book has been written with the explicit purpose of guiding its readers through a contemporary interpretation of all these New Testament documents.

A Literary Approach to the Study of the New Testament

In colleges and universities, biblical scholarship is an academic discipline just like other subjects in the humanities and sciences. Scholars explore the biblical texts like other pieces of world literature for what they can tell us about the history and thought processes of the ancients. However, these particular pieces of literature are also sacred to certain communities of faith. Therefore, most scholars also approach them as texts that nourish the spiritual lives of believers who turn to them as the word of God that reveals God's plan for humankind. As this is a complex task, scholars make use of all the resources at their disposal, including the findings of historians, archaeologists, sociologists, and a number of other disciplines. The goal of biblical scholarship can be explained as **exegesis**. This term is derived from a Greek verb that means "to draw out." The task of exegesis, then, is to draw out from a book or text as accurately as possible the author's intended meaning of its words and phrases and eventually to explain the text as a whole. Exegesis is therefore a technical term used to describe the academic discipline that commits itself to the scholarly interpretation of the Bible. But in the end, it must not be simply regarded as a scholarly discipline. It is a question of "drawing out" meaning from a text written many years ago to stimulate faith in such a way that continues a nourishing process today. As we move through the documents of the New Testament, we must always appreciate both the academic discipline and the tradition of faith these texts serve.

Chapter two of this textbook is devoted to surveying different approaches to the process of interpretation, but here we can say that the task of exegesis is the task of asking relevant questions of the ancient biblical text and seeking answers to those questions through responsible methods. Scholars often regard their method of approaching the biblical text as asking questions about one of three "worlds":

1. The world behind the text
2. The world in the text
3. The world in front of the text

Although responsible interpreters research and analyze all these "worlds," scholars often focus their questions on one of them, while building upon the work of scholars who have focused their questions on another. This will be the case with the textbook we are introducing. Our interpretation *primarily* represents a literary approach, but it stands on the shoulders of the work of others, which will be brought to bear on our final analyses. When an author chooses narrative, or letters, or apocalypse, as the mode of communication, this is itself part of the message. Further, the way an author tells his or her story determines its meaning. More will be said about literary criticism later, but what we have introduced here is sufficient to indicate the direction that this present study will take in order best to serve our audience, perhaps approaching biblical studies and the New Testament for the first time.

The Course of Our Study of the New Testament

We have begun to consider the books of the New Testament and have given some initial pointers to how we will be approaching the interpretation of this literature. Since many students beginning their reflection upon the New Testament books may not have background in the Bible or the study of it academically, the next four chapters provide the necessary background for understanding and interpreting these authors' particular beliefs and teaching on what God did in and through Jesus of Nazareth. As mentioned above, chapter one discusses the Bible as the sacred Scripture of Christianity by introducing the concept of "canon" and surveying the history of "canonization," and chapter two will discuss contemporary methods of biblical interpretation in more detail. Chapter three presents an overview of the story of Israel as it is preserved in the major OT narratives, with a quick nod to the prophets. In this way, both the world of the New Testament authors and the scriptural history they used in composing their books for their communities are also introduced. Chapter four concludes our provision of background material by outlining the story of Jesus of Nazareth and introducing the birth and development of Christianity, as the new covenant through the Jesus movement, and the subsequent writing of the gospel narratives.

The rest of the book focuses on the groups of New Testament books themselves. Chapter five studies the Gospels and Acts as the particular genres of narrative in the New Testament. Chapter six discusses Paul and his letters by studying his world (what we can know of his life and mission) as well as the worlds in and in front of his texts. Chapter seven then focuses on the later letters of the New Testament, often called the Catholic Epistles or General Letters. Chapter eight turns to the one example of an apocalypse in the New Testament, known as the book of Revelation. The conclusion of the course of study discusses the community produced by the New Testament books in the first century and into the present world.

What Have We Learned So Far?

The New Testament books are part of the sacred Scripture of both the early Christians and Christians today. They are ancient texts that reveal the religious experiences of real people who lived almost two thousand years ago, at the beginnings of Christianity. But, as we will see in the next chapter introducing the development of what is called a "canon," this collection of sacred books

Jesus Christ Pantocrator
(Church of the Holy
Sepulchre in Jerusalem)
© Andrew Shiva

has provided and continues to provide authority and guidance for millions of Christians across time, into today and the future. They may have come into existence almost two thousand years ago, but they remain a life-giving word of God for many people in our own time. These people form the world in front of the text, the people whose understanding of God, the world, the Christ, and their place in relationship with all of these is at least partially formed by the New Testament. We say "partially" because the New Testament is only "part" of sacred Scripture. However, it is the literature that will concern us throughout this book. Thus, each chapter will conclude by asking "what have we learned so far?" In answering this question, we will explore what the sacred texts teach audiences about what is known as theology and its various aspects, including cosmology, anthropology, Christology, ethics, ecclesiology, soteriology, and eschatology. Therefore, in this initial section, we will conclude not so much by drawing together what we have learned so far in *this* chapter, since we have largely introduced what is to come, but by presenting these concepts in general so that we can explore them in the context of the texts studied in later chapters.

Let us explain further. **Theology** is the study of God. As an intellectual discipline, theology explores reality from the perspective that God is its origin, its basis, and its goal. More generally, a person's theology is his or her understanding of who God is and how God works in the world. **Cosmology** is the study of the nature and structure of the universe (the *cosmos*)—how it came to be and how it is ordered. The biblical texts, especially Genesis, the first book of the Jewish Scriptures and Christian Old Testament, contain a number of stories that are generally called "etiologies." An etiological story explains origins or the causes of how things are as we know them. Beginning with what actually exists and how things are ordered (or where there is sin and failure—are *dis*ordered), authors speculate about how it all began. A person's cosmology is related to his or her theology and understanding of God's role in creation. Today's environmental crisis leads many to ponder the future of the threatened creation. The choices we make are driven by our cosmology.

Anthropology is the study of human beings and culture. In relation to the study of religion, it refers to the relationship between God, humankind, and creation. Are humans intrinsically good, or bad, or somewhere in between? How do they relate to God? How do they relate to the rest of creation? In the New Testament, anthropology is intimately related to Christology. **Christology** is the study of the Christ. The term "Christ" (from the Greek language) is synonymous with the word "Messiah" (from the Hebrew), and both words mean the "Anointed One." Some religions have a notion of their God (or gods) sending an anointed one (or a prophet) to do something on behalf of humankind. But these religions, and even contrasting voices within the same religion, can have very different ideas about the nature of this anointed one, his role, and his relationship to God and creation. Continuing a theological tradition that can be found in the Old Testament, and in the Judaism of the time of Jesus, the early Christians believed that Jesus of Nazareth was the "Anointed One" of God, a so-called "Christ." Already in the New Testament, he is quickly known as "Jesus Christ," incorporating this title with his name. Given the very name "Christianity," it is easy to see that Christology is central to its belief system and the formation of the community of believers.

The study of **ethics** is the inquiry into the nature of the good, or "right," life in such communities. In this same field, **morality** refers to ways of thinking, feeling, and acting that address considerations of human welfare. On the basis of traditions about right and wrong, the foundation for ethical actions is, therefore, where religious faith and moral decision-making intersect. The biblical texts both directly and indirectly offer ethical guidelines for Christian living. This leads us to **ecclesiology**, which refers to the study of the church. The Greek word *ekklēsia* refers to any assembly of people. The early Christians adopted this term to refer to the gathering of the faithful. The concept of "church" therefore refers first and foremost to the people and their relationship to each other and to God through Christ. It was only much later in the history of Christianity that buildings dedicated to worship also began to be identified as "churches." We will see that the biblical authors present particular understandings of the people of God through their texts.

The biblical authors also have a goal or purpose in mind for the people of God. This leads to our final two components. **Eschatology** is the study of the last things or end times. These ideas are often associated with beliefs concerning life after death, judgment, and the end of the world as we know it. We will see that the biblical authors have particular ideas of when and how the "end time" is understood. **Soteriology** is the study of salvation. One's soteriology is often closely connected to Christology and eschatology. In Christianity, soteriology focuses upon the saving action of God in and through Jesus Christ and subsequently affects what Christians think about the meaning and goal of life.

The New Testament authors have much to teach about their understandings of God, the world God created, Jesus Christ, the human condition, how we are to relate to one another, and our search for meaning in this life and in the next. Each chapter of this textbook explores and interprets the New Testament writings, and we will conclude by seeking an answer to the question "so what?" What does the subject matter of the chapter tell us about what the biblical author teaches audiences about life and the human response to the God who is the primary actor in the story that is reflected in these writings? All the early Christian writings attempt to *persuade* their audiences about God, his Son Jesus Christ, and what God has done for human beings and all creation in and through his Son. Therefore, this book is not only about ancient Christian texts, but also about what we can learn from them about God, humankind, our world, and the way we relate to one another.

Key Terms and Concepts

acts
anthropology
apocalypse
apostles
BC/AD, BCE/CE
Bible
ca.
Christ Event
Christology
cosmology
covenant
disciples
ecclesiology

eschatology
ethics and morality
exegesis
gospels
letters
new covenant
New Testament
Old Testament
Scripture/sacred Scripture
soteriology
testament
theology

Questions for Review

1. What is Scripture and how does it arise in communities of faith?
2. Why is the Bible more like a library than a regular book?
3. What is the relationship between the Old and New Testaments?
4. What is meant by the term "the Christ Event"?
5. Why is it important to discuss theology and all that makes up theology when studying the New Testament?

Bibliography and Further Reading

Alter, Robert, and Frank Kermode, eds. *The Literary Guide to the Bible*. Cambridge: Harvard University Press, 1987.

Lennan, Richard. *An Introduction to Catholic Theology*. New York: Paulist, 1998.

Moloney, Francis J. *Reading the New Testament in the Church. A Primer for Pastors, Religious Educators, and Believers*. Grand Rapids: Baker Academic, 2015.

Powell, Mark A. *What Is Narrative Criticism?* Guides to Biblical Scholarship: New Testament Series. Minneapolis: Fortress, 1990.

The Origins and Development of the Bible

PURPOSE Chapter one discusses the Bible as the sacred Scripture of Christianity by introducing the concept of canon and surveying the history and development of the Jewish and Christian canons. Understanding the complexity of the biblical collection of texts will allow for a more detailed discussion of its contents and their interpretation.

As we introduced in the previous chapter, both the Jewish and Christian traditions use the term "sacred Scripture" to refer to those writings the community of faith has set apart as holy. Scriptures arise in religious communities to serve their particular needs as they struggle to understand their experiences of God and define themselves in relationship to the rest of their society. Since the Christian Scriptures are made up of both the Old and the New Testaments, we can discuss the composition of each part as well as how they came together to form the Bible.

Scripture and the World That Gave Us the Bible

In the ancient world where some 90 percent of the people could neither read nor write, shared history in relationship with God was passed down through the generations by word of mouth. Only particular forces, either internal, external, or both, compel these communities to find the resources to record and preserve their oral traditions in more permanent written forms. As we will see in this chapter, the Jewish people began to pull their traditions together into a written narrative around 1000 BCE, during the reign of King David. This time of peace and prosperity in the kingdom of Israel allowed for reflection and collection of traditions as part of court records. Some five hundred years later, however, the external forces of the Babylonian Empire imposed upon the kingdom, overrunning the land and sending the people into exile from ca. 587–538 BCE. This dark period in the history of the Jewish people was a key factor in solidifying the composition of their Scripture. To keep the hope of their religion alive, the people told stories and recorded them in written form for posterity. Across the next five hundred years, as the people restored their homeland and developed their particular religious sensibility, they continued to preserve their experiences in written form.

Likewise, as Christianity developed, the disciples and apostles of the early movement passed on their experiences of Jesus Christ and his teachings orally as they moved from town to town sharing the good news and founding Christian communities. As we discussed in the previous chapter, Paul began the writing of the Christian tradition with his letters to communities as he traveled through the Roman Empire on missionary journeys. The Gospels, however, were not composed as fully developed narratives until the community felt the need to preserve them. We will discuss this in more detail in chapter four, but we can note here that by 70 CE, about forty years after the crucifixion of Jesus, the community of believers was experiencing the death of their first generation of disciples and leaders. This internal force of loss was compounded by the devastating external consequences of the First Jewish Revolt against Rome, which lasted ca. 65–70 CE. Although the Jewish people led a valiant strike against the empire, the Romans eventually surrounded Jerusalem and, after an extended siege, broke through the city walls and burnt everything in their path. The Jewish Temple was destroyed, and both Judaism and the burgeoning Christian movement were in danger of fading into the shadows of history.

> **Josephus and His Writings**
>
> Flavius Josephus (37–100 CE), a Jewish scholar and eventual military leader who was forced to surrender to the Romans, recorded the many events of the First Jewish Revolt against Rome (66–70 CE). The book is called *The Jewish War* and is a striking record, even though it is written in support of the Roman offensive. He also wrote a long history of Israel called *Jewish Antiquities*. These works aid scholars in studying ancient Judaism.

The Jewish people dealt with this blow in their own way, which we will discuss in the next section, while the Christians began to compose their stories about the life and teachings of Jesus in written form. The Gospels and other writings that eventually became part of the New Testament were written ca. 70–110 CE and circulated throughout the Christian community to share the message and affirm the faith of believers.

The World of the Text and the Canon It Produces

The question of how an authorized collection of these writings known as sacred Scripture developed is a question of the **canon**. In the end, a canon is a list of books that have authority for a given community. The word "canon" comes from a Greek word that means "rod" or "reed." Such canons came to be used for measuring. When the word is applied to a list of books, the implication is that these books are the "standard of measure" for the community. The term "canon" can also suggest a plumb line, a weight on a string used to make sure a wall is straight. A canon of Scripture therefore also ensures that the life and thought of Christians are directed by the word of God to be correct or "straight."

Canons of Scripture develop on the basis of a perceived need for authority. The claim is sometimes made that the Christian canon was imposed by authorities such as bishops or emperors. As we will see below, it worked the other way: Christian people gave authority to the books that made most sense of their attempt to live and believe in a Christian way. As with the writing of Scripture, factors, sometimes internal to the group and sometimes external to it, generated questions in the Christian communities that had to be answered. They eventually became so important that leaders across early Christian communities reflected upon which books were to be "in" the canon and which books would be excluded. This section discusses the formation of the Christian canon by surveying the history of the development of the books as well as the process that led to the acceptance of some books as "inspired Scripture" and the rejection of others. This is called the process of **canonization**. Declaring people "saints" by canonization is a different process. Here we are discussing the establishment of a small library of books that the early Christians considered authoritative and called their canon of sacred Scripture.

The next two chapters will present the narrative history preserved in the Old and New Testaments in more detail. Our task here is to give a rapid overview of the pertinent history and development of the books that became the Christian Bible. The first step in the canonization process in the Jewish and Christian traditions is the grassroots perception of certain writings as sacred—as inspired by God and thus set apart as Scripture. Because of this "grassroots perception" as the starting point of the process of canonization, the idea that the canon was imposed on believers is incorrect. Over time, however, this "grassroots perception" was followed by the felt need to set boundaries on authority. Internal and external factors, such as dissension within the community or pressure or persecution from outside the community, compelled community leaders to determine which texts had authority for the community, which texts might be helpful but did not determine the teachings of the community or status in the community, and which texts were to be rejected as potentially destructive, or at least not helpful, to the community's well-being and belief system. For an overview of the process of canonization of the Bible into the volume well known today, we will begin with the sacred texts of Judaism and then follow with the development of the specifically Christian component of the biblical canon.

The Jewish Scriptures and the Old Testament

The biblical narrative begins in the book of Genesis with the story of God's act of creating the cosmos and everything in it. The first eleven chapters of Genesis deal with what is sometimes described as the "prehistory" of Israel. In Genesis 11, the figure of Abraham appears. Thus, the story narrates the development of the world as we know it, first following the expansion of humankind and the society it forms, then more narrowly focusing on God's choice of Abraham as the righteous man through whom God will form a covenant and through whose descendants a faithful people will form. The faithful descendants of Abraham are traced through their patriarchs and matriarchs, then through prophets, leaders, and judges, like Moses, Joshua, and Samuel, until the people call for a king and the nation of Israel is formed.

These early traditions about their understanding of God and how the world came to be as well as their own history and development as a distinctive ethnic group were preserved by the Israelites through word-of-mouth storytelling as one generation passed on its wisdom to the next. It was likely not until Israel settled into a nation under Kings David and Solomon (ca. 1000 BCE) that its elders and scholars had the luxury and wherewithal to keep a written record. Peace, prosperity, and the construction of a Temple as the house of God and the focus of worship both allowed for and necessitated Israel's entry into the literary world. In addition to the court records, the initial thread of the story of Israel's ancient history and self-understanding as God's chosen people began to be written. The seminomadic people from the time of Abraham (ca. 1800 BCE) through to the time of Moses and the exodus (ca. 1280 BCE) lived in an oral culture and had little time or resources for the written word. A lively memory of this early history, called **oral tradition**, developed, and the scholars of the kingdom incorporated these ancient songs and traditions, during and after the time of King David, into their literary productions.

After a very brief period under David and Solomon as a unified nation, Israel divided into the northern kingdom of Israel (initially ruled over by one of Solomon's servants: Jeroboam) and the southern kingdom of Judah (initially ruled over by one of Solomon's sons: Rehoboam), ca. 920 BCE. From this point, over the succeeding centuries, Judaism traces its heritage through the southern kingdom. Over time, these small kingdoms were threatened by enemies from all sides. These political developments

---

Literacy and Orality in the Ancient World

Most people in the ancient world were not able to read or write. A current estimate is that about 5 percent of the people in the cities could read and write, but it may have been a bit higher. Almost no country or village person, as in many civilizations today, was literate. It was also very expensive to acquire writing materials and books (scrolls). This led to a great deal of "oral" communication: important messages were "spoken" or even "performed" and passed down through the generations by word of mouth.

also led to the rise of a new type of literature in Israel. By the eighth century BCE, prophets, spokespeople for God, began to have their pronouncements and teachings collected and edited into books bearing their names. Prophets such as Isaiah and Jeremiah, among others, called the people and their kings back to covenant with God and warned of the consequences of breaching this covenant. Nonetheless, the northern kingdom fell to the invading Assyrian Empire ca. 721 BCE, and its inhabitants were deported throughout that empire's domain. The southern kingdom withstood this onslaught and even prospered for a time during the seventh century BCE; but eventually it, too, fell to an invading empire. This time it was the Babylonians who overran Judah and destroyed both Jerusalem and the Temple, where worship of God had been centralized. In ca. 587 BCE, the majority of the inhabitants of Judah were deported to the regions of Babylon. This began the period in Israel's history known as the **exile**.

This dark historical period led to prolific literary production as the Israelites kept their faith alive by committing their story to paper, solidifying their identity and their religious tradition in the face of foreign lands and peoples. This community building that took place during the exile also kept hope alive for an eventual return to their land, restoration of the holy city of Jerusalem, and rebuilding of the Temple for the worship of God. By 539 BCE, the empire of Persia became the dominant force in the region, and their king, Cyrus, became the focus of Israel's hope. In 538 BCE, Cyrus issued an edict that allowed the Judeans to return to their land and rebuild both their holy city and its Temple. The new Temple was completed ca. 515 BCE, and, through struggle and perseverance, the people rededicated their Temple to God and rededicated themselves to covenant relationship with that same God. However, the fifty years of the exile meant that two generations of Judeans had lived, and some even prospered, outside their homeland. Therefore, not everyone returned. This phenomenon of Jewish people populating the larger world is known as the **diaspora**, from a Greek word that means "dispersion" or "scattering." God's chosen people were now scattered across the known world and remained connected to their homeland and their Temple through prayer, pilgrimage, and financial support. From this time on, Jewish people living in the diaspora have been an important part of the literary and political history of Israel.

The new interaction of the Judeans with the larger world affected how they understood God, the world, and the literature they produced. Thus, in addition to the historical narratives and prophetic literature discussed above, the last centuries before the Common Era saw the rise of **wisdom literature** and then **apoc-**

Ancient Empires as They Affect Israel and the Jewish People

Egypt	ca. 3000–1000 BCE
Assyria	ca. 900–605 BCE
Babylon	ca. 605–539 BCE
Persia	ca. 539–332 BCE
Greece	ca. 332–141 BCE
Rome	ca. 63 BCE–600 CE

alyptic literature in Israel. Wisdom literature and the sages who contemplated wisdom focus on the individual. They were typically unconcerned with history or even God's action in history. The major interest of the wisdom writers was the problem of human existence and the lived experiences that are common to all human beings. As with those of many other ancient cultures, Jewish families created ways of passing on the collective wisdom of the ancients about life, from generation to generation. Examples of this literature from the Jewish Scriptures include Proverbs and Job. Apocalyptic literature finds its classic expression in the Jewish Scriptures in the book of Daniel. Contrary to popular usage, the term "apocalypse" means *revelation*, and in Judaism, the genre of apocalyptic literature refers to the belief that God *reveals* to certain faithful individuals truths that transcend the immediate experience of suffering and hardship and tell of God's ultimate victory over evil. These individuals then share this information in literary form in order to comfort those who are suffering and give them hope to endure until God's eventual victory. This type of literature appeared regularly and remained dominant in Judaism into the Common Era, such that it also became a popular component of early Christian literature.

Over time, all this literature began to be regarded as Scripture and collected in groups for use in teaching and worship. By ca. 400 BCE, the material that became the first five books of the Bible was published together as the "Instruction" or "**Law**," and was accepted in Judaism as the written word of God. The Hebrew word for this collection is *Torah*, a word that means "instruction." These early books, believed to contain the teaching of Moses and the record of the self-understanding of the formation of Israel as God's chosen people, gained their place as the primary Scriptures of Judaism. To this day, *Torah* lies at the heart of the Jewish understanding of Scriptures. Meanwhile, the later stories of Israel as a people and a nation with a king grew in stature as the definitive record of Israel's history, and the collection of books that bear the names of God's prophets began to appear. By ca. 200 BCE, these books came to be accepted as the part of the Jewish Scriptures known as the "**Prophets**." The Hebrew word for Prophets is *Nebi'im*. We should note here that this group of books included narratives of the story of Israel as well as the sayings of the prophets, which is different from the way these books were eventually collected by Christians. By the turn of the era, the wisdom literature and other writings from the post-exilic period were being referred to with the catchall term "**Writings**." The Hebrew word for Writings is *Khetubim*. The authority of this last group of books was still in dispute at the time of Jesus and the development of Christianity across the first century CE. This last collection of books continues to be accepted somewhat differently among Jews, Roman Catholic, Orthodox, and Protestant Christians today. We will return to this issue, but for the moment we can see how these three groups of books came to make up the three parts of the Jewish canon. The name of the corpus of Jewish Scripture is formed by the first letters of the names of each of these segments in Hebrew: **TaNaKh** (*Torah, Nebi'im, Khetubim*).

Returning to a discussion of the broader process of canonization, we should first note the differences in the Christian Old Testament (OT) canons. The Christian OT is not identical to the three-part Jewish canon, and in fact, there is more than one Christian OT canon. In addition to the thirty-nine books in the Tanakh revered by both Jews and Protestant Christians as inspired, the Catholic tradition includes seven other books. Thus, a Catholic Bible will contain forty-six books in its OT canon. The additional books are 1 and 2 Maccabees, Tobit, Judith, Sirach (also known as Ben Sira and Ecclesiasticus), Wisdom, and Baruch. In addition to these extra books, the Catholic OT canon contains expanded versions of the books of Daniel and Esther. These books are known in the Catholic tradition as the **Deuterocanon** or "deuterocanonical" books, which means "second canon" to acknowledge their absence from the Tanakh. In the Protestant tradition, these books are part of the **Apocrypha** or "apocryphal" books, terms that indicate that their authority is "hidden" and that they are absent from the Jewish canon.

The mention of the Jewish canon reminds us that this was not originally a Christian debate. The differences we have today stem from the unsettled state of the Jewish canon until the second century CE. This is not to say that the Jewish people did not have Scriptures at the time: The law was revered as the Torah of God by ca. 400 BCE, and the Prophets were in place as sacred Scripture by ca. 200 BCE, but the authority of the Writings remained unsettled for many years, even into the period after Jesus and the earliest church. They were widely used in teaching, worship, and writing for years, but for a long time there was no urgency within Jewish life and practice to rank them beside the Torah and the Prophets as Scripture. The **rabbis**, or teachers, began to do so late in the first century CE, not just because they had their own internal convictions that these books should be regarded as Scripture, but also because of the external pressure of early Christian usage. The early Christian movement had begun quoting these texts as Scripture, and the relationship between Judaism and the burgeoning Christian movement was deteriorating to the point of separation.

At this stage, we can look back over what we have discussed to better understand how this separation took place. Here we will delve deeper into some of the later post-exilic political and historical world events and how they affected Judaism. Linguistic, cultural, and political developments in world history had given rise to various distinctions within Jewish practice. By the time

---

Extracanonical Jewish and Christian Literature

In addition to the books found in Bibles, there were many other interesting texts written about the same time, or slightly later, that provide information about the history and thought of the time. Some of them come from Judaism and others come from Christian authors. Examples of the former include the Letter of Aristeas, mentioned in the text as emerging in the Greek period, as well as the Mishnah, which emerged well after the First Jewish Revolt against Rome (66–70 CE). Examples of the latter are the many Gospels that appeared, including the Gospel of Thomas and the Gospel of Mary Magdalene, that were not included in the NT canon.

of the exile in the sixth century BCE, the Israelites began to lose their common language and culture. During the period of the Persian Empire (547–333 BCE), Aramaic, a Semitic dialect related to Hebrew, became the common language of the people of the empire. Indeed, Aramaic remained the native language of the people of Judea for some five hundred years, into the Common Era. Alexander the Great ended Persian rule in 333 BCE by means of a stunning military campaign that took him and his conquering armies as far as the western reaches of today's India. He established Greek rule and cultural influence by setting up military colonies and scholastic academies and founding Greek-style cities, the most important of which was Alexandria in Egypt. This process is known as **Hellenization**, from the Greek word *hellenismos*, meaning "Greek." Hellenization, the actual political, social and religious practice of imposing Greek ways on all the conquered countries and civilizations, and its resulting phenomenon, **Hellenism**, were extremely successful and pervaded this part of the ancient world.

Greek became the common language for most people of the empire, and the language of literature and commerce for all. This process produced a cultural and linguistic unity that had never been known before this time. For the Jewish people, the Hebrew Scriptures became inaccessible to many in the now Greek-speaking world. Therefore, a Greek translation of the Hebrew Scriptures began to appear in Alexandria in the late second century BCE. First, the Torah, and later, all the books circulating in the Alexandrian community as Scripture were translated into Greek and collected. This work eventually became known as the **Septuagint**, a term derived from the Latin word for seventy. This name comes from the legend preserved in an extracanonical Jewish work known as the Letter of Aristeas. That "letter" claimed that separate translations from the Hebrew were made by seventy-two scholars—six from each of the twelve tribes of Israel—and all the translations proved to be identical. This legend sought to give a divine authority to the Greek translation of the Hebrew Scriptures. When discussing the Septuagint, scholars often abbreviate this somewhat difficult word with the Roman numeral for 70: LXX.

This Greek translation, the Septuagint (from now on: LXX), moved away from the three-part division of the Jewish Tanakh into a four-part division that saw the Scriptures from a different perspective: the **Pentateuch**, the **Historical Books**, the **Wisdom Books**, and the **Prophets**. The LXX became the authoritative edition of the Scriptures for the Greek-speaking Jews in the diaspora. It was later adopted by the early Christians who took the good news of Jesus Christ, based in God's covenant with Israel, into the larger Greek-speaking world. As we can see, the LXX was formed during the period when the inclusion of the Writings into the canon of Scripture was still being debated. This meant that the LXX included books and expanded versions of books that were not in circulation in Hebrew. It was used freely by both Jews and Christians in the Greek-speaking world, side-by-side with the use of the Hebrew Scriptures in Judea. It is gener-

The Septuagint

Many myths surround the origins of this Greek translation of the Jewish Scriptures, indicated by the Latin for "seventy" (LXX). The Letter of Aristeas, a document from the middle of the second century BCE, claims a miraculous origin for the Greek translation. The Septuagint was most likely produced in various stages—and in various versions—in Egypt around 280 CE. As many Jewish people living and worshiping in Egypt, and especially Alexandria, no longer knew Hebrew, a Greek translation gradually emerged. Early Christian writers, including the writers of the Gospels, used the Septuagint as the Word of God when they cited Jewish Scriptures in their writings.

ally thought that the Hebrew collection in Judea did not contain these books. Although all the Writings were considered sacred, they were not given the same reverence as Torah, and there was initially no felt need to authorize their canonicity.

As history moved forward, the Jewish people eventually gained independence from the remnants of the Greek Empire as a result of the Maccabean Revolt in 167–164 BCE. Although a key moment in Jewish history, this period had little effect on the canonization process. Nonetheless, several books now found in the LXX were produced in this era, for example, the two books of the Maccabees. Over time, the Roman Empire came to power in the Mediterranean world. The Roman general Pompey marched south down the east coast of the Mediterranean Sea, and Judea and its surrounding regions fell under the iron fist of Roman control in 63 BCE. The region remained a part of the Roman Empire until the latter's fall centuries later. The *pax Romana*, or Roman peace, facilitated a great deal of travel and communication, but the simultaneous suppression of autonomy also facilitated a rebellious spirit, and hopes for a Messiah who would throw off the yoke of Roman control became stronger.

The Jewish canon did not take final form until the early second century CE, but the process began in the first century CE with both the rise of Christianity and the destruction of the Temple in Jerusalem as a result of the rise and failure of the First Jewish Revolt against Rome (65–70 CE). The first Christians, better identified at this point as the **Jesus movement**, were observant Jews and, as the books of the NT attest, initially just one of several Jewish sects that formed in the Judaism of the time, including the **Pharisees**, **Sadducees**, **Essenes**, and **Zealots**.

After the destruction of the Temple and the fall of Jerusalem to the Romans in 70 CE, this diversity in both belief and practice began to be a cause of concern. The Sadducees, Essenes, and Zealots did not survive these tumultuous decades as distinctive groups, although there were no doubt still priests and angry revolutionaries present in Jewish society. The rabbis, the heirs of the Pharisees, arose as the new leaders of Judaism since there was no longer a centralized worship in the Temple. They eventually gathered at Jamnia, a city west of Jerusalem near the Mediterranean Sea, slightly south of the present-day international airport in Israel, to establish a center for rebuilding the battered Jewish religion and people. The diversity, or **heterodoxy**, of the previous generations was no longer understood as helpful or even possible, and a stricter **orthodoxy** ("right thinking or belief") and **orthopraxy** ("right practice") were sought to unify the battered people and their religion. The rabbis began to put in place a clearer system of belief, based in a canon of Hebrew Scripture. What emerged over time was Judaism as a religion oriented toward the written "word of God" and the Jewish people as a "people of the book." Therefore, the Tanakh, as introduced above, was formed as canon. In addition, the **synagogues**, community centers that developed in the diaspora, were reoriented as houses of worship for the practice of the Jewish faith. Jewish Christians, those who understood that the long-awaited Messiah of Israel had come in the person of Jesus, were identified as unorthodox, and their place within Judaism was eventually no longer possible, since mainstream Judaism held the position that God's Messiah had not yet come. There are several places in the New Testament (especially the Gospels of Matthew and John) where the tension between these two streams of Judaism is evident. The sad separation into Judaism and Christianity is often called "the parting of the ways."

By the end of the Second Jewish Revolt against Rome in the mid-130s CE, the two groups, Judaism and Christianity, began to develop their distinct identities and characteristics along separate paths. The newly formed Christians did not initially establish their OT canon. Their attention was more focused on the canon of specifically Christian Scriptures that would eventually form the New Testament, but they made use of the Septuagint they inherited from Greek-speaking Judaism. In this way, the first generation of Christians used the LXX version of the Jewish Scriptures as their "Old Testament" to understand the story of God working in

---

Jewish Groups: Sadducees, Pharisees, Essenes, Zealots, Jesus Movement

Prior to the First Jewish Revolt against Rome, there were several ways of living as a Jew. The Jewish author Josephus describes four:

The **Sadducees** are the more traditional priestly group who adhered strictly to the first five books of the Bible (the Torah). They were closely allied to the Temple, its organization, and influence.

The **Pharisees** are a more recent Jewish movement that was broader in its acceptance of Scripture, looking beyond Torah. They were teachers and scholars who survived the Revolt of 65–70 CE because they were more dynamic in adapting to the changed conditions, and were not bound to the Temple, as were the Sadducees.

The **Essenes**, closely associated with the Dead Sea scrolls found at Qumran, sought to live an uncontaminated Jewish life. They largely withdrew from society, which they saw as corrupt, and lived a more ascetic life.

The **Zealots** formed a revolutionary group that struggled against Rome, sometimes violently, for the liberation of Israel as God's land and people.

Alongside these four, the **Jesus movement**, before it became universally inclusive, was also a Jewish group who believed Jesus of Nazareth to be the long-awaited Messiah through whom God put in place a new covenant. They eventually became known as Christians for these beliefs.

The Jewish Canon and the Two Western Christian Old Testament Canons

Jewish Canon: The Tanakh	Roman Catholic OT Canon	Protestant OT Canon
Law: Torah	**Pentateuch**	**Pentateuch**
Genesis	Genesis	Genesis
Exodus	Exodus	Exodus
Leviticus	Leviticus	Leviticus
Numbers	Numbers	Numbers
Deuteronomy	Deuteronomy	Deuteronomy
Prophets: Nebi'im	**Historical Books**	**Historical Books**
Former Prophets	Joshua	Joshua
Joshua	Judges	Judges
Judges	Ruth	Ruth
1 Samuel	1 Samuel	1 Samuel
2 Samuel	2 Samuel	2 Samuel
1 Kings	1 Kings	1 Kings
2 Kings	2 Kings	2 Kings
	1 Chronicles	1 Chronicles
	2 Chronicles	2 Chronicles
Latter Prophets	Ezra	Ezra
Major Isaiah	Nehemiah	Nehemiah
Jeremiah	Tobit	Esther
Ezekiel	Judith	
Minor Hosea	Esther	
Joel	1 Maccabees	
Amos	2 Maccabees	
Obadiah		
Jonah	**Wisdom/Poetic Books**	**Wisdom/Poetic Books**
Micah	Job	Job
Nahum	Psalms	Psalms
Habakkuk	Proverbs	Proverbs
Zephaniah	Ecclesiastes	Ecclesiastes
Haggai	Song of Songs	Song of Songs
Zechariah	Wisdom	
Malachi	Sirach	
Writings: Khetubim	**Prophets**	**Prophets**
Psalms	Isaiah	Isaiah
Proverbs	Jeremiah	Jeremiah
Job	Lamentations	Lamentations
Song of Songs	Baruch	Ezekiel
Ruth	Ezekiel	Daniel
Lamentations	Daniel	Hosea
Ecclesiastes	Hosea	Joel
Esther	Joel	Amos
Daniel	Amos	Obadiah
Ezra	Obadiah	Jonah
Nehemiah	Jonah	Micah
1 Chronicles	Micah	Nahum
2 Chronicles	Nahum	Habakkuk
	Habakkuk	Zephaniah
	Zephaniah	Haggai
	Haggai	Zechariah
	Zechariah	Malachi
	Malachi	

history through Israel and the promises of a Messiah. When the eventual books of the Christian NT were written, their authors generally used the text of the LXX and referred to it as "Scripture."

As the Roman Empire flourished, Latin replaced Greek as the language of the Mediterranean world. The fourth century CE church leader and scholar Jerome was commissioned to translate all of Scripture, what the Christian church by then called the Old and New Testaments, into Latin. Jerome's translation, popularly called the **Vulgate** (from the Latin *vulgata*, meaning "vulgar" or "common" with regard to the language), became the standard for Christianity, and its version of the OT contained all the books, and the expanded versions of books, that were present in the Septuagint. Without ever taking an explicit "vote" on the matter, the question of the OT canon was thereafter hardly discussed in the Christian church for some one thousand years, until the era of the Protestant Reformation when the reformers raised it again in the sixteenth century. In his translation of the Bible into German in 1534, Martin Luther grouped the seven books and expansions found in the Christian OT but not in the Jewish Hebrew

> **The Vulgate**
>
> The Jewish Scriptures were available in Hebrew (with some Aramaic) and Greek (the Septuagint) long before Christianity emerged. As the Mediterranean world was increasingly dominated by Rome and the Christian church became more focused upon Rome, Latin became an important language. The Jewish and Christian Scriptures were available in a number of Latin translations, known as the Old Latin versions. In 382 CE, Pope Damasus commissioned Jerome to produce a unified Latin translation. A great linguist, working in Bethlehem, he produced a Latin version known as the Vulgate (for the masses) in 405 CE. For many centuries, the Roman Catholic Church regarded the Latin Vulgate as a sacred text.

canon at the end of his version of the OT. He called this group "Apocrypha," as mentioned earlier. He claimed they were "not held equal to the sacred Scriptures and yet are useful and good for reading." It seems Luther mistakenly understood the Jewish canon to have been solidly in place in the time of the first Christians, and he wanted to get back to those origins. The OT canon he formed contains the same books as the Tanakh but still follows the four-part structure of the Septuagint/Catholic OT. In the counter-reformation response, the Roman Catholic Church defined their existing OT as officially part of its canon at the Council of Trent in 1546. The result of these reformation issues is the existence of different Christian OT canons. Debates over the "correctness" of these canons have raged at various points in Christian history since the Reformation, but in today's more collaborative climate they have faded. Scholars, clergy, and lay people alike are more interested in learning from all the ancient texts available to us.

The Christian Scriptures and the New Testament

The process of the formation of the New Testament (NT) is comparable to that of the OT, though taking place across a far briefer timeline. To the best of our knowledge, Jesus of Nazareth left no written records. He lived ca. 4 BCE–30 CE and was an itinerant teacher, not a writer or a historian. The Scriptures that he and his disciples lived by and quoted as the basis for their teaching were the Jewish Scriptures we have just been discussing. These Jewish Scriptures would have been passed on to Jesus orally. Instead of reading and quoting from a written text, he would have used the Scriptures on the basis of his memory of what he had been taught. Even though Jesus would have spoken Aramaic, and likely was familiar with the Hebrew Scriptures read in the Synagogue (see Luke 4:16–20), once the Christians began to write, they wrote in Greek and almost always used the LXX as their "Scripture."

It was some years before written Christian documents appeared. The first complete Christian document has been dated some twenty years after Jesus's lifetime. Scholars suggest the apostle Paul's first letter to the churches in Thessalonica (1 Thessalonians) has this distinction. Paul was not a disciple of Jesus and did not become a believer in Jesus as the Christ until several years after Jesus's death by crucifixion. Another decade passed before he became a prominent apostle and leading voice of early Christianity. Therefore, most interpreters agree that 1 Thessalonians was written ca. 50–51 CE. It was another twenty years before a gospel appeared. By that time, all the letters that we can certainly claim that Paul wrote had been completed, and Paul had most likely been martyred or executed for testifying to his faith (64–65 CE). Although church tradition has long regarded the Gospel of Matthew as the first and fullest expression of the gospel and placed it as the first of the Gospels in the Christian canon, there is a general scholarly consensus today that the Gospel of Mark was the first full narrative of the good news of Jesus Christ, composed sometime between 65 and 70 CE. The remaining books that eventually became part of the NT emerged over the course of the next thirty years or so. These books include three more gospels, one example of a type of historical narrative called an acts (The Acts of the Apostles), a total of twenty-one letters, and one example of apocalyptic literature (Revelation). All the writings that eventually became the New Testament were written by the turn of the first century of the Common Era, or ca. 100–110 CE.

The NT literature, like that of the OT, emerged within the community of believers. There were many Christian writings that appeared across the first centuries of the existence of the Christian community, but some seem to respond more immediately to their understanding of Jesus and to their own need to understand and

---

The Luther Bible

Even prior to the sixteenth-century Reformation of the Christian church, many wished to have the Bible in their native language, rather than in Latin. The greatest of the Reformation Bibles came from Martin Luther (1483–1546). He published his translation of the New Testament in 1522 and, along with others, translated the Old Testament. Luther published a complete German Bible in 1534. He continued to work on this translation. It eventually became an important work of literature that played a role in the formation of German religion and culture, widely available because of the invention of the printing machine in the 1450s by Johannes Gutenberg.

live by what he had left them. Under the guidance of the Holy Spirit, they reflected upon and responded to what they understood to have been made available by God as salvation in Jesus Christ, the long-awaited Messiah of God for Israel. Of course, these twenty-seven books are by no means the only early Christian works, and the writing did not stop after the turn of the century. In fact, it is still going on as Christians continue to interpret and write books about how God has worked and is still working in the world throughout history. However, Christians believe that the life, death, and resurrection of Jesus, the Christ and Son of God, was the final public revelation of God to the world, and thus the early records of this event and the church it formed have a particular significance for Christian faith and teachings.

In the first years after the life of Jesus, even though the early believers were convinced of Jesus's resurrection from the dead as an action of God, little thought was given to the production of Christian writings, no doubt because Jesus himself, like the rabbis of the time, taught solely by the spoken word. This teaching was remembered and discussed by his disciples, who in turn passed it on by word of mouth. Thus, the disciples' recollection of these teachings and memories of the events of Jesus's life were communicated to new audiences and second-generation disciples. This is why all the early Christian writings are in Greek, understood by everyone in the Mediterranean world and beyond. As this teaching and community building by spoken word carried on, an early Jesus movement, or loose network of believers, formed, and an oral tradition developed. Again, like with the OT, there was most likely some writing going on from the earliest years: The developing Christian **liturgy**, or worship service, included hymns (songs of praise), creeds (statements of belief), and prayers. Some of these early snippets of worship were eventually incorporated into the written texts, as was the case with the inclusion of the hymn about Jesus found in Paul's letter to the community in Philippi (see Phil 2:6–11).

> ### Gnosticism
>
> In the second century CE a very speculative form of Christianity emerged, influenced by Eastern religions and Greek philosophy. It was called "Gnosticism" because—although it had many forms—its main belief was that the physical reality of the human Jesus and the bloody event of Jesus's death, followed by God's action in the resurrection, were not "salvific." People were saved by "knowledge" (Greek: *gnōsis*), not by Jesus's life, teaching, death, and resurrection.

As we have already seen, the first Christian writings to come to us are the letters of Paul. They were attempts to bridge distances as the apostle traveled from town to town in Asia Minor (modern-day Turkey), Greece, and eventually modern-day Europe. He founded and instructed communities in the good news of Christ and then moved on to new areas to do the same. In fact, Paul is the first to call this message "gospel." Once he left his communities, he would stay in touch, mediate disputes, continue the teaching process, and affirm his authority by way of these letters, which were initially treasured and preserved by their recipients. From these beginnings, the letters of Paul have been part of Christian literature through the ages. Although most scholars today do not think that the apostle Paul wrote all the letters attributed to him, those who eventually established the NT canon understood all thirteen to be authentic reflections of this early church figure. In addition, the canon includes the so-called Letter to the Hebrews, which is not really a letter at all but a sermon or religious treatise. Although this text does not claim to be written by Paul, early tradition collected it with the rest of Paul's letters for a total of fourteen.

Near the end of Paul's ministry, scholars suggest the writing of the Gospels began. The memory of Jesus's life and ministry had been kept alive in the intervening decades by Paul and the other early preachers, teachers, and storytellers in the various Christian communities. We will discuss the genre of gospel in greater detail in later chapters, but for now we can note that the First Jewish Revolt against Rome, which began to rage across Judea in 65 CE and climaxed with the burning of Jerusalem and the destruction of the Temple in 70 CE, must have been part of the impetus behind some early Christians feeling compelled to commit their understanding of the good news of God's action in Jesus Christ to the written word in story form. In addition, the first generation of apostles and disciples had largely disappeared off the scene, martyred for their faith, by the late 60s. This would certainly have been another factor in the felt need to capture both the story and the authority in its telling in literary form. A new generation of Christians was emerging that no longer retained the experiences and the memories that were so closely associated with Jesus of Nazareth and the beginnings of the community. The gospel accounts differed slightly as the story was told with a different emphasis or theological agenda in Rome, in Jerusalem, in Ephesus, etc. Thus, from among the many stories about Jesus, and most likely collections of his sayings, we have the four distinct Gospels of Matthew, Mark, Luke, and John, which made their way into the Christian canon in the second and third century.

The New Testament letters outside the Paul collection are often grouped together as the "Catholic" or "General Epistles," because they are addressed to various forms of the universal church body instead of particular communities and are thus known by their authors. These include letters attributed to James, Jude, two attributed to Peter, and three letters attributed to John. Finally, we have the book of Revelation, the one NT piece of apocalyptic literature.

For the early Christians, like the Jews, the process of canonizing, or giving official author-

Muratorian Canon Fragment

In the eighteenth century, scholar L. A. Muratori was studying an eighth-century manuscript in the Ambrosian Library in Milan, Italy, when he discovered another document tucked between the pages. Upon further investigation, he determined it to be a kind of catalogue of books for a New Testament canon. He published the text in 1740, naming it for himself: *Canon Muratori*. The text itself was written in Latin, but scholars believe it comes from a Greek original. The composition has been dated to the late second century CE. Although the beginning and likely the ending of the document are missing, it is considered the earliest draft of the NT canon that has been preserved, and it gives a great deal of information about the issues at stake for the church leaders and how they argued for the inclusion of some books as well as the exclusion of others.

ity to these writings, and rejecting the many others of the new movement came about due to conflict. In particular, in the middle of the second century CE, about 150, a Christian leader by the name of **Marcion** began to advocate a particular way of being Christian and writings that supported that way of life. Marcion was the first to indicate "books" that should be regarded as authoritative, but some of his "books" were very different from the books that we have just described. Marcion's teachings were more like a popular Greek philosophy called Gnosticism than Paul's understanding of the new covenant and God's union of all Israel. Therefore, other church leaders began to advocate a clearer idea of what Christianity was and what writings represented that way of life and faith practice. One of the most important figures from the second century in this quest to establish a canon that best represented the heart of Christianity was the church leader **Irenaeus**, the bishop of Lyons, in modern-day France, but there were many others. This process took a long time and did not reach a final consensus for another two hundred years. It appears to have been finalized about the middle of the fourth century. A document known as the **Muratorian Canon fragment** was discovered in the nineteenth century and has been dated to the late second or early third century. It shows the extensive conflict and debates that arose over this process of canonization.

For our purposes, it is sufficient to note three major criteria for inclusion in the canon, which developed and led to the acceptance and establishment of the twenty-seven books that now make up the NT canon. They are the following:

1. Apostolic authority (a book is connected to the authority of an apostle)
2. Usefulness for moral and spiritual encouragement and instruction in the faith
3. Popularity and extent of use in the early communities and in their worship services

The year 367 CE seems to have been a milestone for publication of a "final draft" of the canon. In his Easter letter of that year, a very significant and influential early church leader, **Athanasius** (296–373 CE), included the list of twenty-seven books that was eventually accepted by the whole church and became the New Testament canon. This letter

---

Athanasius

Saint Athanasius of Alexandria (296–373 CE) was one of the most influential figures in the troubled fourth century CE. He stood for what eventually became accepted Christian doctrine, articulating in his many works and homilies what became the orthodox teaching of the church on the Trinity and the role of Jesus Christ. Despite much suffering, he was highly respected. For that reason, his list of the books that should be accepted as Christian Scriptures, named in an Easter Letter of 367, was quickly accepted as the authoritative word on a discussion that had been unresolved since late in the second century.

---

can still be found in its original Greek, and in Syriac and Coptic translations. The existence of this letter in the languages that came from dominant churches *in the East* at that time (Syriac came from Palestine and parts of Asia Minor, and Coptic from Egypt) is an indication of the authority of Athanasius and the widespread acceptance of his list. He includes the four Gospels, followed by Acts and the Catholic Epistles (James, 1–2 Peter, 1–3 John, and Jude), then fourteen Pauline Epistles (Hebrews is listed after 2 Thessalonians, before the Pastorals and Philemon).

In the Latin tradition *in the West*, Pope Innocent I (Pope from 401–417), in response to a question from the Gallic bishops concerning the canon, named the list of Athanasius in 405 CE. He was most likely under the influence of the great fathers of the Latin-speaking church, Jerome (ca. 347–420) and Augustine (354–430), who had already accepted the Athanasian canon. This is the canon that was finally and universally adopted by the early Christian church. It remains the authoritative NT canon for all Christians around the world today.

The Christian New Testament Canon

Gospels	Letters of Paul	Catholic Epistles
Matthew	Romans	James
Mark	1 Corinthians	1 Peter
Luke	2 Corinthians	2 Peter
John	Galatians	1 John
	Ephesians	2 John
Acts	Philippians	3 John
Acts of the Apostles	Colossians	Jude
	1 Thessalonians	
	2 Thessalonians	**Apocalypse**
	1 Timothy	Revelation
	2 Timothy	
	Titus	
	Philemon	
	Hebrews	

What Have We Learned So Far? The Canon of Sacred Scripture

As we first discussed in the introduction, this section of each chapter will reflect upon the ground we have covered and explore the theological components that have risen to the surface. Since this chapter has provided a rapid historical overview of the development of the Bible as the canon of sacred Scripture of Christianity, there has been little focus on theology. However, we must remember that in the ancient world, there was no separation between the religious, political, social, and literary worlds. The hand of God (or the gods, depending upon one's religious system) was understood to be involved in every natural and human-created phenomenon. Further, as the people of faith reflected upon the story of their relationship with God and God's action in the world in relationship to them, they understood the traditions they developed and the texts their authors composed as inspired by that God. The formation of the

Jesus Christ as Teacher
(St. Catherine's Monastery,
Mount Sinai, Egypt)

© carulmare

canon of Christian Scripture is thus theological from beginning to end, as well as historical and literary. Therefore, although our task in this course is largely academic—historical and literary—it is also by nature theological as we seek answers that the Christian faithful have been seeking and will continue to seek of the New Testament. The succeeding chapters will have much more to add to this component of our study.

Key Terms and Concepts

apocalyptic literature

Apocrypha

Athanasius

canon/canonization

Deuterocanon

diaspora

Essenes

exile

Hellenization/Hellenism

heterodoxy

historical books

Irenaeus

Jesus movement

Law/*Torah*

liturgy

Marcion

Muratorian Canon fragment

oral tradition

orthodoxy

orthopraxy

pax Romana

Pentateuch

Pharisees

Prophets/*Nebi'im*

rabbis

Sadducees

Septuagint (LXX)

synagogues

Tanakh

Vulgate

wisdom literature

Writings/*Khetubim*

Zealots

Questions for Review

1. What is generally meant by the expression "sacred Scripture"?
2. What is meant by the expression "canon"?
3. What were the most important factors that led to the development of the Jewish canon known as the Tanakh? What is the origin of this name?
4. What role did "oral" transmission of stories and teachings play in formation of both the OT and the NT?
5. Who is the earliest preserved Christian author? Why is understanding the role of this apostle as well as the texts he did (or did not) write important to understanding early Christianity and its canon?
6. What were the key factors that led to the development of the NT canon?

Bibliography and Further Reading

Dawes, Gregory. *Introduction to the Bible.* New Collegeville Bible Commentary: Old Testament. Vol. 1. Collegeville, MN: Liturgical, 2007.

Frigge, Marielle. *Beginning Biblical Studies.* Rev. ed. Winona: Anselm Academic, 2013.

Law, Timothy M. *When God Spoke Greek: The Septuagint and the Making of the Christian Bible.* New York: Oxford University Press, 2013.

Miller, John W. *How the Bible Came to Be: Exploring the Narrative and Message.* New York: Paulist, 2004.

Moloney, Francis J. *Reading the New Testament in the Church: A Primer for Pastors, Religious Educators, and Believers.* Grand Rapids: Baker Academic, 2015.

Methodology for Biblical Interpretation

PURPOSE Chapter two presents the basis for biblical interpretation as well as a brief overview of the development of contemporary methodologies. We will focus attention on approaching interpretation through the "worlds" of the biblical text.

As we pointed out in the introduction, the goal of biblical scholarship can be explained as the task of **exegesis**. This term is derived from a Greek verb that means "to draw out." From that primary meaning, it thus also denotes "to explain," or even "to unfold the story" in the sense of interpreting its meaning. The verb form of this word is "to exegete." However, the word "exegete" is also sometimes used as a noun to indicate the one who exegetes the text. For example, we might say that Dr. Jones is an exegete of the biblical text. One of the tasks of exegesis, then, is to draw out from a book or passage the author's intended meaning of its words or phrases and to explain the text as a whole. As we will see, it is not the only task for the biblical interpreter, or exegete, as this activity includes not only the *textual* meaning (the sense of its words and phrases), but also its *contextual* meaning (the sense of its words or phrases in the framework of the given passage or book around it) and its *relational* meaning (their sense in relation to the body of works and faith as a whole). Therefore, we might say that once we have exegeted the text, we then have to answer the question, "so what?" So what does this text mean, and how is it relevant to people's lives?

Methods for Interpreting the Bible: The Worlds of the Text

The mode of interpretation that has been dominant in the twentieth and early twenty-first centuries is called the **historical-critical method**. This exegetical method seeks to establish the original meaning of the text by using techniques of historical and literary criticism to trace the ancient foundations of the people of God and of the Christian church. It is called a **critical** method not because it criticizes the Bible in the sense of faultfinding or that it seeks to be skeptical about the ancient text, but because it compares and analyzes the details of the text in an effort to arrive at a historical and literary judgment about it. The method recognizes that the Bible, though it is considered by Christians to be the inspired written word of God, is an ancient record, composed by many human authors over a long period of time. As such, it should be read, studied, and analyzed as other ancient records of history. The historical-critical method attempts to reach back into the past to understand the meaning of the ancient records of God's dealing with his people and of the ministry of Jesus of Nazareth and of the emerging communities that believed they continued his ministry and presence "in the Spirit." These critical techniques are geared to one end: to determine the meaning of the sacred text as it was intended by the human author, understood by the Christian faithful to be inspired by God, who composed it long ago. Traditionally, this is where historical criticism ceased, but more recent times have seen a demand from both scholars and Christian believers for exegetes also to attempt to ascertain what the text is saying to readers today.

Nowadays, again as we indicated in the introduction, it is common for biblical interpreters to speak of investigating **the "worlds" of the texts** of Scripture in an effort to form a more complete picture of their meaning. These worlds include the historical background, which is often identified as the **world behind the text**. This is the world of the author, his or her social and belief systems, the larger political, cultural, and economic systems around the author, as well as any needs in this regard that the author's intended audience might have. When approaching the world behind the text, scholars attempt to discover the ancient foundations for a people of God and to understand what was meant by the ancient records of God's dealing with that people. What is most important is the reconstruction and the interpretation of *the past*, including the events, people, places, and time that produced the composition. This approach is very important to ensure that we approach the real-life experiences and possibilities of both the biblical authors and the people and events portrayed by these authors. A book written hundreds of years ago must be read on its own terms and not as if it were written in the twenty-first century. In other words, we must seek to understand *their* world and how *they* experienced God in that world in order to make sense of how *they* expressed those experiences in their writings. Only then can we begin to apply what they teach our contemporary world. All these elements come together for the author to conceive and compose the content of the text.

The latter half of the twentieth century, however, began to look more closely at the way the text itself has been assembled by the author, to analyze its literary characteristics and style. This approach attends to the **world in the text**. This is the world of literary genres and forms, of the symbols and metaphors the author uses, and of how the author develops and orders all these elements into the plot of the narrative, the direction of the letter, or the imperatives of the essay. In this approach, the interpreter explores the content, literary characteristics, and themes present within the final composition, the writing as a whole. With narratives, this includes all the storytelling techniques the author may employ, such as plot, setting, the passing of time, places where events take place, and characterization, to mention just some of the important elements that can be found in any "story." When it comes to letters, the approach must be different. The interpreter must trace rhetorical devices the author uses to communicate a message and to persuade readers. The letters that are found in the New Testament (and many letters throughout history) were written to "persuade." Many interpreters claim that what they must discover is the author's "rhetoric of persuasion."

In addition, more recently, interpreters have begun to ask about the effect that a biblical text has upon audiences and readers. While they must never ignore the historical and literary interpretations of the text, interpreters who follow these more audience-focused methods attend to the **world in front of the text**. They focus on the emotional and intellectual effect that compositions have upon their audiences, be they readers or watchers and hearers of oral performances of written texts. All authors have agendas, or reasons for putting pen to paper (or quill to parchment in the case of the ancients), and the task of interpretation is discovering what authors want their audiences to take away from their encounter with these writings. This approach to a text can have a number of objectives. For example, the interpreter can use parallel documents from the past to try to understand how the original author may or may not have perceived his text to impact original readers. However, nowadays there is increasing interest in how these ancient texts make an impact upon an audience (reader/hearer, etc.) literally sitting *in front of the text* then and now. This, in many ways, is the world the text produces as it persuades certain beliefs in people who read or hear it and leads them to live accordingly, either in agreement with or in reaction to it.

As we also indicated in the introduction, our primary focus in this book will be literary. We will be interested in uncovering what the New Testament says to readers and listeners of today. However, as you will see, we cannot ignore the other worlds. The brief historical background and the description of how we came to have a biblical canon, provided in the previous chapter, already indicate that we want our readers to understand from where all these texts came. Therefore, we will inquire about all the worlds of the text. We introduced this chapter by saying that the goal of biblical scholarship is the task of exegesis. In that same vein, the process of exegesis is the task of asking questions of the ancient biblical text and seeking answers to those questions through responsible methods. When we analyze the text by asking and answering these questions, this is **criticism**. The term "criticism" in this context means a systematic analysis of data (in our case ancient texts) with the aim of making decisions and drawing conclusions. In popular language, criticism

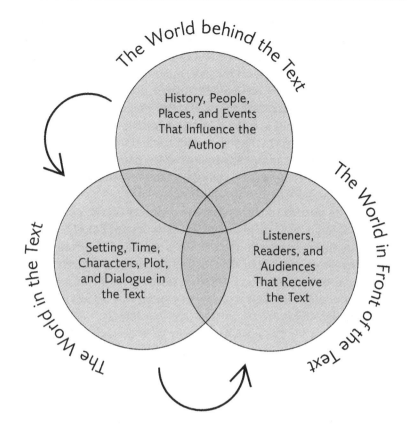

often indicates tearing down or finding fault, but this is not necessarily the case and never the goal of a good biblical scholar. Rather, the focus here is on analysis and decision-making about meaning. What type of criticism we are doing depends upon what type of questions we are asking. Although there are a number of sometimes complex types of criticism, in the sections that follow we will introduce several basic areas of criticism within their respective worlds of the text. We will utilize these approaches later on as we introduce the exegesis of the New Testament.

The World behind the Text

In order to begin interpreting any biblical text, we must understand its context in the world from which it came. The world behind the text is the world of its author and the writing he or she produced. If we establish as best as we can how the text was composed and preserved and what was important in those communities in the ancient world, then we can move forward on more solid ground as we explore how it is important in our own time. **Textual criticism** is a fundamental step in asking and answering questions about the world behind any biblical text. Textual criticism is concerned with the transmission of the biblical text in its original language and in ancient translations through the many copies made over the years and determines what the best-preserved text is. Scholars of the early Jewish and Christian eras were called "**scribes**," and part of their role was to transmit the early texts by hand. They had no printing presses or copy machines or any other way to distribute the gospels, letters, and other important texts to the widespread communities. These scribes were very good at their jobs, and this hand-copying was done remarkably well, with precision and care. Nonetheless, changes in the text seeped in, sometimes by mistake and other times as a result of scribes trying to clarify what they perceived to be unclear thoughts or poor grammar on the part of authors. Therefore, although there are no originals of any of our biblical texts, we have thousands of ancient copies in the form of scrolls, papyrus fragments, and parchment codexes, and few of these copies are identical. So, the task of the textual critic is to determine, as a result of studying all the possible options, what the best or most original text is. By this we mean the most likely text the author originally wrote.

Fortunately for us, this work has already been done and continues to be done as we read the Bible in English, based on the work of skilled textual critics and translators. Nonetheless, textual criticism is a crucial component of biblical interpretation. Some of these discrepancies are still a matter of debate. Very often, English study Bibles will indicate serious textual issues (places where the ancient manuscripts have conflicting readings of the text) by retaining the word or phrases in question in the final text, but enclosing them in square brackets. Other times, they will include superscript indicators and

---

Example of Textual Criticism

The basis of English-language New Testaments is a Greek text that has been constructed into a printed edition from thousands of manuscripts and ancient translations, some of which come from the second century and others from the early Middle Ages. Textual criticism is a branch of New Testament studies that attempts to establish the most original text possible from these many sources. A good example of textual criticism is found in John 20:30–31, where scholars ask whether John wishes to call people to faith when he ends his Gospel claiming that he wrote "so that you may believe" (*pisteusēte*) or to exhort them to continue and deepen their faith "so that you may go on believing" (*pisteuēte*). Only the Greek letter for "s" differs between these two texts, and both forms are found in ancient manuscripts. The text critic assesses which represents the earliest text. Issues like this are found on every page of the New Testament.

corresponding notes outlining the textual issues. This practice allows readers to identify the scholarly concern while continuing to read a smooth translation of the text. We will discuss some relevant examples as they arise in our study of the New Testament.

Once we have completed textual criticism and decided what the best form of our text is, we turn to **historical criticism** to attempt to reconstruct the world the text relates to us. We use all the resources at our disposal, including archaeology, anthropology, and numerous other academic disciplines to learn as much as possible about the world in which the authors and audiences of our text lived. We have already begun to do this in chapter one of this textbook and will continue to delve into that history in the next two chapters. We must always remember that the biblical world is very different from our own, and we must respect that world and its culture. This includes the geography and climate, but also the ruling people and their governments alongside subjected peoples and their ideals, as well as religious beliefs, cultural norms, and societal standards. All of this helps us understand the events that take place, the concerns people have, the symbols and images the writers use, as well as the expectations those writers place on both people in the texts and audiences of them.

Regardless of the historical reality that produced a text, however, we must also take seriously that the author has chosen to transmit the message in a literary form. Just like authors today, ancient authors sometimes wrote from their own experiences, sometimes wrote from the shared wisdom of their community, identified as oral tradition, and sometimes used other literary sources.

Example of Historical Criticism

The interpretation of the New Testament must include analyzing the historical background of events reported in narratives and the possible historical background of the life of the early church reflected in the non-narrative texts. For example, there is evidence from early non-Christian literature that Jesus of Nazareth healed the sick and had power over evil spirits (see, e.g., Matt 4:24; Mark 5:1–20). At that time sickness, for example epilepsy, was often regarded as evidence of a demonic possession. In the Gospels, the early church told these stories as reflections of God's presence in Jesus's ministry (interpretation), based on something that actually happened (historical criticism). Likewise, when Paul writes to the Romans that nothing can separate us from the love of God made visible in Jesus Christ (Rom 8:31–39), he lists in vv. 35–37 many possible conflicts that Christians may have to face. A recognition of the authentic historical experiences of the early Christians (historical criticism) enriches Paul's teaching on what God has done for humankind in Christ (interpretation).

Source criticism therefore seeks to determine the literary prehistory of a biblical book. Exegetes ask the question, what sources did the author use in composing the book? This type of criticism therefore tries to construct what we today would call a "bibliography" of sorts after the fact for a text that did not originally cite its sources. Answering this question can tell us a great deal about why the author included some information but omitted other events or data. Source criticism can also tell us what was important for authors as they shaped their own tellings of the tradition.

Textual, historical, and source criticisms are three basic types of questions and answers that help exegetes construct the world behind the text. There are others, but these will be most useful for our purposes in this textbook. We will highlight their use in the coming chapters.

The World in the Text

The notion of addressing the situation the New Testament's first readers and hearers encounter is the driving principle behind the analysis of the "world in the text." The task of exegesis does not come to an end once we have identified the final form of the text and the possible historical background of its component parts. Next, we must ask and answer questions about how these component parts are woven together to form the text as we now have it. The

---

Example of Source Criticism

The term "source criticism" is classically applied to the search for the sources used by biblical authors in composing their books. With regard to the Gospel of John, Rudolf Bultmann famously suggested that behind the Gospel's Prologue (1:1–18) and many of Jesus's lengthy discourses he could trace original discourses that came from early Gnostic literature. Similarly, many scholars claim that behind the series of events in John 6 (multiplication of the loaves and fishes, boat journey, Peter's confession) lies Mark 6:31–8:29. Others claim that John is using Luke's passion account (Luke 22–23; John 18–19). Source critics attempt to discover "sources" for the text they are analyzing and explain it in terms of a "reworking" of an original source. Although views are not unanimous, most critics think that John is using his own sources, many of which come out of oral tradition and certainly have contacts with the Synoptic tradition; but he does not use them as, for example, Matthew and Luke used Mark. When applied to the Gospels of Mark, Matthew, and Luke, the expression "source criticism" has traditionally described investigations of the literary dependence that might have existed between the three very similar, yet still different, lives of Jesus.

fundamental approach to reconstructing this world is **literary criticism**. Literary criticism analyzes the form and stylistic character of the text. We ask questions about genre, word choice, symbolism, and style of writing. The answers to these questions are crucial because they can set parameters for a judgment on the historical aspects of a text. If we see that the writer has employed poetry for a certain effect, or certain persuasive techniques to make a point, then we may realize that the historicity of the writing may not have been the writer's primary concern. We can also make decisions about the author's background and theological concerns as well as those of his intended audiences. With the New Testament, we know we are working with four gospels, an acts, twenty-one letters, and one apocalypse. All of these genres of literature have conventions of form and content. The authors adopt these generic customs and adapt them to their own personal styles. Literary critics then explore these stylistic characteristics to learn more about the author and what he is trying to teach through this medium.

We will discuss genre and the literary characteristics of the various New Testament books in more detail in later chapters. In addition, we will say more about the literary approach later on in this chapter, as it is our primary area of inquiry in this textbook.

Form criticism is a further step in literary criticism as it seeks to specify the literary form or subform of a given biblical passage. The questions an

---

Example of Literary Criticism

Several different things are indicated by the term "literary criticism." For many early critics, it meant source criticism as scholars debated the literary origins of each Gospel tradition. Nowadays, it is often used by scholars to refer to the parallels that exist between the literary style and unity of a passage, in comparison with great literature. For example, the Johannine Prologue (1:1–18) has the same literary function as the prologues used in Greek dramas: to inform the audience, before the action began, about the central features of the drama that they were about to witness. For others, it refers to the literary techniques used to analyze a passage. For example, another of John's literary traits is his tendency to state and restate the same message (John 6:25–51; 14:1–16:33). Literary criticism involves asking questions about these "literary features." Literary criticism is also used in the interpretation of the Synoptic Gospels (Mark, Matthew, and Luke) and the Letters of Paul. Literary critics identify structures such as repetitions used to capture the audience's attention and larger literary structures that enable an interpreter to define the beginning and end of a certain argument. A well-known example is Mark's use of two stories of the curing of blind men, in Mark 8:22–26 and 10:46–52, to open and close his account of Jesus's journey to Jerusalem with his disciples.

exegete asks in this type of criticism include whether the text is, for example, a hymn or psalm. If so, what kind? Is the text prophetic? Apocalyptic? Is a given gospel episode a parable? A miracle story? A pronouncement story? A historical narrative? The answers to all these questions set boundaries for the text and allow exegetes to make use of the customs and conventions of those forms to help them make sense of and interpret the text. Forms in the New Testament include poetry, narratives, miracles, discourses where Jesus gives extended teachings, and prayers, among others.

Redaction criticism is the final type of interaction with the world in the text that we will discuss. The verb "to redact" means to put into a suitable literary form for the author's purposes. The terms we may use more commonly include "to revise" or "to edit." Redaction criticism, therefore, seeks to determine how biblical writers have shaped, modified, developed, or "redacted" the source material they have inherited from other writers or from community traditions before them in the interest of their own literary or theological goals. If we have a strong sense of the sources writers used, we can ask questions about how they revised those sources and traditions and why they may have left some information in, taken some out, or tweaked

---

The Development of Form Criticism

Late in the nineteenth century and early in the twentieth, Gospel scholars devoted great attention and serious research into possible literary forms, situations in the life of Jesus, and the Christian community that determined the story. One of these was Rudolf Bultmann, who wrote a major handbook, heavily used to this day, called *The History of the Synoptic Tradition* (1921). His focus was upon the history that produced the Gospel texts. Bultmann wrote a significant commentary on the Gospel of John (1943) and made a major contribution to Pauline studies in various works.

Example of Form Criticism

A major development in biblical scholarship was to recognize that the material in the New Testament, and especially in the Gospels, repeated well-known "forms" of literature: miracle stories, parables, discourses, prayers, farewell speeches, hymns, and apocalyptic visions, to give a few examples. Every NT text is made up of these and other forms. John uses a number of these (miracle stories, discourses, a farewell speech) but other "forms" are absent (e.g., there are no parables). However much John may use literary forms, he often uses them in an unexpected fashion. Contemporary Johannine scholar Harold Attridge argues that the author practices "genre bending." He may use a "farewell discourse," but he uses it in a unique fashion, determined by his unique theology and rhetoric. We will suggest that a different John, the author of Revelation, also "bent" the use of the apocalyptic literary form. By contrast, the Synoptic Gospels reveal more conventional forms, such as the miracle story (e.g., Mark 1:29–3:1), the parable (e.g., Luke 15:11–32), the pronouncement story (e.g., Mark 2:15–17), the prophetic or apocalyptic saying (e.g., Matt 23:13–39; 25:1–13), and the similitude (e.g., Luke 17:7–10).

other aspects. The answers to these questions can shed light on the authors' concerns about the theological, political, or social situations that have compelled them to write in the first place. We can then suggest how these concerns might be relevant to our own times and situations.

Literary, form, and redaction criticisms are three basic approaches to the world in the text. These techniques help exegetes know how and why the Jesus movement and the authors of the New Testament generated the unified texts as they have been preserved for us. There are a number of features *within the text* that indicate why authors gathered the material in the ways they did. These are the elements that guide an interpreter attempting to uncover the world in the text. We will make use of these critical methods and note these features as we explore the New Testament books.

The World in Front of the Text

As we approach our final "world," it is important to recognize that the interpreter should always be aware that she or he depends upon all the different methods of approach. No one method should regard itself as the only way to understand the biblical text. We stand on the shoulders of those who went before us. This is very much the case as we turn our focus to the world in front of the text. This textbook's main concern will be the presentation of the New Testament from this perspective. But at no stage will we neglect the fact that our

---

The Development of Redaction Criticism

Many earlier interpreters suggested that each Gospel was driven by a unified theological point of view. However, the use of so-called redaction criticism became a part of the interpreter's trade after the work on the Gospel of Luke by Hans Conzelmann, *Die Mitte der Zeit* (*The Midpoint of Time*), in 1954. He asked that scholars continue to trace the traditions that formed the Gospels but focus their attention upon how an evangelist uses those traditions, placing them side by side in a deliberate sequence. What does the story as a whole proclaim?

Example of Redaction Criticism

Redaction critics classically trace the original source of any given passage (e.g., Mark 8:27–33) and examine how a later author has "redacted" the source, giving new meaning (e.g., how Matt 16:13–20 reshapes that passage from Mark 8:27–33). This is not easy for the Gospel of John, as its distinctiveness may prevent the discovery of his sources, but he has told a story that resulted from a deliberate choice of only some of the "signs that Jesus did in the presence of his disciples" (20:30), using this collection to tell a story that might lead his audience to ever great faith (v. 31). All the documents in the New Testament, especially the Gospels and the book of Revelation, have been "shaped" by an author to communicate a message to an audience. Not all authors are as clear as John 20:30-31, but interpretation strives to understand the overall theological argument of every document.

understanding of the New Testament depends upon the historical and literary studies that have been pursued for centuries by many great and hard-working scholars. Nor should we ignore the fact that the New Testament has been the source of reflection and commentary in the life of the Christian churches for almost two thousand years. What follows as an introduction to learning about the world in front of the texts builds upon what we have seen in the worlds behind and in the text. But it transposes them into another key. Now this message is not only in a printed text, but in the eyes, ears, and hearts of people who are reading this text, hearing it read, or even seeing it performed.

As we work our way through the good news of Jesus recorded in the New Testament, we will find that it makes a strong impression upon its readers and hearers because of patterns of repetition. We read or hear the central message of the New Testament articulated in various ways and by means of different literary forms, over and over again. It has often been said that the message of the New Testament is very simple, but very deep. Its simplicity comes from the fact that it is the same message, stated and restated throughout the telling of the stories and the commentaries of the letters. Building upon what we have seen in our reflections upon the worlds behind and in the text, we suggest that the world in front of the text can be discovered through narrative criticism, rhetorical criticism, and what we call audience-response criticism.

Narrative criticism concentrates on the communicative power of stories as a means of transmitting the word of God. Throughout history, people have often passed on messages or made argumentative points by telling a story. When an author chooses narrative as the mode of communication, this is itself part of the message. Telling a story resonates with the lived experience of audiences and al-

---

The Development of Narrative Criticism

A significant event in the appreciation of the Gospel of John as a unique literary contribution was the publication of *Anatomy of the Fourth Gospel: A Study in Literary Design* by R. Alan Culpepper (1983). Guided by Frank Kermode, a renowned literary critic, Culpepper analyzed such elements as the use of plot, time, characters, etc. in the Gospel of John, using the methods of contemporary literary criticism. This approach to the text, which is similar to redaction criticism in focusing upon the whole of the narrative as a single utterance, but which does not follow redaction criticism into an identification of sources, has led to the approach known as narrative criticism. Interpretation does not depend upon sources but on the narrative appeal of the story itself to audiences. All of this was made possible by a volume called *Mark as Story: An Introduction to the Narrative of a Gospel* by David Rhoads, Joanna Dewey, and Donald Michie (1982, 1999, 2012), which formally introduced biblical studies to the discipline of narrative criticism.

lows these readers to identify with or distance themselves from various aspects of and characters in the story. Further, within the narrative, authors select from among so many events that could be shared, how they will be narrated, and in what order. This selection is made so that an author can best communicate the message as he or she intends it to be received. Thus, the way an author tells his or her story determines its meaning. When we ask questions that approach the biblical texts only as compilations of data, we fail to take seriously the power of storytelling and the agency of the authors who chose to share their messages as narratives. Interpreters who use this technique, therefore, seek to reckon with the Bible's narrative accounts: stories with plots, characters, and climaxes. The Gospels are stories about the good news of Jesus that are intended to be read from beginning to end. Narrative critics therefore ask questions about plot and storylines as well as how authors shape characters and develop stories to achieve a certain outcome by the conclusion.

Similarly, **rhetorical criticism** analyzes the persuasive character of the text. The term "rhetoric" refers to using language effectively through word choice and figures of speech in order to influence an audience. These techniques, sometimes called "rhetorical devices," are used by authors and speakers to affect audiences and to arouse in them certain reactions, emotions, values, and inter-

---

Example of Narrative Criticism

Narrative critics devote great attention to the inner workings, the flow, and the communication process that goes on *inside the narrative*. Although not without interest in the historical setting that generated the narrative, the workings of the narrative itself are most important. In John 20, for example, the author leads the audience from one episode to another, as people respond to the empty tomb, the message that Jesus has been raised, and the appearances of Jesus. Tension mounts as Mary Magdalene, Simon Peter, and the Beloved Disciple from the Gospel demonstrate no faith, partial faith, and true faith. The reader is being led from one episode to another, until Jesus issues his final words to the characters in the story: "Blessed are those who have not seen, and yet have come to believe" (v. 29).

The reader recalls that the Beloved Disciple believed (v. 8) but did not see the risen Jesus. The stage is now set for the author to tell the reader why he wrote his Gospel: "that you may go on believing" (AT: v. 31). By means of this narrative, the implied author has persuaded the implied reader about the need for strong faith to have life in the name of Jesus. Likewise, in the first half of the Gospel of Mark, a series of episodes are placed side by side to enable the audience to follow a narrative from one bread miracle (Mark 6:31–44) to another (8:1–10). Between those two "bookends," the audience follows a series of encounters in 6:45–7:37 between Jesus and others that often deal with the question of "eating"—for better or for worse in the relationship between the characters in the story and Jesus.

ests. Rhetorical critics ask questions in an effort to uncover the author's agenda and determine the message of the writing as a whole. While narrative criticism is particularly helpful with biblical books like the Gospels, rhetorical criticism is largely used with the letters and more essay-oriented texts. For example, when an author chooses to write a letter, that is part of the message. As we will see in the letters of the New Testament, the communication often becomes personal as the author makes various appeals to the recipients of his story. Nonetheless, the techniques of both of these types of criticism can be used across genres to great benefit. Further, these critical approaches also cross the worlds in and in front of the text. We gather our data about the narrative and its rhetoric from the texts; this information has its most profound effect on the world in front of the text as audiences respond to its influence.

What we are calling **audience-response criticism** is really a combination of two other types of analysis that have developed in recent years: reader-response

---

Example of Rhetorical Criticism

The sidebar on narrative criticism indicates that the Gospels have their own "rhetoric." They are all written to "persuade" readers to accept truths about God, Jesus Christ, and what it means to have life from faith in him. Thus, one of their rhetorical aims is to "communicate truths of faith." There are other "rhetorics," and many elements in a written document are rhetorical, i.e., written in order to have a desired effect (e.g., a letter written to a loved one always has rhetorical impact). This is especially clear in 1 John. It is clear that the community has divided (see 1 John 2:19). There are varying understandings of God and Jesus Christ, and the letter is written to confirm the correct understanding of what God has done in Jesus and the fact that the human person of Jesus was indeed the Christ and the Son of God. The same can be said of every document in the New Testament, from some of the longest (e.g., Hebrews) to the shortest (e.g., Jude). Indeed, powerful Pauline rhetoric is found in the deeply moving passages that address the audience at the end of his reflections on life in the Spirit (Rom 8:31–39) and his appeal to God's wisdom as he closes his questioning of the relationship between Judaism and the coming of Jesus Christ (Rom 11:33–36).

A good example of the rhetoric used by the author of 1 John can be found at the letter's beginning. After affirming the truth of what the community learned "from the beginning" of their lives as Johannine Christians, in a series of accusations, he points out that there are now some who have a different opinion. They are pointedly described: "If we say that we have fellowship with him while we are walking in darkness . . ." (1:6); "If we say that we have no sin . . ." (1:8); "Whoever says 'I have come to know him,' and does not obey his commandments . . ." (2:4); "Whoever says 'I am in the light,' while hating a brother and sister . . ." (2:9). They are wrong! The author is rhetorically indicating that certain people have strayed from the truth. Their teaching must not be accepted, while that of the author continues what they learned "in the beginning." Rhetoric is a way of writing (and speaking) that makes a point strongly and clearly by means of different techniques.

criticism and performance criticism. Which type of audience-response criticism one is investigating depends upon whether the interpreter envisions the audience of the text as an individual reader or a group who is seeing and hearing a storyteller sharing the text orally. Both types of transmission certainly occur in our world, which includes individual silent readings as well as multimedia productions on stage and screen. Scholars have also shown that both types of transmission occurred in the ancient world as well. **Reader-response criticism** focuses on the act of reading itself. Different readers and groups of readers will have different responses to a given text. This approach asks what those might be and how the author may have been envisioning and using potential responses in the construction of his story. In recent years, some scholars have also begun to argue for the centrality of performance in the early life of the church. Therefore, **performance criticism** has emerged as a discipline to inquire about the impact of this oral and aural culture. Performance critics ask questions about the multifaceted sensory experience that develops between storytellers and audiences in the oral culture of formal and informal story and letter sharing that sustained the early Christian traditions. Realizing that authors knew that their works

---

Example of Audience Response Criticism

In recent years, critics have become more aware that most early Christians were not literate—they either heard these texts read or saw them performed. There are often signs that a narrative was deliberately constructed for oral communication and for performance. The text, as we have it written, was to make an impact in an oral world, drawing an intellectual and emotional response from the audience. A fine example of this is found in John 18:28–19:16a: Jesus's trial before Pilate. After setting the scene (very dramatically, as the light of day opens, in v. 28), the so-called trial takes place "outside" and "inside" the praetorium. Pilate comes out, Pilate and Jesus go in, Pilate and Jesus come out, Pilate and Jesus go in, etc. Verbs of motion mark changes of location. Outside, Pilate presents Jesus as innocent and the King of the Jews. Inside, Pilate becomes increasingly under the impact of Jesus, finally asking the key Johannine question: "Where are you from?" (19:9).

At the center of this dramatic change of location, associated with the gradual recognition as a rejected king, Jesus is ironically and mockingly crowned and dressed as a king (19:1–3). An audience follows the movement, the different voices, abuse, ironic confessions of the truth, and the rejection of that truth. This audience is both intellectually and emotionally involved as it responds to a story that ends: "Then he handed him over to them to be crucified" (19:16a). Although not as dramatically sophisticated as John 18–19, a case can be made that the final verses of Mark, ending with the failure of the women to communicate the message of Jesus's resurrection and the need to go to Galilee (Mark 16:6–8), were deliberately written to shock the audience into examining their own belief in the resurrection in the midst of their failures. Such examples are found at every turn of the narrative texts of the New Testament.

would be seen and heard as well as read, performance critical techniques focus on the cues they may have embedded in their texts as "stage directions" or how seeing and hearing the spoken text may affect how it is received by audiences and how they may respond to it.

Narrative, rhetorical, and audience-response criticisms are three widely used approaches to discovering the world in front of the text. This world is expansive and marked by great diversity. Engaging this world can, in many ways, be the most creative and satisfying aspect of biblical scholarship. This means, however, that these types of criticism can also lead to irresponsible methods and unfounded, even dangerous conclusions. We must caution, one more time then, to explore all the worlds of the text in conjunction with each other in order to preserve the ancient meanings while also answering the questions of inquiring audiences today.

As we bring this foray into the worlds of biblical interpretation—exegesis—to a conclusion, we can suggest that these critical techniques are all geared to one end: to determine the meaning of the sacred text as it was intended by the human author, moved long ago to compose it, and to ascertain what it is saying to readers today. Stories and letters of the good news of Jesus, written almost two thousand years ago, made sense to its readers and listeners *then* (the world behind and in the text). It continues to make sense to believing readers and listeners *today* (the world in front of the text). We will ask a variety of questions of these sorts across the rest of the course as we uncover the complexity and beauty of the New Testament.

Exegeting Biblical Texts

When biblical scholars discuss using different critical approaches to the text, the concept of **hermeneutics** often arises. The term "hermeneutics" comes from the Greek word for "interpretation" and is used in biblical scholarship to refer to a particular interpretive approach. Although, as we discussed above, it is crucial for exegetes to incorporate critical techniques from all the worlds of the text, it is difficult—if not impossible—for a single interpreter to responsibly address every angle a complex text presents. Indeed, a scholar may not be interested in answering every possible question that may arise when studying a text. Therefore, biblical scholars often have a particular hermeneutic, that is, specific concerns or interpretive interests, when inquiring into a text. Various important hermeneutics have developed in biblical scholarship that have added a great deal to the discussion and brought to light many important components of this literature, including feminist, liberation, and cultural criticisms.

Feminist criticism seeks the historical and literary recovery of the role of women in the ancient world in general and the biblical story in particular and tries to point out the dangers of interpretation. **Liberationist criticism**

approaches the text from the perspective that God opposes all aspects of human oppression and seeks to realize here on earth the reality that all people are created equally. **Cultural criticism** approaches the text with the desire to undercut the monopolization of culture by the elite in community and makes room for cultural expressions of the masses. These hermeneutics allow more emphasis on subjectivity, that is, how a given text affects the interpreter as well as specific groups and periods of time of which the interpreter is knowledgeable. These approaches add many more important voices to the discussion of the exegesis of the biblical literature—voices that have often been ignored or even suppressed in the past. For the Bible and biblical study to remain relevant in our contemporary world and into the future, these voices must have a place at the table and be heard. In addition to what it adds to the exegesis of a text, the key in taking any hermeneutical stance is for the interpreter to be self-aware of his or her position. This will allow for a more responsible, balanced approach to the text. Whether one has a feminist, a historic, a literary, or any other hermeneutic, acknowledging this interest and focus will further the discussion in an open and explicit manner. As we have indicated already in this chapter, the hermeneutic of this textbook and its authors is primarily literary. We find questions about genre, plot, narrative structure, symbolism, language choice, themes, and characteristics more important to explore and answer than questions about historical facticity, sources, layers of composition, or the like. We build upon the world behind the text in order to explore the worlds in and in front of it.

This literary critical hermeneutic results in a continuous two-level reading of the text. Again, as exegetes, we are always asking questions of the text. We can introduce these two levels in terms of asking questions about the author and what the author is trying to do. We can ask, what does the author say, and what is the author trying to teach? When we are working with narratives, these are clearly two distinct questions, and across our study of the narratives of the New Testament, we will make both types of inquiry. When, however, we are working with letters, the distinction is not so strong. Often what the authors say and what they are trying to teach are the same. Indeed, they may not be trying to teach anything. Instead, they are simply giving travel plans or personal health wishes. At other times, they are explicitly teaching, that is, articulating what the recipients should or should not believe

Other Types of Biblical Criticism

In the twentieth and twenty-first centuries, a number of additional critical methods have developed to give voice to the variety of contexts in our global culture and the particular questions that emerge from these experiences. They include but are not limited to:

anthropological criticism
black criticism
canonical criticism
de-colonial and post-colonial criticism
Jewish traditions criticism
minoritized criticism
psychological/psychoanalytic criticism
reception criticism
semiotic criticism
sociological criticism
womanist criticism

or do. Therefore, we will not make this distinction in our questions so often when we study the letters of the New Testament. That said, even letter writers sometimes tell stories to make a point, or quote Scripture or some other source to teach a lesson. In those cases, we attend to both levels of the text.

In narratives in general, and the Gospels, Acts, and Revelation in particular, storytellers create plots, characters, and settings. They reveal information about the world of their story while they entertain or inform. Characters move from place to place, encounter other characters, are faced with crises and decisions, etc., all as the plot unfolds to a climax and eventual resolution. This is what we can call the **narrative level of the text**. In the Gospels, for example, Jesus, his disciples, and potential opponents are introduced early, they move through the regions of Galilee, Judea, and Samaria in the eastern Roman Empire along the Mediterranean coast, meet new people, face opposition, etc., all leading to the climax of Jesus's arrest, death, and resurrection. This narrative level of the text tells something about Jesus and his disciples, as well as Judaism and the Greco-Roman world in the first half of the first century CE. However, the Gospels do not and cannot tell everything about these people or their world. They are also not objective tellings in the sense of a camera following these people around simply showing what happens without comment. In fact, what we have are authors who themselves do not know everything about the life of Jesus, who further select from what they do know to shape the story they want to tell. They then further insert themselves as narrators to shape and comment upon what they do tell.

All storytellers shape their traditions and information in such a way to evoke responses from their intended audiences. This is certainly true for fictional narratives that derive largely from an author's imagination, but it is also the case for stories that render actual historical events and people. Whether an author is telling a bedtime story to a small child or sharing the news of the day, that author shapes the story or events to give a message, to teach a lesson, or to evoke a response to or from that intended audience. We can call this message sharing, on the part of authors through the stories they tell, the **discourse level of the text**. The term "discourse" can mean different things in different contexts, but its basic definition refers to written or spoken communication. Through the discourse level of the text, therefore, the author is communicating something beyond the content of the story. In the New Testament, in addition to telling us something about Jesus and his mission (the narrative level), the authors are also continually teaching us what all this means and how we should and should not act accordingly. This discourse level is strongly determined by the world of the author and the events and crises he or she may be facing. The evangelists write their stories of Jesus several decades after the events of Jesus's life and several decades into the Christian movement spawned by Jesus's mission. We will discuss this world of the evangelists in more detail in later chapters, but for now we can say that they write from their *particular* perspectives for communities that need to be told a *particular* story in a *particular* way. They infuse their messages to their intended audiences throughout the narratives. Therefore, we can also call this discourse level the teaching level of the text, and we must attend to what the evangelists are trying to *teach* us about what Jesus and the life that results from his mission mean right alongside our attention to what they *tell* us

about who Jesus was, where he went, what happened to him, etc. In exegeting Revelation, tracing the discourse or teaching level of the text is also important and rendered more complex because it is more universal, and symbols are used: God, angels and other heavenly beings, satanic characters, prophets, women, cities, the author John, etc., all play their part in the narrative.

The narrative level of the text is the story that the biblical authors tell, and the discourse level of the text is the meaning of these people and events that the biblical authors teach. Thorough exegesis draws out both levels of any text. What this means for our project in this textbook is that, as we move into a closer exegesis of the books of the New Testament, we will both *summarize* what happens in each text (the narrative level) and *analyze* the meaning of each text. We will therefore ask both what the biblical authors are saying and what they are teaching by saying what they say *in the way they do.*

> **Narrative and Discourse Levels of the Text**
>
> Central to a critical interpretation of narratives is the distinction between what is said as the story (the narrative) unfolds, step by step, and the overall message that the author wants to communicate (the discourse) by telling the story in a particular fashion. Although this has long been recognized, the work of Seymour Chatman, *Story and Discourse: Narrative Structure in Fiction and Film* (1978), has been influential upon New Testament narrative critics. As the title of the book indicates, Chatman did not focus upon New Testament narratives. However, his theoretical understanding of the way narrative works remains important for biblical scholars today.

The **methodology of exegesis** provides a fairly standard process for exegeting a text along these lines. We begin with a broad knowledge of the world behind the text and then move to more specifics. We then turn to the world in the text. The first step here has to do with structure and literary flow of the narrative. By establishing a broad outline of the text, we are respecting the fact that the author chose to write, for example, a story as opposed to a letter, a sermon, or any other genre of literature. Particular genres unfold in certain manners, and knowing where we are in those genres helps us exegete any particular passage. Thereafter, we explore and exegete the text along this structure. In this way, we can make sense of what happens when. Once we discuss and develop the literary context of a given passage or narrative unit, we then explore in greater detail what occurs in it (the narrative level). This will lead us to suggest what it reveals about the world behind the text and what the author may intend audiences to do as a result (the discourse level and the world in front of the text). In the end, we draw all this together to answer what we might call the "so what?" question. So what have we learned, and what does it all mean? This, of course, is the goal of exegesis.

This process is customary in exegeting any passage, with adaptations particular to a scholar's context or needs. A "to-do" list of the exegesis of a given passage could therefore look like this:

1. Introduction and Thesis: Here an exegete might introduce the overall text and context as well as establish the thesis for this particular exegetical project. The questions this thesis might want to answer are, "Why does the author tell this story/write this letter in this way? Why is this passage important in the overall text? And what is the author teaching audiences by presenting this passage in this manner?"

2. Context and Structure: Here an exegete might ask and answer relevant questions about the world behind the text. The exegete might also establish where audiences are in the larger text and what this means for interpretation. In other words, are we at the beginning of the text? The middle? The end? How might establishing this location in the flow of the narrative/letter/apocalypse help us interpret it? The exegete could provide a detailed structure for the outline of the text in question. Again, how we understand the way authors structure passages helps us understand what they intend to narrate and teach.

3. Exegetical Analysis: Here an exegete might take on each component of the outline established in the previous section to provide a close analysis of the constituent parts of the overall passage. Exegetes gather data from all the worlds of the text and bring them to bear from their particular hermeneutics in order to draw out the author's intended meaning.

4. Conclusion: Here an exegete brings it all together to answer that "so what?" question. The thesis that was introduced and has been threaded through the exegesis is concluded in terms of what the passage means for people of both the first century and today.

The content of this to-do list is not a novel idea. Rather, it reflects a process that will allow for a strong, responsible exegesis from a particular hermeneutic. The succeeding chapters in this textbook will exegete the books of the New Testament, following this pattern through a literary-critical hermeneutic. In this way, we hope to bring to life the texts in terms of their meaning for both first-century and twenty-first-century audiences.

What Have We Learned So Far? The Worlds That Created and Are Created by the Text

Much like the previous chapter, this chapter has not focused on new information regarding the components of theology as expressed in the New Testament. Since this chapter has provided a brief overview of the methodology for scholarly exegesis of the Bible, there has been little focus on theology. We mentioned in the previous chapter that in the ancient world, there was no separation between the religious, political, social, and literary worlds. In this same vein, the endeavor of biblical interpretation was first engaged by people of faith inquiring about God's message to them and interaction with their lives and the lives of their communities. This continues to be the case today. The succeeding chapters will therefore have much more to add to this component of our study.

Key Terms and Concepts

audience-response criticism

criticism

cultural criticism

discourse level of the text

exegesis

feminist criticism

form criticism

hermeneutics

historical-critical method

historical criticism

liberationist criticism

literary criticism

methodology of exegesis

narrative criticism

narrative level of the text

performance criticism

reader-response criticism

redaction criticism

rhetorical criticism

scribes

source criticism

textual criticism

world behind the text

world in front of the text

world in the text

worlds of the text

Questions for Review

1. What is meant by the term "exegesis"?
2. Briefly describe what is meant by the approaches of biblical interpretation that consider "the world behind the text," "the world in the text," and "the world in front of the text."
3. What is textual criticism, and why is it important in establishing the text of the Bible?
4. What is literary criticism, and why is understanding genres and literary forms so important in interpreting the Bible?

5. How do audiences shape and how are they shaped by the biblical text? Why might understanding these potential responses aid in biblical interpretation?

6. What is meant by the narrative and discourse levels of a biblical text? Why must an exegete always keep an eye on each of these levels?

7. How should an exegete approach his or her task with a particular biblical text? What might a to-do list look like?

Bibliography and Further Reading

Adam, A. K. M. *What Is Post-Modern Biblical Criticism?* Edited by by Dan O. Via Jr. Guides to Biblical Scholarship. New Testament Series. Minneapolis: Fortress, 1995.

Carvalho, Corrine. *Primer on Biblical Methods.* Winona, MN: Anselm Academic, 2009.

Cone, James. *God of the Oppressed.* Maryknoll, NY: Orbis Books, 1997.

Dawes, Gregory. *Introduction to the Bible.* New Collegeville Bible Commentary: Old Testament. Vol. 1. Collegeville, MN: Liturgical, 2007.

Fitzmyer, Joseph A. *Scripture, the Soul of Theology.* New York: Paulist, 1994.

Gutiérrez, Gustavo. *A Theology of Liberation: History, Politics, and Salvation* (15th Anniversary Edition with New Introduction by Author). Maryknoll, NY: Orbis Books, 1988.

Iverson, Kelly, ed. *From Text to Performance: Narrative and Performance Criticisms in Dialogue and Debate.* Biblical Performance Criticism 10. Eugene, OR: Wipf & Stock, 2014.

Junior, Nyasha. *An Introduction to Womanist Biblical Interpretation.* Louisville: Westminster John Knox, 2015.

Perry, Peter S. *Insights from Performance Criticism.* Reading the Bible in the Twenty-First Century: Insights. Minneapolis: Fortress, 2016.

Powell, Mark A. *What Is Narrative Criticism?* Guides to Biblical Scholarship: New Testament Series. Minneapolis: Fortress, 1990.

Reid, Barbara E., O.P. *Wisdom's Feast: An Invitation to Feminist Interpretation of the Scriptures.* Grand Rapids: Eerdmans, 2016.

Rhoads, David. "Performance Criticism: An Emerging Methodology in Second Testament Studies." *Biblical Theological Bulletin* 36 (2006): 118–40, 164–88.

Wasserman, Tommy, and Peter J. Gurry. *A New Approach to Textual Criticism: An Introduction to the Coherence-Based Genealogical Method.* Atlanta: SBL Press; Stuttgart: Deutsche Bibelgesellschaft, 2017.

The Old Testament Story: Israel and Covenant with God

PURPOSE Chapter three presents an overview of the story of Israel as it is preserved in the Christian Old Testament. In this way, both the world of the New Testament authors and the world behind the texts they composed on behalf of their communities are also introduced.

In this chapter, we will trace the thread of the narrative of the history and development of Judaism as it is woven through the Jewish Scriptures. The many books that tell the story of Israel were written at different times and places and by authors who sometimes report events in different ways. That need not bother us, as the final product of this complex history of writing tells its own story. The biblical story of Israel can be traced by following the accounts in the OT books in the way they have come down to us. Indeed, this was the way that Jesus, the early church, the NT authors, and their audiences understood the story of God's people. Therefore, we will not overly concern ourselves with the world behind these texts, but rather focus on the worlds in and in front of them so that we can get a sense of how first-century CE Jewish people might have understood their history in relationship with God, with each other, and with the rest of the world. We can also begin to form a picture of how some Jewish people, including the NT authors and their communities, might have understood God to be acting in and through Jesus to offer a new development in that relationship. What follows is thus not close, technical exegesis of the Old Testament—that is an entire course in its own right!—but a broad overview of the story, highlighting key figures and their roles in the history and theology of Judaism. As a result, when we come across these people and concepts in the New Testament, we will have a better understanding of who and what they are and why they are important in these NT texts.

The Story of Israel

As we read through the OT, a basic component of the narrative history that emerges is that a single God is creator and ruler of all. This is known as **monotheism**. Further, this God interacts with the created world in a relationship that is described as a **covenant**. The Jewish people trace their story to the beginning of creation and come to understand themselves as having a unique covenant relationship with God. As this story develops, some basic characteristics of what is meant by a covenant relationship also materialize: one party of the covenant (God) is vastly more knowledgeable, more powerful, and more "sighted" than the other (humans). In every instance, then, God *knows*, can *do*, and can *see* things in creation and history that the human parties do not and cannot know, do, or see. This constant feature of the relationship between God and humankind means God is always the initiating agent of these covenants. This gives God encompassing *authority* in this relationship, while the human participants are always called to some form of *obedience*. There are always binding promises and obligations at play. In the first century CE when the earliest Christians—who were Jewish people—described their experiences of Jesus, they understood God to be acting in and through Jesus in this same fashion. When the evangelists set out to compose their gospel stories, they saw them as the continuation of this same story of God's relationship with humankind. To prepare ourselves for their stories, therefore, we must begin at the beginning—the *genesis*—of their people Israel's story as they would have understood it.

Monotheism

The belief in only one deity is called monotheism. In the ancient world, the major religions were polytheistic, meaning they had several, and often many, deities. Ancient Israel was exceptional in its firm belief in one Sovereign Creator God. This was still the case as Judaism developed in the first century CE. Today the world's major monotheistic religions—Judaism, Christianity, and Islam—profess belief in the same God.

The Beginnings of God's Work in Creation as Preserved in Genesis 1–11 (Primeval History)

The Old Testament narrative begins with the book of Genesis, which, as its name indicates, tells the story of the creation of the world by the one sovereign creator God and then the story of the birth of Judaism. The text can be divided in the broadest sense into two parts. Genesis 1–11 is, in this sense, an account of the primordial history of the known world. The text then moves into the more specific account of the ancestry of the people of Israel in Genesis 12–50. Even though Israel did not yet exist as God's people, the first part narrates several key episodes in how the Jewish people understand who God is and how God

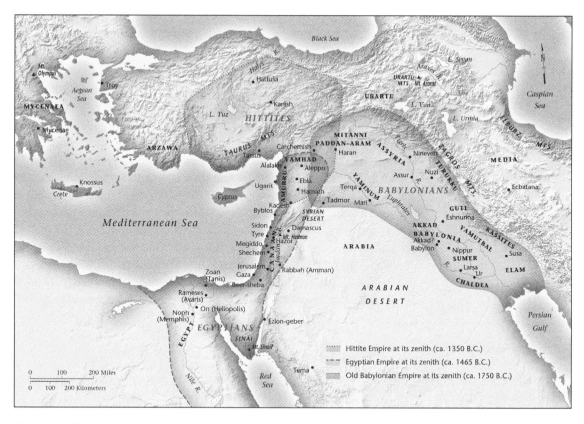

Hittite Empire at its zenith (ca. 1350 B.C.)

Egyptian Empire at its zenith (ca. 1465 B.C.)

Old Babylonian Empire at its zenith (ca. 1750 B.C.)

REGION OF MESOPOTAMIA

works in the world in relationship to creation and all humankind. These and other narratives across the Old Testament give what are called **etiologies**. An etiology is a study of causes or origins. Therefore, an **etiological story** explains in narrative form how something or some custom or practice came to be in the world or in a particular community. Genesis 1–3 tells the story of creation itself as well as the story of the first human beings and their relationship with God. These first chapters of Genesis are a good example of an "etiological story." Written during difficult times in Israel's history, the authors want to show that in the *beginning* everything was good and that the evil and division experienced by the people did not *begin* with God's creation. It came about because of the disobedience of human beings. After a lengthy genealogy in Genesis 5 that moves us several centuries forward in history, Genesis 6–9 tells the story of Noah, his ark, and the flood that God sends over the earth. Another genealogy in Genesis 10 is sometimes called the Table of Nations and lays out the diversity of peoples who have developed over the millennia and leads to the story of the Tower of Babel in Genesis 11. This event becomes a catalyst in God's choosing of Abraham as the eventual father of the Jewish people. The following paragraphs will give a bit more detail on these initial chapters of Jewish Scripture as they set the pattern for how God works in the world, how the world itself works, and how humankind is created to respond to God.

The beginning of Israel's story tells of God's word of creation. God literally spoke creation into being (1:1–2:4a). Communication thus becomes the basis of relationship, and relationship becomes the basis of God's interaction with creation. God creates the world as we know it in a pattern of days that systematically expands the creative act until God can rest and reflect on its goodness on the seventh day. God gives **Adam**, the first human and pinnacle of creation, life and food and shelter and then culminates this relationship in the gift of community with the creation of Adam's partner, the woman who is eventually named Eve. The promise of this relationship is Eden, the garden that represents the ideal dwelling place in peace with the created order. In return, God demands obedience. Living in harmony with God and the rest of creation is dependent upon their refraining from eating from the tree of the knowledge of good and evil. In short order, however, Adam and Eve fail: they disobey when Eve is lured by the serpent, the cleverest of all creatures, into eating from

---

Literary Forms in the OT

In addition to **etiologies** (short narratives that serve to explain the origin or meaning of elements of daily life such as customs, names, or rituals), several other literary forms are prominent in the OT. Examples include:

Myth: a narrative that explains profound human truths through the interaction of the divine with the earthly or human. Myths typically express a group's self-understanding of identity and serve to bond the community members together. Scholars speak of the creation myth or the Exodus myth in the OT without judgment about their historicity.

Legend: a narrative, typically of exaggerated history from a core historical event. Legends usually develop around larger-than-life community heroes and tend to magnify their accomplishments. Scholars can speak of legends of the patriarchs or the David legend.

Law code: a series of behavioral precepts concerning interpersonal ethics and/or ritual worship life in the community. In this vein, Exodus 20:19–23:33 is often referred to as the Covenant Code, while Deuteronomy 12–26 is called the Deuteronomic Code.

Call story: a brief narrative that portrays the call of an important person by God. Typically, (1) God appears in some form, (2) God commissions a person to a task, (3) the person responds, often offering an objection, and (4) then God insists and reassures the one called. Call stories are typical in the prophets but occur across the Scriptures.

Psalms: brief songs or hymns that typically fall into one of several categories: praise, laments, thanksgiving, repentance, royal celebration, wisdom, or historical memory.

Proverbs: short popular sayings that communicate a practical truth, observation, or guide to good living in a pithy, easily remembered form.

the fruit of the tree. The lesson here has to do not with serpents and apples but with forgoing immediate gratification and looking to long-term rewards, as well as taking responsibility for one's own decisions. As a result of Adam and Eve's disobedience, the perfect union of their relationship with God is broken. The reestablishment of right relationship with God becomes the guiding force of the rest of the Jewish Scriptures.

Sin and death enter the world through this disobedience and quickly spread as humankind grows. The story of Adam and Eve's first children, Cain and Abel, and Cain's falling into sin in killing his brother out of jealousy establishes how quickly disorder takes root in creation (Gen 4). The narrative is careful to illustrate, however, that God never breaks fidelity to his promises. Even as Adam and Eve lose their right to Eden, God clothes and prepares them for the life they have chosen (Gen 3:21). Likewise, God protects Cain even as Cain has to live out his life in the consequences of his actions. Further, God gives Adam and Eve a third son, Seth, to continue the line of humankind in creation, which leads to the founding of Judaism. God begins to rectify this relationship with creation by making a covenant with Noah.

The story of **Noah** and his experience of covenant with God makes up Genesis 6–9. Genesis 6 opens with a strange and provocative story of the spread of humankind that is consonant with the multiplication of evil across the earth. Humankind, to whom the earth was given and whose inclination was to be for God, is focused only on evil. God's heart was aggrieved, and he determined to "un-create" through the flood. But Noah found favor in the eyes of God (Gen 6:8), ensuring that "re-creation" would follow. Noah is characterized immediately as a father who is "righteous," "blameless," and who "walked with God" (Gen 6:9–10). Because of this character, God chooses Noah and through him and his obedient action saves the best of what was already created. God gives Noah his reasoning for re-creation through a coming flood and then instructs Noah to build an ark—a boat in the middle of the desert. This command emphasizes the obedience that is demanded of Noah, and Noah's unyielding response in action confirms his integrity. In response, God establishes a covenant with Noah. Genesis 7–8 details the flood itself as God does as promised, allowing the waters of the deep and the heavens to burst forth. God then begins to speak to Noah again and once more opens with another command, this time, "Go out." Noah again responds in full obedience to God's call. This second act of response in action is followed by Noah's first initiating action as he builds an altar and offers a burnt sacrifice. God gives his blessing to Noah and affirms the sanctity of life, particularly human life, however limited and transient. Genesis 9 then turns to God's covenant with Noah. What was promised before the flood comes to fruition as part of the re-creative communication. God makes his covenant with Noah and his offspring as well as with all of the re-created order. The covenant is eternal, and creation will never again be destroyed. Noah, the primary human character

Adam and Eve
by Albrecht Dürer

of this account, is silent throughout. God initiates all the action and does all
the speaking. Noah's response is in his action, and by his obedient action he
accepts God's word of covenant and lives in accord with that relationship, thus
facilitating God's covenant with all creation.

Genesis 6–9 therefore tells the story of God's work in creation, beginning
anew through Noah. God's relationship with humankind, however, needs more
story as the early chapters of Genesis close with the confusion and scattering of
humankind following the attempted construction of the **Tower of Babel** (Gen
11). The people of God's creation continue to show that although they have an

The Tower of Babel by
Pieter Bruegel the Elder

innate desire to live in right relationship with God, they also have tendencies to look for other means of fulfillment. They often follow human authority and the desires of this world. The culmination of these latter tendencies is narrated as the people determine to build a tower to get to the heavens and God and "make a name" for themselves. The narrative of Genesis thus far has shown us that the people are meant to be "calling on the name" of God. God therefore thwarts these attempts by "confusing" their language and "scattering" the people over the face of the earth. This scattering symbolizes the radical break in the relationship between God and humankind as the opposite of the unity for which it was created. This entire episode also becomes an etiological story for the many languages of humankind as well as how people came to populate the entire earth.

The narrative then moves forward several hundred years by way of a genealogy, further symbolizing this breakdown in the relationship. From this point forward, God will never again walk with his creation in the garden, or anywhere else for that matter. The distance between God and his creation only grows. The characterization of the fearsome and awesome power of God also expands. From what we have shared from Genesis 1–11, we can see how this profound story informs Israel about God, creation, sin, blessing and protection from God, and the divisions among peoples, nations, and languages. This is how it all began.

Abraham and the Jewish Ancestors as Preserved
in Genesis 12–50 (ca. 1800 BCE)

The second part of the book of Genesis, chapters 12–50, covers the ancestral period of the history of Israel. It begins with a man called Abram, whom God eventually renames **Abraham** (Gen 17:5). We will devote several pages to this portion of the story, since it is foundational to the story that follows. The Abraham cycle of stories begins at Genesis 12 and runs through Genesis 23. Scholars tend to call these stories of the patriarchs—a term that means something like "father-leader"—cycles. They are called cycles because they are repetitive and spiral into the next one. Genesis 12 is traditionally understood to recount the call of Abraham. After several centuries of apparent silence, God calls out to one person: "Now God said to Abram, 'Go . . .'" (v. 1). And that one person responds, taking his family and all that he owns with him: "So Abram went . . ." (v. 4). Once again, the narrative recounts God's call in terms of command and the chosen one's response in action in terms of precise obedience. And for his obedience Abram receives the assurance of blessing—a great nation and a great name—along with the covenantal obligation of invoking the name of the Lord in blessing or cursing those he encounters (vv. 2–3). After the radical break with all creation at Genesis 11, God chooses to work in terms of one man—of individual faith and practice. From this action, we find the new basis for a people of God. In response to God's call at Genesis 12, Abram moves his wife, Sarai (eventually renamed Sarah), and his nephew, Lot, to Canaan.

Crucial for our study is not only God's covenant with Abraham, but also the journey, of both body and spirit, which is integral to the content and the purpose of that relationship. In the narrative, God's relationship with Abraham grows as Abraham grows. Abraham's movement, therefore, is not only physical but spiritual as well, as he moves from pure response in action accompanied by a faith riddled with doubt to a response in action that is grounded in the fullness of faith. Doubt overtakes Abraham almost immediately as he endangers Sarah, the promised matriarch, to the hands of Pharaoh (12:10–20). This doubt continues to hinder Abraham's faith even as he continues to respond in action. Thus, his is a move from strict obedience to obedience in faith. And this is what is eventually credited as righteousness (15:6).

In Genesis 13, God once again commands Abraham to go, and Abraham complies. This new act of obedience is followed by Abraham's overwhelming success in rescuing Lot from eastern kings, exemplifying his ability to protect his people and overcome his enemies (14:1–24). The proof of this blessing, and Abraham's acknowledgment of it, brings him to the first full expression of God's covenantal action: the promise of descendants (15:1–6) and land (15:7–21). For the first time in the biblical narrative, the human party responds to God verbally (vv. 2–3). Further, Abraham enters into full dialogue with God by expressing his doubt about God's ability to carry out his promise, given the reality of his

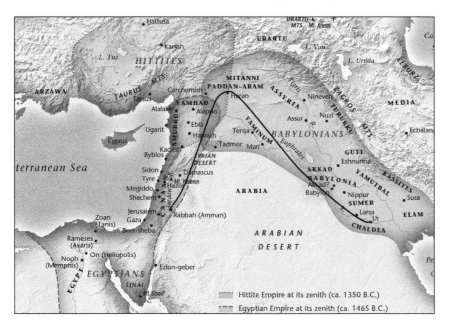

**REGION OF MESOPOTAMIA AND ABRAHAM'S JOURNEY
FROM UR TO THE PROMISED LAND**

aging situation. Even more remarkably, God responds not in anger, but in the openness of relationship in communication, bringing Abraham outside and giving the visual confirmation of the stars as the gauge by which his offspring will be numbered (vv. 4–5). Abraham then takes the first step from mere obedience in action to active obedience in faith when "he believed" God. And here God first credits his faith (v. 6).

This is not the end of Abraham's journey, however. The very next chapter describes the doubt that persists when Abraham "listened to the voice" of another human being, in this case Sarah (16:2), when he has been called time and again to "listen to the voice" of God. This leads to strife in the family and the endangerment of Abraham's own child Ishmael by his concubine Hagar (16:3–6). God must intervene, rectifying the wrong done to Hagar, saving the unborn child, and presenting the child Ishmael with a divine commitment of his own (vv. 7–16). God then goes to Abraham and recommits them both to the covenanted promises. Scholars generally consider Genesis 15 and 17 to be varying traditions of the same event told from different perspectives. On reading the final form of the narrative, however, we see the ups and downs of Abraham's journey of faith. In Genesis 17, Abraham is renamed in the process to represent this divine commitment. The eternal nature of the covenant is clarified, and the promise of land is once again brought to bear. Distinctive in this episode is the sign of the covenant that God introduces. Circumcision will henceforth mark God's

Sacrifice of Isaac
by Rembrandt

covenant with Abraham and all that are his. Sarai, too, is renamed Sarah, and the child from her womb is identified as Isaac. Thus, as the story progresses, the covenant develops further. Its sheer magnitude comes to the fore. When God finishes speaking, he departs. Abraham's agency as a participant is reduced; he simply receives the promise in silent awe. His ensuing action, however, is once again full obedience as he takes his entire house to be circumcised (vv. 23–27).

Abraham's agency is then reasserted in the following chapters, and his journey comes to its climax at Genesis 22. His winding path of growth and development over the last ten chapters of narrative has been leading to this ultimate point of decision where "God puts Abraham to the test," and Abraham must confront not only his own true nature, but also that of the God with whom he is covenanted. In this encounter, God, for the first time in their relationship, calls Abraham by name. In fact, Abraham is called three times by three different characters, denoting the crucial nature of his role: first by God ("Abraham!" v. 1), then by Isaac ("my Father!" v. 7), and finally by the angel of God ("Abraham!" v. 11). Each time, Abraham answers in the same fundamental manner. With this simple particle of existence, best translated as "Here I am," Abraham places himself before God in a direct way. This episode thus embodies a profound personal experience with God. The command to sacrifice his "only son," the beloved son of the promise, puts Abraham, who has been so obedient in action, to the ultimate test of faith. For his part, Abraham responds in word as well as deed, exemplifying that his faith in God's promise has finally matured with his obedience. By raising his hand to kill his son, Abraham's journey of faith reaches its goal, and he is rewarded. Isaac is spared (as is Abraham), and a ram is given for the sacrifice. It is this sacrifice, the result of Abraham passing God's test, that ultimately seals his covenant with God. Abraham's story quickly comes to a close, his place in God's covenantal action in history assured. The remainder of Genesis details the fruition of God's promises as the descendants of Abraham eventually become the Israelites, a great clan that eventually makes its way down into Egypt. Abraham thus becomes the father of Judaism and the model of faith for his descendants across history.

> **Israel**
>
> The name Israel comes from the Hebrew "he strives with God" or possibly "may God rule." It was first given to Jacob in Genesis 32:28. The name is later extended to the twelve tribes descended from Jacob/Israel. The people come to be called "the children of Israel" or "the Israelites." The earliest occurrence of the name outside Israel is in Egypt ca. 1230 BCE. The name was extended to the nation ca. 1000 BCE. After the division of the nation, "Israel" is usually preserved for the northern nation. Following the fall of the northern nation ca. 721 BCE, the ideal of a greater Israel persisted in the Scriptures. Over time, the name came to encompass not only an ethnic and political designation but also a theological description for the people of God in any age.

Abraham's son Isaac marries Rebekah, and they have two sons, Jacob and Esau (Gen 24:67; 25:25–26). Jacob becomes the son of God's promise over a lengthy cycle of stories that show that he is manipulative and a bit duplicitous in his efforts to get his father's blessing and the wife he desires (Gen 25–47). Nonetheless, Jacob proves his mettle with God and is renamed **Israel**, which means "he strives with God" (Gen 32:28). Jacob eventually becomes the father of many sons, who develop into the twelve tribes of Israel. One of these sons is Joseph, with whom many are familiar because of the "coat of many colors" given to him by his father (Gen 37:3). Joseph becomes successful in the pharaoh's court in Egypt and eventually brings his entire family there to escape famine in the land promised to them by God (Gen 41–50). This "Joseph story" is one of the most beautiful stories in the Bible, especially when we recognize that it was written more than three thousand years ago. The book of Genesis ends with the "twelve tribes of Israel" successful and content in Egypt. They have received the blessing of their covenant with God, but they are outside the land promised to them by God's covenant with Abraham. This situation becomes the setting for the book of Exodus and the next major narrative episode in Israel's history.

Moses and the Sinai Covenant as Preserved in Exodus, Leviticus, Numbers, and Deuteronomy (ca. 1280 BCE)

The book of Exodus opens by narrating the passing of a number of generations. The Israelites, as they are now identified, are successful for some time in Egypt. However, once a new pharaoh comes to power, they fall out of favor and are forced into labor camps for the royal building projects. This situation sets the stage for the next major events in Israel's history: the exodus and the Sinai covenant, which is forged in its aftermath. We are also introduced to arguably the most important figure in Israel's history, **Moses**. The magnitude of this period in Israelite history is matched by the amount of narrative devoted to its telling. While the early millennia of the history of the world were narrated in the first eleven chapters of Genesis, the fifty to one hundred years of the time of Moses, the exodus, and the Sinai covenant are narrated across the next four books of the Bible: Exodus, Leviticus, Numbers, and Deuteronomy.

Moses is called by God and, despite all his efforts to get out of God's call, becomes God's greatest prophet. Exodus 3 tells the famous story of Moses out tending the flocks of his father-in-law and seeing a bush on fire but not burning up. Once he investigates, he encounters God, who calls him to be both the leader of the Israelites and God's spokesperson. This portion of the narrative also shares the sacred name of God (Exod 3:14). This name is so revered that it is never spoken aloud. Even today, it is never uttered, and we cannot be sure how it should be spoken. The Hebrew word can be written in English as **YHWH**. Even in Hebrew this is an odd formulation, but scholars agree it is some form of the Hebrew verb for "to be," and English translations render it as something like "I am who am." The divine name is therefore connected to the very essence of being. Because the Israelites revere this word, they develop the custom of saying "Lord," a more common word of honor, when they see it. The tradition of honoring the sacred name of God by never vocalizing persists today.

The Tetragrammaton

The sacred name of the God of Israel is written in Hebrew as יהוה and is transliterated into English as YHWH. Scholars sometimes refer to it as the **tetragrammaton**, a term that comes from the Greek and means "the four-letter word." Since out of reverence for God it is not to be uttered, we do not know how it would be pronounced. The ancient Jews developed the practice of saying the title "Lord" when they read the sacred name. Therefore, to indicate where the Jewish Scriptures use the tetragrammaton, many modern Bibles and textbooks use "Lord" with small capital letters.

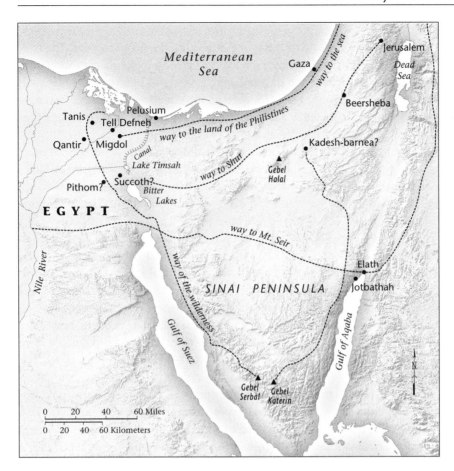

SINAI PENINSULA AND POTENTIAL EXODUS ROUTES

For his part, Moses takes this divine name and the authority God gives him as God's **prophet**, or spokesperson, and challenges the pharaoh to let the descendants of Abraham, Isaac, and Jacob (whom we now know as the Israelites) go to worship God in the wilderness. The book of **Exodus** is named for the events of the rest of its first half, as Moses proves the wondrous power of God and eventually leads the people out of Egypt from under the pharaoh's control. Moses continually wields the power of God, and the Israelites make their way into the desert of the Sinai Peninsula where they encounter God in a new way. The miracles Moses performs are identified as **signs** because they point to the wonders of God's awesome power.

Exodus 19–24 provides the narrative of the next step in God's relationship with the descendants of Abraham, which scholars generally call the **Sinai covenant**. This new covenantal development is marked by a call and response. Crucial to sealing this covenant is God's promise, "if you will obey my voice and keep my covenant, you shall be my own possession among all the peoples" (19:5). And it is an offer that is not operative until the people accept. The Israelites, who had fallen into slavery, have struggled to make their exodus from Egypt under the leadership of Moses and now stand before God in the wilderness of the Sinai Peninsula. The solemn introduction to the Sinai covenant affirms that this covenant is different from those that God has established thus far. God uses Moses as a mediator to offer a conditional covenant to an entire people and has them respond first by word and then, only when the covenant is sealed, by deed. This is a development of the covenantal nature of God's relationship with the children of Israel. The divine commitment remains, but the human obligation in word and deed—in *relationship*—comes to the fore. The people must "obey the voice" of God and "keep the covenant." They must remain in active relationship with God and God alone. Abraham "hearkened to the voice" of another on occasion and caused his own stumbling on his journey, but his covenant was never at stake. In the conditional nature of this covenant, God presents its maintenance as dependent on this obedience. Moses does as he is commanded, and the people respond positively in full voice, "All that God has said, we will do" (19:8). The people are then instructed to consecrate themselves for two days to prepare themselves, for "on the third day the Lord will come down upon Mount Sinai in the sight of all the people" (19:11). The appearance of God occurs on the third day, as promised (19:16–25).

The purpose of the consecration and appearance, or **theophany**, is so that God may initiate the covenant-making process through the giving of his words. Exodus 20 is devoted to the narration of these **Ten Commandments**, the Decalogue, in covenant form. God is identified as the covenant giver, and, after a brief history of their relationship, the people are given the obligations of the covenant in the Ten Commandments. Witnessing to the theophany strikes fear in the people, leading them to ask Moses to be the official mediator, thus formalizing his role as God's prophet. Moses agrees and urges the people not to fear but to understand the curses that are integral to the covenant relationship. He then draws near to God to receive further instruction, resulting in the laws that are often called the Covenant Collection or "book of the covenant." Exodus 20:22–23:19 begins and ends with legislation regarding ritual and the worship of God, so that all social interaction as the people of God is framed in worship, while Exodus 24 narrates the completion and ratification of the covenant in two rituals. In order for the covenant to be completed, it seems necessary for the people to give a twofold reiteration of their commitment to exclusive relationship with God through keeping the covenant stipulations laid before them in the Ten Commandments.

Across the rest of Israel's Scriptures, this Sinai covenant is the covenant necessary for the people to understand how to live in right relationship with God. This is also the foundation of the covenant that lies behind the thinking of the early Christians. The rest of these early books are dedicated to God giv-

Moses by Michelangelo

© Alvesgaspar

ing his people all the obligations of this covenant (Exod 20–31; Lev 1–27; Num 28–36; Deut 4–30), as well as the events that lead a new generation of Israelites, forged in the wilderness under the direction of Moses and the Sinai covenant, back to the land promised to their ancestor Abraham. For their part, God's chosen people struggle with the covenant's demands, but this law, the *Torah* in Hebrew, is given as the gift that guides the people into right relationship with God. The book of Deuteronomy closes with the death of the great prophet and leader Moses, and the people, under the leadership of Joshua, poised to retake the land they understand to be theirs through this covenantal history.

The Conquest and Settlement of Canaan as Preserved in Joshua and Judges (ca. 1200 BCE)

The book of Joshua describes the conquest of Canaan, the land promised first to Abraham and then to the children of Israel at Sinai, in epic pageantry. The tribal assembly at Shechem is a covenant-making event, in terms of a renewal of the Sinai covenant, to form a twelve-tribe league of crucial importance to the creation of a unified people. By reaffirming the Sinai covenant, this new generation of people render themselves personal participants in that same covenant.

Joshua 23 recounts the farewell speech of Joshua himself. Therefore, bringing the tribes together in covenant renewal to form a confederation is Joshua's final act as prophetic leader of the people of God. The final verses of Joshua 24, and the final verses of the book as a whole, recount Joshua's death and the faithfulness of Israel that he facilitated. When Joshua recites the sacred history of Israel, he dwells on God's action on Israel's behalf in the exodus and the wilderness but begins with the divine promises to the patriarchs. The purpose of the recitation comes in the call to decision made to the current generation that follows. Joshua 24:14–24 is marked, as are all the covenant-making passages, by

---

Joshua 24:14–24

"Now therefore revere the Lord, and serve him in sincerity and in faithfulness; put away the gods that your ancestors served beyond the River and in Egypt, and serve the Lord. Now if you are unwilling to serve the Lord, choose this day whom you will serve, whether the gods your ancestors served in the region beyond the River or the gods of the Amorites in whose land you are living; but as for me and my household, we will serve the Lord."

Then the people answered, "Far be it from us that we should forsake the Lord to serve other gods; for it is the Lord our God who brought us and our ancestors up from the land of Egypt, out of the house of slavery, and who did those great signs in our sight. He protected us along all the way that we went, and among all the peoples through whom we passed; and the Lord drove out before us all the peoples, the Amorites who lived in the land. Therefore we also will serve the Lord, for he is our God."

But Joshua said to the people, "You cannot serve the Lord, for he is a holy God. He is a jealous God; he will not forgive your transgressions or your sins. If you forsake the Lord and serve foreign gods, then he will turn and do you harm, and consume you, after having done you good."

And the people said to Joshua, "No, we will serve the Lord!"

Then Joshua said to the people, "You are witnesses against yourselves that you have chosen the Lord, to serve him."

And they said, "We are witnesses."

He said, "Then put away the foreign gods that are among you, and incline your hearts to the Lord, the God of Israel."

The people said to Joshua, "The Lord our God we will serve, and him we will obey."

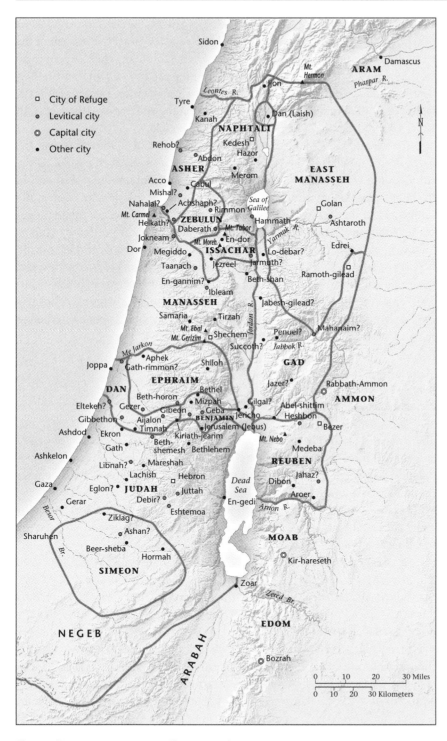

□ City of Refuge
● Levitical city
◎ Capital city
• Other city

TRIBAL DISTRIBUTION IN THE PROMISED LAND

call and response. The first commandment of Sinai is here reiterated in terms of service. God has already chosen Israel; it is now for Israel in the form of the tribal confederation to respond with their choice for God. And the people do so, three times. When they give their final response to the call, they affirm their determination to serve God by also vowing their obedience. Therefore, it is the demands of the Sinai covenant that determine the success or failure of both Israel as a whole and the lives of its individual people.

The book of Judges takes us from this ideal period of all the tribes working together to a time when the leaders call for a king and a unified nation. As the story continues, we learn that, despite the magnificent conquest narrated in the book of Joshua, the Israelites continue to contend with peoples, such as the Philistines, in the land of Canaan. The early leaders of Israel are called judges because they are local military or judicial leaders who are called by God to liberate the people from their enemies. They do not form dynasties, nor do they act as sovereign leaders over all the tribes. The events of this period and the leadership of twelve judges against powerful odds are narrated across this text. Over time, however, the Israelites contend not only with outsiders but also with each other, and they begin to clamor for a king who will not only go before them in battle but also unite them as a nation.

King David and the Nation as Preserved in the Books of Samuel and Kings (ca. 1000–587 BCE)

The story of **David**, the shepherd-turned-king of Israel, spans the books of Samuel and continues into the first chapters of the books of Kings. If Moses is the ideal prophet of Israel and the primary figure of the Torah, David becomes the ideal king and the figure who looms largest over the books known as the Prophets and much of the remaining Jewish Scriptures. The story of the monarchy does not begin with David, but with Samuel, the last judge, and Saul, the first king anointed by Samuel.

As 1 Samuel opens, the birth and development of Samuel as a man of God and just judge, following the model of Moses, is narrated alongside evidence that this organizational structure for the expanding tribes of Israel is not sustainable. The elders of the tribes come to Samuel and call for a king "like the other nations"; but Samuel gives voice to the potential negative consequences to living under a monarchy, reminding the Israelites that as God's chosen people, they are not meant to be "like the other nations." Nonetheless, God accedes to the people's wishes and directs Samuel to anoint Saul, who ruled in the late eleventh century BCE, ca. 1020. Saul seems to have been a more effective military leader than a governor. Even his military expertise faded, however, once he lost God's favor by overstepping the bounds of his role as king. He commanded a citadel at Gibeah, a few miles northwest of Jerusalem, but never controlled all

David by Michelangelo
© Jörg Bittner Unna

the tribes. He did, however, create some sort of union stable enough to endure the external threat from the Philistines and form a basis for the national developments to come.

David enters the narrative of Israel's history at 1 Samuel 16 as a boy tending his father's flock in Bethlehem, from the tribe of Judah. Even at the first mention of his name, readers begin to understand the powerful role he will have in the national and religious developments to come: "And Samuel took the horn of oil and anointed him in the midst of his brothers; and the Spirit of

God came mightily upon David from that day forward" (1 Sam 16:13). David's rise to power is swift and direct from the moment he enters public life, first as a musician in King Saul's court, then as the king's armor bearer and the champion who slays the giant Philistine warrior Goliath. His special relationship with God is foreshadowed even in these early verses. By the time David becomes king (2 Samuel 2), and certainly by the time of his death (1 Kings 2), this relationship had become one of the most complex and intricately drawn in all of Israel's Scriptures.

David is anointed king prior to the death of Saul, who is then presented more or less as a tragic character, who falls to the growing power of a supposed ally (David) and the rejection of the prophet who anointed him (Samuel). For his part, David becomes a larger than life figure in Israelite tradition, becoming the model for anointed leaders from that point forward. David marries Saul's daughter, Michal, and becomes beloved friends with Saul's heir apparent, Jonathan. Saul's fear and jealousy of David forced the latter into exile among the Philistines. Jonathan eventually dies in battle, as does King Saul, tragically, by his own sword. David then moves quickly to solidify his power and establish his kingship at Hebron. The Philistines see their former accomplice as a new enemy of dangerous proportions and attack in force. David deals them a decisive defeat and further consolidates his power by capturing Jerusalem from the Jebusites. The city was naturally well suited for defense and lay neither in Saul's ancestral land of Benjamin nor David's home of Judah, so he quickly transferred his capital there. At its greatest extent, David's kingdom possibly stretched as far north as the Lebanon mountain range to deep into the Sinai desert in the south, and from the Mediterranean in the west to the desert in the east. He ruled across the early tenth century BCE, ca. 1000–960.

Second Samuel 7–8 provides a crux to the David story, which underscores his personal relationship with God and his role as God's king and anointed one, or **Messiah**. David's initiative to build a house for God is presented as the impetus for God to make a new covenant with him and, through him, with the Israelites as a nation. The theme of "dwelling" runs through this passage, such that the concepts of "house" and "dynasty" are interwoven to make up the divine promise and commitment. God's promise of future glory and unmatched greatness in name is given to David through the prophet Nathan as a reaffirmation of a land for the people, in which they may live in peace and security. God then assures David's dynasty by establishing an everlasting relationship. David is promised offspring who will build a house for God, and God likens their relationship to a father-son kinship of obedience and discipline as well as steadfast love and blessing. For his part, David enters the tent in which the ark of the covenant (the container that holds the Ten Commandments from the Sinai covenant) dwells. In prayer, David extols the greatness and uniqueness of God, who has made the divine presence known, and then recounts God's redeeming action on Israel's behalf through the exodus, when the people were

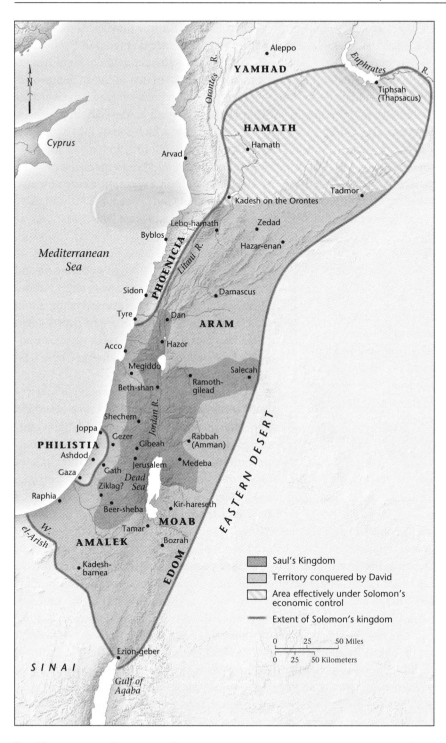

THE KINGDOM OF DAVID AND SOLOMON

set apart in God's name, into his own time. With this prayer, David accepts God's promise, including the blessing and obedience that it entails.

Through this covenant, God promises that a descendent of David will always be king over God's people. Since kings are anointed in the ancient world, this king would be God's "anointed one." In the Hebrew language, the word for "anointed one" is *mashiach*, which comes into English as **Messiah**. In the Greek language, the word for "anointed one" is *christos*, which comes into English as **Christ**. The words "Messiah" and "Christ" are therefore synonyms. A messiah, then, is a term used for kings in ancient Israel, and God's messiahs rule the people in God's name. What scholars call **messianic expectations** are now also introduced into the hope of Israel. As a result of God's covenant with King David, whenever they find themselves suffering and oppressed by outsiders, God's people can expect that God will send a Messiah, whom they understand to be a descendant of David, to liberate them from this oppression and become king over them as a sovereign nation. This Davidic covenant adds a new component to God's covenantal relationship with Israel. Jerusalem becomes the holy city, and a royal component of the nation and God's anointed one, who will lead it, comes into play.

David's military and governing expertise mark a sharp contrast to his relative weakness in personal and family relations. A lengthy narrative running through the remainder of 2 Samuel and into 1 Kings tells of the darker side of David and the limits of his power. The intrigue that follows over David's successor hints at the problems that would only heighten during his son Solomon's reign and lead to the eventual split of the kingdom. As King Solomon takes the throne, we see the strengths of his character in his wisdom as well as his determination to complete the Temple as the house of God. Like his father before him, Solomon also shows weaknesses as he marries numerous foreign wives and subjects his people to conscription into the military, forced labor, and a heavy tax burden. Solomon preserved and even further consolidated David's kingdom throughout a long and relatively peaceful reign (ca. 960–920 BCE). In the midst of all this prosperity, however, the solidity of the kingdom was beginning to show signs of wear and tear. Solomon's foreign wives brought with them the religions and cultic worship of their homelands, and the king did little to prevent their influence on the worship of the God of Israel. Solomon's successful commercial ventures were still not enough to fund his bureaucracy, and he divided the nation into twelve administrative districts across tribal lines in an attempt to streamline management as well as break

---

Messiah/Christ

The expression "Christ" is the Greek form of the Hebrew/Aramaic expression "Messiah." It means "anointed one" and was used in the ancient world to refer to any king who was understood by his subjects to be "anointed" to the role. Israelites referred to all their kings as messiahs and understood them to be anointed by God. Even the Persian King Cyrus, who allowed the Israelites to return home from Babylon, is called "messiah" for his beneficence to the people (Isa 45:1).

Beirut

Sidon

Damascus

PHOENICIA

Litani R.

Mt. Hermon

Pharpar R.

Abana R.

Tyre

Dan

Kedesh

ARAM

Hazor

J. Jarmuk

Acco

Sea of
Galilee

Mt. Carmel

Ashtaroth

Kishon

Mt.
Tabor

Yarmuk R.

Edrei

*Mediterranean
Sea*

Megiddo

Mt. Moreh

Beth-shan

Ramoth-gilead

Taanach

R.

Ibleam

Mt.
Gilboa

Jabesh-gilead?

Samaria

Tirzah

Jordan R.

Mt. Ebal

Succoth?

Penuel?

Mahanaim?

Yarkon R.

Mt. Gerizim

Shechem

Jabbok

R.

Joppa

Aphek

Shiloh

ISRAEL

Bethel

Rabbah (Amman)

Gezer

Jericho

AMMON

Aijalon

Mt. Nebo

Heshbon

Ashdod

Gath

Jerusalem

Medeba

Ashkelon

Mareshah

Bethlehem

Gaza

Gerar

Hebron

*Dead
Sea*

Dibon

Besor Br.

JUDAH

Amon R.

Raphia

Beer-sheba

MOAB

PHILISTIA

Kir-hareseth

Zered Br.

WILDERNESS

*Region
periodically
contested
by Judah
and Edom*

Bozrah

WILDERNESS

Kadesh-
barnea

EDOM

| 0 | 10 | 20 | 30 Miles |
| 0 | 10 | 20 | 30 Kilometers |

THE DIVIDED KINGDOM

down tribal allegiances. These measures were most successful at producing resentment toward the monarchy, especially in the north, which felt it bore the major burden of supporting the extravagance of the court in the south with little benefit. Although the kingdom remained intact at Solomon's death, the edifice was beginning to shake and would soon crack apart.

Rehoboam succeeded Solomon as king ca. 922 BCE and went to Shechem to solidify the allegiance of the northern tribes. Failing to grasp the fragility of the alliance, however, he refused the northern leaders' demand for easing the burdens of taxation and forced labor. This failed summit resulted in a revolt of the northern tribes under Jeroboam I. Therefore, what had been the united kingdom of Israel under David and Solomon was divided into the northern kingdom of Israel (ten tribes) and the southern kingdom of **Judah** (two tribes). The secession of the northern tribes from the united kingdom is understood by the biblical authors to be a "sin," and the resulting southern kingdom of Judah is presented as maintaining right relationship with God through the covenants with Abraham, Moses, and David as well as worship at the Temple in Jerusalem. It is through Judah that the story will continue and through which the people and religion of Judaism eventually develop.

Jeroboam I was the first king of the northern kingdom, and he took measures to divert attention away from Jerusalem and the Temple as the focus of the faith by establishing sanctuaries at the ancient religious sites at Dan and Bethel. This northern kingdom of Israel eventually established its capital at Samaria and survived for two hundred years until it fell ca. 721 BCE to an onslaught by the Assyrian Empire from the east. From the time of the division forward, the narrative of 2 Kings switches back and forth between the two kingdoms as it traces their history until the northern kingdom falls; then it turns its focus solely on the southern kingdom of Judah, which remained more stable under the dynasty of David, such that it withstood the Assyrian aggression. Good, strong kings like Hezekiah and Josiah come to the fore, but many kings struggle under the external pressure of powerful enemies as well as the internal concerns of a small monotheistic people in a larger polytheistic society.

In the sixth century BCE, a new powerful empire arises centered in Babylon, and like those who came before, the Babylonians set their sights on the key route from the east down into Egypt along the east coast of the Mediterranean Sea. The tiny nation of Judah sat squarely in their path. This time, Judah could not withstand the attacks, and the Babylonians captured Jerusalem in 597 BCE. They deported the king and many of the people into Babylon. The Babylonian King Nebuchadnezzar placed a weak and vacillating King Zedekiah on the throne in Judah, who staged an ill-fated revolt against Babylon. This time, Nebuchadnezzar destroyed the city completely—razing the Temple and deporting most of the remaining people into exile in Babylon by 587–586 BCE. 2 Kings 25 (the last chapter of the book) recounts this tragic event, telling that he left only "some of the country's poor." The beginning of this dark histori-

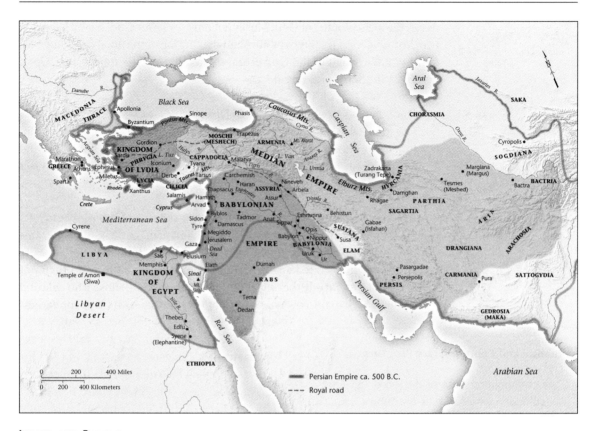

Israel and Babylon

cal period, known as the **Babylonian exile**, brings us to the end of what the Jewish Scriptures call the Former Prophets. It also brings us to a break in what the Christian OT calls the Historical Books and allows us to take a look at key figures in the story of Israel, called prophets, as well as touch upon the many books that bear their names.

The Rise of the Prophets (ca. 800–400 BCE)

Since our primary concern in this chapter is to bring to light the theological and historical world behind the text of the New Testament, even a brief overview of all the OT prophets is beyond our scope. We can, however, note the rise of this important group in Israel's history, known as the "classical prophets," as well as the body of literature their schools produced. In the Scriptures of Judaism, a **prophet** is one who speaks for another, and the term is generally used for one who relates the messages of the divine. A true prophet in Israel, therefore, is one who speaks for God. We already noted that Moses is the figure who encompasses the ideal prophet of God. Moses not only spoke for God, but he led God's people out of bondage in Egypt, through the forging of the Sinai covenant, and to the boundary of the land God promised to them as their inheritance. Upon his death, the Scriptures reveal,

> Since then no prophet has arisen in Israel like Moses, whom the LORD knew face to face. He had no equal in all the signs and wonders the LORD sent him to perform in the land of Egypt against Pharaoh and all his servants and against all his land, and for the might and the terrifying power that Moses exhibited in the sight of all Israel. (Deut 34:10–12)

Once Israel enters the period of the monarchy, the role of the prophet shifts from that of the primary leader to the "right-hand man" of the king. For example, the prophet Nathan was integral to David's rule. However, over time the role of the prophet shifted again, and the true prophets more often than not found themselves outside the circles of power, confronting those who rule and calling them back to the covenant and right relationship with God. The earliest example of this sort of prophet is Elijah, whose story is contained within 2 Kings. Elijah speaks out against the kings of the north and risks his life in so doing. Once he appoints his successor Elisha, God takes him directly into heaven by way of a fiery chariot. Elijah becomes the only prophet in Israel's biblical history who does not die. Therefore, over time he becomes identified with the people's messianic expectations, and they begin to look to his return as the sign of the advent of the messianic era.

Biblical and Contemporary Prophets

The contemporary use of the word "prophet" as someone who foretells the future is quite different from the biblical understanding of prophecy. In the Bible, a true prophet is "one who speaks for God," sharing God's message with all who would listen. In this sense, future events are merely the result of acceptance or refusal of the given message. We must bear this in mind as we exegete the biblical texts.

The work of the latter prophets is preserved in books that bear their names. The books of Isaiah, Jeremiah, and Ezekiel are the longest and are thus referred to as the "major prophets." Much less is preserved about the twelve "minor prophets," and their books are briefer. Nonetheless, prophets like Amos, Hosea, Micah, and Zechariah have much to say about social justice, God's people's covenantal duty to God and each other, and their hopes for a Messiah. The earliest of these literary prophets appear in the eighth century BCE. Amos and Hosea worked in the northern kingdom, while Isaiah and Micah worked in the southern kingdom. The idea of "knowing God" begins to appear in prophetic texts to reflect being in covenant with God, while the concept of "truth" is found throughout the literature to signify the origin and nature of this relationship as well as the fidelity inherent in maintaining it. For example, the prophet Hosea teaches that the lack of knowledge is tantamount to a breach of covenant with God.

> Hear the word of God, O people of Israel; for God has an indictment against
> the inhabitants of the land. There is no faithfulness or loyalty, and no knowl-
> edge of God in the land. (Hos 4:1)

The prophet Isaiah likewise describes life in Israel in breach of covenant as the
failure of truth:

> Justice is turned back, and righteousness stands at a distance; for truth stum-
> bles in the public square, and uprightness cannot enter. Truth is lacking, and
> whoever turns from evil is despoiled. (Isa 59:14–15)

The seventh- and sixth-century prophets Jeremiah and Ezekiel build upon
this symbolism and understanding of knowledge and truth. God's relationship
with Israel is intimate, grounded in its Sinai role as God's chosen people and
the obligatory response of absolute fidelity. In describing the hope for the future
repentance of the people, Jeremiah reports:

> I will give them a heart to know that I am God; and they shall be my people
> and I will be their God, for they shall return to me with their whole heart.
> (Jer 24:7)

Jeremiah's famous "new covenant" passage is probably the most telling—and
the most beautiful—example of God's desire for the knowledge of the people
in terms of their heart as well as their walk:

> See, the days are coming, says God, when I will make a new covenant with
> the house of Israel and the house of Judah, not like the covenant which …
> they broke, though I was their husband, says God. But this is the covenant
> which I will make … I will put my law within them, and I will write it upon
> their hearts; and I will be their God, and they shall be my people. And no
> longer shall each man teach his neighbor and each his brother, saying, "Know
> God," for they shall all know me, from the least of them to the greatest, says
> God; for I will forgive their iniquity, and I will remember their sin no more.
> (Jer 31:31–34)

What is striking about this passage is not just the connection between knowing
God and living in covenant but also the promise of a new covenant, built upon
the old, which will be expressed and lived in a distinctive way. Like Jeremiah
before him, Ezekiel believed that the covenant that God will establish with his
people in the future will have a distinctive character yet be built solidly upon
the old. This new covenant of peace will encompass both the action and the
very being of those counted among God's sheep yet remain lived intimately in
the knowledge of God. Even after the exile, the prophets continue to employ the

concept of "truth" to express the essential nature of this relationship. Through Zechariah, God commands the people:

> Render true judgments, show kindness and mercy to one another, do not oppress the widow, the orphan, the alien, or the poor; and do not devise evil in your hearts against one another. (Zech 7:9–10; see also 8:16–17)

Likewise, God commands the people to express their worship with the simple command: "Love truth and peace" (Zech 8:19).

The writing of prophetic literature gradually declined in the fifth and fourth centuries BCE. The oracles of Malachi, Joel, Obadiah, and Jonah are the final works of prophecy to be included in the canon. The body of prophetic books is traditionally understood to come to a close by 400 BCE as they begin to be collected as Scripture. They serve as the moral compass of the people and, alongside Torah, as both the heart of and the guidebook for the preserved relationship between God and the chosen people. The prophets, therefore, are not seers of the future; rather they "look back" to covenant and call God's people to faithfulness.

The Exile and Post-Exilic Era as Preserved in Ezra and Nehemiah (ca. 538–333 BCE)

We can now take up our overview of the biblical narrative once again. The holy city of Jerusalem was overrun by the Babylonians ca. 587 BCE. The Temple was destroyed, and the people of Judah were exiled across the Babylonian Empire. The return to Jerusalem occurred in 538 BCE under Cyrus, the king of the newly rising Persian Empire. Interestingly, King Cyrus is the first non-Israelite in the Bible to be called "messiah," indicating that the biblical authors looked to him as a king who was God's "anointed one" to restore the people. The books of Ezra and Nehemiah recount the end of the exile and the return and restoration of the land, following the Edict of Cyrus. Many faithful Judeans returned to their promised land, and the rebuilding of the city and Temple commenced, full of hope and tension and conflict. However, after fifty years living outside the land, many faithful Judeans also decided not to return but to continue to live as God's people outside their homeland while supporting those who returned however they could. This situation inaugurates the phenomenon in Judaism known as the **diaspora**, a term that means "dispersion" or "scattering" and refers to the reality that ethnic and religious Jews now live "dispersed" across the known world, gathering and worshiping in synagogues and other communal environments.

The period of the return and restoration through the end of the Persian reign is known as the **Post-Exilic Era**. After much struggle, the people of Judah rebuilt their Temple ca. 515 BCE. Nehemiah 8 records that at the consecration

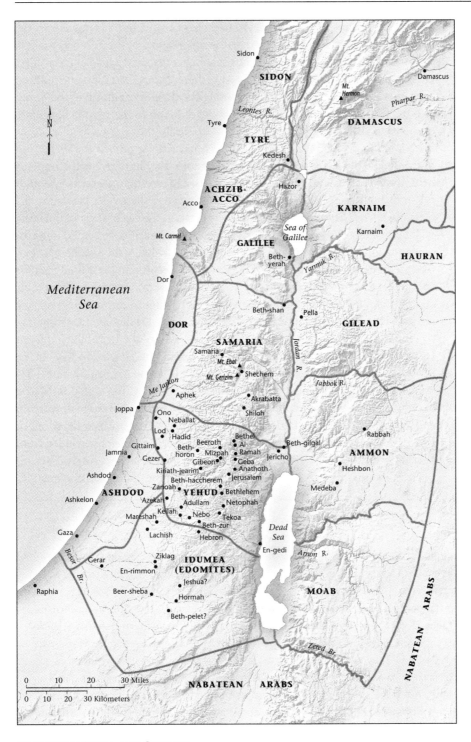

Post-Exilic Judea and Samaria

of the Temple for the feast of Tabernacles, Ezra read a book of the law in the hearing of all Jerusalem. This could be the first reading of the Torah as we now have it. Further, Nehemiah 10 recounts that Ezra organized a formal ratification of the covenant of Moses after the Feast of Tabernacles. Later Jewish tradition considers Ezra a second Moses, attributing the definitive editing of the Torah to him. The restoration of the exiled people of Judah to their land culminates in the momentous event of rededication to Torah, thus paralleling the covenant-making events in the wilderness at Sinai with regard to the formation of the people of God. All the people gather, and their initiative is the impetus behind the reading and renewal. The narrative is careful to assert the people's full understanding of the Torah they heard, as well as their verbal assent to the blessing of God. The Torah is then implemented in the celebration of the Feast of Tabernacles as prescribed. The covenant renewal itself is presented in terms of confession and commitment. The people acknowledge the steadfast love of God as the integral component of his covenant-keeping in their final plea for continued protection in relationship. They close in prayer and confirm their commitment to God in writing. The communal pledge of commitment reflects the stipulations of covenantal behavior that the people take upon themselves.

Judah was relatively self-enclosed from the rest of the world during these years, but it was still a part of the Persian Empire and was affected by its policies. It was at this time that Hebrew began to be displaced by Aramaic, a fellow Semitic language that had become normative in the empire. The high priests gave in only reluctantly, and Hebrew was still preserved as the language of worship and study. Those who remained in what had been the northern kingdom of Israel were now known as **Samaritans**, and they were completely excluded from Jewish life and worship. They eventually built a temple of their own on Mount Gerizim in the latter part of the fourth century, and the opposition and hostility

Jews and Samaritans

When the united kingdom of Israel divided, the southern kingdom was known as Judah and maintained its capital at Jerusalem. Judaism traces its story through the happenings in Judah. The northern kingdom takes the name Israel and eventually locates its capital at Samaria with a temple built on Mount Gerizim. They were strict Torah observers and looked to Moses as the teacher of the true faith. After the destruction of the northern kingdom of Israel in 722 BCE (see 2 Kgs 17), the conquering Assyrians introduced various other races into the region and deported many originally Israelite people elsewhere. By the time of Judah's restoration in 538 BCE, these were known as Samaritans. The people of Judah understood their northern neighbors to be "apostates" (they had fallen away from the true faith). The feeling was mutual. As often happens with peoples of a shared ancestry who have diverged due to historical events and religious beliefs, anger against each other is often stronger than that for complete outsiders.

between the two former tribal siblings of Judeans and Samaritans grows as they are both confronted by a new era of civilization.

The Jewish People and the Greek Empire as Preserved in 1 and 2 Maccabees (333–63 BCE)

In the late fourth century BCE, a new set of influences began to affect the Jewish people. In 336 BCE, Alexander, who would be called the Great, ascended to the throne in Macedonia. After imposing unity on Greece, he turned to the east. In 333 BCE, at the decisive battle of Issus (in present-day Turkey), he defeated the Persian army and began the period of Greek domination in the known world. **Judea** (as the region is now known) thus came under Alexander's control at this time as he marched down the Mediterranean coast from Syria, through Palestine, and into Egypt. He established the city of Alexandria in Egypt in 332 BCE. As we introduced in the last chapter, Alexander's strong hellenizing program began immediately. His practice of infusing conquered lands with Greek language—or Hellenization—became a threat to the worship of God, just as Baal worship had been in the past. The resulting phenomenon of **Hellenism** pervaded the Mediterranean region for centuries thereafter.

A short ten years later, in 323 BCE, Alexander died, and his kingdom divided among his warring generals. Ptolemy seized control of Egypt. Seleucus took Babylon and the regions west to Syria. The region of Judea was thus first controlled by the Ptolemies, who were fairly noninterventionist. In 198 BCE, however, the east coast of the Mediterranean Sea came under Seleucid rule. The Seleucid ruler, Antiochus III, accorded the inhabitants of Judea the same privileges they had been receiving for some time, but his star began to fade, and he was assassinated by his son, Seleucus IV, who took over (187–175 BCE), and his subjects began to feel a tax burden. He was eventually assassinated and succeeded by his brother Antiochus IV Epiphanes (175–163 BCE). The adoption of Greek culture no longer remained benign as Antiochus IV determined to crush the worship of Israel's God. This severe religious persecution provoked the **Maccabean Revolt** in 167–164 BCE. Accounts of this event are given in 1 and 2 Maccabees.

The book of Daniel was also composed during this time to encourage hope and faithfulness. Even though the book of Daniel is associated with the great prophets in Christian Bibles (normally located after Ezekiel), the author makes extensive use of apocalyptic language and imagery. In the face of hopeless odds,

> **The Books of Maccabees and the Canon**
>
> Remember that the two books of the Maccabees are not found in all Bibles. This is the result of the development of the Septuagint (LXX) alongside the Tanakh in Jewish tradition. These books are found in the LXX and therefore in the Roman Catholic OT. Because they are not found in the Tanakh, they are not in many Protestant editions of the OT. Refer to chapter one for more detail.

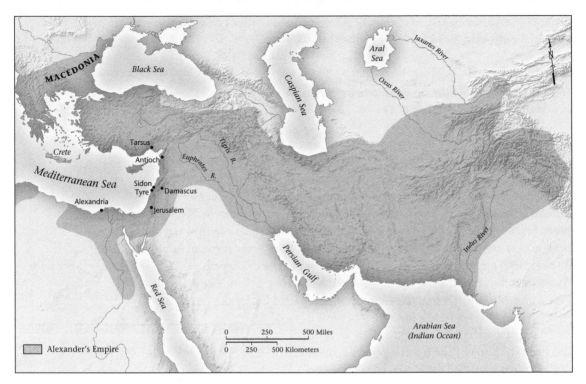

THE GREEK EMPIRE

by means of narratives and visionary experiences, the author of the book of Daniel encourages Israel to believe that God will ultimately be victorious over evil.

According to 1 Maccabees 1, Antiochus IV imposed universal Hellenism in an effort to unify his empire for defense, including emperor worship as well as that of Zeus and the rest of the Greek pantheon. This policy put him on a collision course with Judaism. He appointed high priests supportive of his policies and eventually forbade circumcision and other Jewish observances, using Temple funds for his own projects. 2 Maccabees 6 reports that the last straw was the erection of an altar to Zeus in the Temple. This is the "horrible abomination" also mentioned in Daniel 9. Rebellion erupted when the head of a faithful Jewish family, Mattathias, refused to offer sacrifice to Zeus and rallied a band of revolutionaries in the Judean hills. When Mattathias died in 166 BCE, leadership fell to his son, known as Judah the Hammer, or the Maccabee. Judah led a full-scale revolt against the forces of Antiochus, and his group became known as the Maccabees. He was eventually victorious, pushing the Seleucids out of Jerusalem and purifying the Temple in 164 BCE. These faithful Jews first rededicated the Temple to the worship of Israel's God—a celebration that is commemorated every year in the Festival of Dedication, more commonly known by its Hebrew name, Hanukkah. Judah continued his campaign for complete independence and finally fell in battle in 160. He was succeeded by his younger brother Jonathan, who was the first of the family to be named high priest by the current Seleucid ruler. Jonathan was succeeded by his brother Simon, who managed to get an official decree of independence from the Seleucid Demetrius II in 142 BCE.

First Maccabees 14 records that the people decreed that Simon would be accepted as their ruler and high priest until "a true prophet arises." Nonetheless, the Maccabees, however heroic, were not of the Davidic line of kings or of the Zadokite line of high priests, and this angered some of the purists. The Jewish separatist movement known as the Essenes is thought to date from this time. Simon was eventually succeeded by his son John Hyrcanus. This dynasty became known as the Hasmoneans after an ancestor of Mattathias. John solidified his rule and expanded north, ultimately destroying the Samaritan temple at Mount Gerizim. The other Jewish groups known from the NT, the Sadducees and the Pharisees, seem to have emerged during this reign, with the Pharisees eventually breaking with the Hasmoneans in protest over the secular nature of their rule. As political power corrupted the Judean leaders over time, many faithful Jews once again found themselves suffering persecution and the inability to worship effectively. The beleaguered people found itself in turmoil once again, and messianic expectations began to rise.

> **The Zadokite Line of High Priests**
>
> Zadok served as a priest under King David and was traditionally understood to be a descendant of Moses's brother Aaron of the tribe of Levi. In the succession struggle, Zadok supported Solomon and became his sole priest once Solomon took the throne. His descendants controlled the priesthood in Jerusalem until the exile. Even then the prophet Ezekiel declared that only Zadokite priests should minister in the rebuilt Temple. They continued to serve in the high priesthood until 171 BCE, when others—first Hellenizers, then the Hasmoneans—took over the position. Scholars suggest that the Jewish groups known as the Essenes and the Sadducees could have formed during this time in protest over the outsiders usurping this key role in the worship life of the Temple.

The Jewish People and the Roman Empire (ca. 63 BCE into New Testament Times)

The wrangling for rule that arose in the years that followed eventually brought about the intervention of **Rome**. In 63 BCE, the Roman general Pompey marched on Jerusalem, and the independence won by the Maccabees came to an end. Pompey made Palestine part of the Roman province of Syria. The major cities were Antioch and Damascus. When Julius Caesar defeated Pompey and visited Syria in 47 BCE, he appointed a Roman prefect, or governor, and a series of rulers from the resident ethnic groups. Herod governed over Judea and remained in Rome's favor during the tumult that followed the assassination of Caesar. Herod was eventually named king of Judea (and later also Samaria) by

Marc Antony and Octavian. He solidified his rule in 37 BCE and reigned until his death in 4 BCE. His reign is noted for vicious acts of brutality, as well as for major building projects. He supported an early form of Roman emperor worship, which added to the resentment the Jews felt toward him. To curry favor, in 20 BCE he began the restoration of the Temple that had been completed ca. 515 BCE. This work continued during the lifetime of Jesus and was not finished until 63 CE, just seven short years before the Temple was destroyed forever in 70 CE. Historically, this brings us to the tumultuous times of Jesus of Nazareth and the events of the NT as messianic expectations among faithful Jewish people reached a fever pitch.

What Have We Learned So Far? The Story of God, Creation, and God's Chosen People

Our relatively brief and rapid overview of the story of Israel has presented not only the birth and development of Judaism, but has also shed a great deal of light on the people of Israel's relationship with God and therefore on the components of Jewish theology. The most fundamental of these is, of course, theology itself: the Jewish understanding of who God is and how God works in the world. As we introduced earlier in the chapter, Judaism is monotheistic. **Monotheism** is the belief in a sovereign creator God who is both transcendent (exists beyond creation) and immanent (is intimately involved in creation through relationships). The hallmark of this belief is found in the Torah and is known as the Great Shema, or the great call to hear: "Hear O Israel, the LORD is our God, the LORD alone. You shall love the LORD your God with all your heart, and with all your soul, and with all your might" (Deut 6:4–5). Judaism is understood to have invented monotheism in the sense that it is the earliest religion to advocate this theology. Further, the strength and tenacity of the religion was built upon sustaining and developing this faith in a singular God in the midst of polytheistic cultures that often demanded obedience in their own right.

As is typically the case, Jewish cosmology and anthropology are compatible with Jewish theology. In other words, the belief in God is somewhat determinative of the understanding of how the world came to be and the role of humankind within that world and in relationship with God. The book of Genesis narrates the creation of the heavens and the earth in a six-day period of goodness, with rest on the seventh day. In terms of cosmology, the key takeaway from this story is the all-encompassing power, authority, and knowledge of God in this creative act as well as the inherent goodness of the result. In addition, however, we learn that the world is not how it was intended to be due to an early act of disobedience that results in a *dis*order of the perfectly ordered world. Creation, therefore, is in a constant struggle to live to its true nature in relationship with God in the face of the challenges presented by disorder and chaos. This leads directly into anthropology and the biblical understanding of people. Genesis shows that humankind is the pinnacle of God's creation in the image of God. Perfect relationship with God is breached by disobedience and breakdown of this relationship, resulting in the ongoing struggle in the human will between good and evil. Nonetheless, God continues to work with all humankind through the period of the flood until the climactic event of the Tower of Babel. From this point forward, God works in relationship only with the descendants of Abraham, who first become the Israelites and then are eventually known as the Jewish people.

By the time we arrive at the end of the OT narrative, these people understand themselves to be in special relationship with God. This means, of course, that the vast majority of humankind does not enjoy this special relationship. Further, the Jewish people have reason to expect things from God, including the sending of a Messiah to redeem them from their current suffering at the hands of these other peoples (the Romans) and to rectify their status in the world. This, then, is mainstream Jewish Christology: God will send a Messiah who is a descendant of David and who will become a king like David, a military ruler who will lead the people once again out of bondage and into a sovereign nation.

The story of the Jewish people's developing understanding of God, the world, and their role in it leads to a clear position on morality and ethics. The foundation for Jewish values and right actions is based in Torah and the guidelines given in the Sinai covenant. Loving God and humankind, as God's creation, and living in a socially just society is essential to the Jewish worldview and finds its impetus in the Ten Commandments. These commandments, however, are moral ideals, and the reality of life in this disordered world is complex. Therefore, Torah, as a "full-service" manual for life in relationship with God, offers a complete set of contingency plans for ethical action in every eventuality. Further, Torah demands **sacrifice** as a means of **atonement** for sin and straying from the right path of relationship with God. When one turns away from God to pursue more immediate gratification, this results in a breakdown of communication, which in turn results in a breakdown of the intended union within that relationship. To "atone" means to become "at one" once again. Torah dictates the offering of some sort of sacrifice—something important to one's life and well-being—in

> ## Sin, Sacrifice, and Atonement
>
> Broadly speaking, **sin** is anything that is in opposition to God's purposes for creation. In the Scriptures sin is detailed as missing the mark, conscious rebellious action, and abomination. Sin, then, is any turning away from God. Repentance, or turning back, is often the counter to sin. The Jewish people developed a system of sacrifice to atone for sin. **Sacrifice** is the offering or surrender of something precious for the sake of something else. Ideal sacrificial worship is described in the Priestly writings, especially the book of Leviticus. Sacrifices could be burnt offerings, peace offerings, sin offerings, guilt offerings, or cereal offerings. The burnt, guilt, and cereal offerings were done to atone for sin. **Atonement** is the means by which the chain of sin is broken resulting in reconciliation. "At-one-ment" indicates the restoration of one's relationship with God.

order to bring the individual or, at times, the entire people back into union with God.

The final components that we want to bring to the fore are eschatology and soteriology. As these portions of the theological worldview often overlap, it is helpful to discuss them together. Judaism offers a linear view of history that posits a clear understanding of a beginning, middle, and future end. This, like the other foundational beliefs of Judaism, is quite distinctive in the ancient world. Eschatology, by nature, focuses on that future end, and Judaism, through the particular contributions of the prophetic and apocalyptic texts, developed a belief in a "day of the Lord," on which God would judge everyone based upon the theological and ethical decisions they have made. Apocalyptic literature also provided an additional development of the potential for reward and punishment in a next life. The book of Daniel speaks of a life after death through the resurrection of the body, in which the good will be rewarded with eternal life in perfect union with God and the wicked will be destined to a life of suffering outside the presence of God.

By the first century CE, Judaism was complex and multifaceted. This means that the theological worldview we have just presented took on a variety of expressions. The rabbis and other Jewish leaders and followers take both pleasure and pride in debating the potentialities of God's offerings. The more archaeologists and other scholars unearth about this period and the more we take in from the literature it produced, the more we can appreciate the beauty and profundity of first-century Judaism. We also learn, however, that this complex history and theology has several valid interpretations. The Jewish people have been living and struggling in relationship with God for millennia by the time we find ourselves in the first-century Roman oppression. They have learned to adapt, but they are tenacious and ever hopeful that their God will intervene on their behalf to make right the world and facilitate right relationship. We must take this reality seriously, for the worlds in and in front of the texts of what Christians call the Old Testament form a major portion of the world behind the texts of the New Testament. We can now turn our attention to the events of the life and literature of Jesus of Nazareth.

Key Terms and Concepts

Abraham/Abrahamic covenant	etiology/etiological stories
Adam	Exodus
atonement	Hellenism
Babylonian exile	Israel
covenant	Judah
David/Davidic covenant	Judea
diaspora	Maccabean Revolt

Messiah/Christ	sacrifice
messianic expectations	Samaritans
monotheism	Sinai covenant
Moses	the Temple
Noah	Ten Commandments
Post-Exilic Era	theophany
prophet	Tower of Babel
Rome	YHWH

Questions for Review

1. Who are the major figures in Israel's history? Trace a brief chronological overview of the development of this story.
2. What are the major covenantal stories of the Old Testament narrative? Who are the mediators of this developing relationship, and how might they come into play in the gospel story of the new covenant?
3. What is a messiah? From where does this concept come, and how does it develop in Judaism? How might this affect the development of a religion called Christianity?
4. How do concepts such as obedience, knowledge, and truth help us understand the Jewish understanding of the relationship between humankind and God?
5. What are the political, social, and theological elements of Jewish life in the Roman Empire in the first century CE that lead to extreme messianic expectations?

Bibliography and Further Reading

Anderson, Bernhard W., Steven Bishop, and Judith H. Newman. *Understanding the Old Testament.* 5th ed. Upper Saddle River, NJ: Pearson, 2007.

Brown, Sherri. *God's Promise: Covenant in John.* New York: Paulist, 2014.

Carvalho, Corrine. *Encountering Ancient Voices: A Guide to Reading the Old Testament.* Winona, MN: Anselm Academic, 2006.

Green, Barbara. *From Earth's Creation to John's Revelation: The INTERFACES Biblical Storyline Companion.* Collegeville, MN: Liturgical, 2003.

Hillers, D. R. *Covenant: The History of a Biblical Idea.* Seminars in the History of Ideas. Baltimore: Johns Hopkins Press, 1969.

Knight, Douglas A., and Amy-Jill Levine. *The Meaning of the Bible: What the Jewish Scriptures and Christian Old Testament Can Teach Us.* New York: HarperOne, 2011.

The New Testament Story:
Jesus and the New Covenant

PURPOSE Chapter four outlines the story of Jesus of Nazareth and introduces the birth and development of Christianity through the Jesus movement as the new covenant.

Now that we have established the "big picture" of the world behind the New Testament authors and their texts, in terms of Judaism and the Old Testament story, we can turn our attention to the larger world in which they lived and worked. The world of the Roman Empire is the sociocultural milieu that was familiar to them. It is also the world in which they understood God to have acted and to continue to act in and through Jesus Christ. This is the contextual background that ultimately compelled them to write their understandings of the good news.

The World of the New Testament Story

Once we arrive in the first century of the Common Era on the east coast of the Mediterranean Sea in the regions of Judea, Samaria, and Galilee, we are in the midst of a complex world indeed. Biblical scholar Luke Timothy Johnson discusses social environments in terms of "**symbolic worlds.**" He suggests that we all get along in our cultures by forming symbolic worlds through which we live, learn, work, and pass on wisdom to the next generation. These symbolic worlds influence, but more importantly are influenced by, the larger world around us. Thus, a symbolic world is made up of the social structures in which people live, and of the symbols attached to and supporting those structures.

Johnson also claims that in the case of the eastern Roman Empire in the first century, it might be better to speak of *symbolic worlds*, so complex and pluralistic was this setting. This diverse climate was constituted by the combination of four distinctive elements: Jewish religion, Mediterranean culture, Hellenistic civilization, and Roman rule. It is from these elements in their life-setting

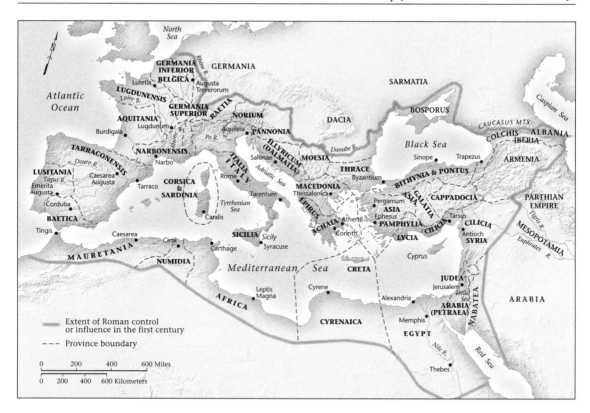

PALESTINE IN THE FIRST-CENTURY ROMAN EMPIRE

that first-century Jewish people in general, Jesus and his disciples in particular, as well as the later writers of the New Testament, were given symbols with which to develop their worldviews and understand how God was working in their world.

Jewish Religion

We have already said a great deal about the world of Judaism in the previous chapter. Here it will serve us well simply to draw some major points together in terms of the Jewish self-understanding of Jesus and those around him. The Judaism of the first century was complex. As we saw in the last

> **The North American Symbolic World**
>
> The North American symbolic world is diverse and multifaceted. It includes constitutional issues such as freedom of religion and expression, the right to vote, and the right to privacy. It also includes more esoteric concerns such as individualism and the pursuit of happiness. The list goes on for the varying race, ethnic, gender, sexual orientation, and familial identities that make up the ever-evolving society. Readers should cultivate an understanding of their own symbolic make-ups.

chapter, it was the product of a long history of covenantal relationship with the one God, which looked back to Abraham, as the father of the nation, and to Moses, as the one who freed Israel from the slavery of Egypt and to whom

The Second Temple
(often called Herod's
Temple in the first
century)

God gave the law. King David was the remembered hero, and a hoped-for Messiah—or "anointed one" who would defeat any who would oppress the Jewish people—would rise from the house of David. But the royal line had disappeared over time, and the nation had suffered great losses and exile. The land, which they understood to be theirs by divine right, was, in reality, no longer theirs, as it was occupied by a foreign regime. Acts of heroism on the part of the Maccabees and their descendants a few centuries earlier led to the reestablishment of Israel, but it soon fell into division and turmoil. Diverse groups such as the Pharisees, Sadducees, and Essenes had emerged, and their various ways of approaching the contemporary situation sometimes put them in conflict with each other. In the time of Jesus and the early Christians, there was no independent Israel. The land was ruled by Rome through the agency of a puppet royalty and local governors. Eventually, Jewish conflict with the Roman occupiers was so intense that it led to the First Jewish Revolt of 65–70 CE. This uprising held on for a surprising length of time, but the Romans eventually broke through the city walls, burning and leaving devastation in their wake, including the destruction of the Temple. Judaism has always been marked by people of great holiness and fidelity. However, there were times when the God of Israel and his commandments were remembered only by a remnant. The first century CE was, therefore, a time of change and challenge for the Jewish people.

In the time of Jesus and the earliest Christians, there were many ways of being Jewish, just as today there are many ways in which people accept the Christian faith. In those days, Sadducees, Pharisees, Zealots, Essenes, and Christians, to mention only the best-known groups, lived side by side and practiced a common faith. Belief in the one true God, worshiping God in the Temple, and the observance of God's commandments stood at the center of this faith. But that observance was understood in different ways, often shaped by the history that gave birth to those various expressions of Judaism. Nevertheless, Judaism had its history (interpreted and told in its Scriptures), its law (Torah), its traditions, and its land. Jesus lived and died at a time when these fundamentals of the Jewish way of life and hope were under threat.

There were different ways of understanding how God would resolve this threat and restore the land, the observance of the law, and a community that lived by the law and its traditions. One way was known as "messianism," that is, the hope for a Messiah. But not everyone expected a Messiah. The hopes for a saving figure whom God would raise up from among the people fluctuated, depending upon the sociopolitical situation of Israel at any given time. At the time of Jesus, there were hopes for a Messiah who might be a soldier Messiah of the line of David; but there were also hopes for a messianic priest or prophet like Moses. Some hoped for a combination of both. Above all, Jewish hope was based on the unshakeable belief that God would intervene, destroying all evil and restoring the original glory and beauty of his creation, lost because of human sin and disorder. In the end, God would reign over all. We must keep all this in mind when we read or hear the words "the kingdom of God" in New Testament books.

Mediterranean Culture

The Jewish world described above did not exist in a vacuum. The larger Mediterranean culture had always served as the backdrop of the development of these religious symbols and beliefs. Although this world was deeply affected by the empires that swept through it over time, the patterns of the Mediterra-

---

Messianic Expectations

Recall that the expression "Christ" is the Greek form of the Hebrew/Aramaic expression "Messiah." It means "anointed one" and was used before Christian times to refer to an anointed king. The Jewish people believed that God's covenant with David insured that one of his descendants would be their Messiah. Historical events, including subjugation by the Romans, resulted in conflicting expectations about the Messiah. In the first century CE, some thought he would be a priest; others expected a prophet like Moses; others hoped for a royal and military figure. Not all Jews hoped for a Messiah, but most looked to a figure who would release Israel from its service to the Roman Empire. Several individuals arose who claimed to be such a messiah. Jesus and the Gospels have a very different, more God-oriented idea of Jesus as the Messiah, or Christ.

Elijah and the Prophet as Messianic Figures

In John 1:20–21, after John the Baptist rejects any notion that he is the Messiah, his interrogators ask if he is Elijah or the Prophet. The story of the prophet Elijah is found in 1 Kings 17:1–2 Kings 2:18. In the early verses of 2 Kings 2, Elijah is taken up into heaven in a chariot of fire. Elijah was considered God's true prophet who does not die but is taken directly to God, and many expectations of Elijah's return developed over time. The later prophet Malachi refers to Elijah as a messianic precursor who will prepare the way for the Day of the Lord (4:5). By the first century CE, great hopes were in place for Elijah's return. "The Prophet" is a reference to a prophet like Moses. In Deuteronomy 18:18, God tells Moses, "I will raise up for them a prophet like you from among their own people; I will put my words in the mouth of the prophet, who shall speak to them everything that I command." Since the death of Moses, the people had been hoping for a "prophet like Moses" as part of their messianic expectations. Later in the Gospel of John, the people even wonder if Jesus has taken this role (6:14; 7:40).

nean culture were deeply infused in the Jewish way of life. The larger economy was still primarily agricultural and based in rural villages, but the trade of the sea was booming, and the diversity of languages, philosophies, and religions allowed for growth and the development of new ideas. This world of large households run by patriarchs with slaves facilitated a culture of severe disparities between the elites and the majority of the population. A system of patronage developed as benefactors, and beneficiaries sought honor and avoided shame at all costs. This world of land and sea, food and wine, agriculture and trade, and haves and have-nots also provided the setting for the multifaceted civilization of the Greeks.

Hellenistic Civilization

As we have already discussed, the Jewish people of the first century CE had a history, whether as a nation or as an occupied ethnic group, of being forever under siege and conquered by the Assyrians and the Babylonians. Prior to the Roman occupation of the first century, the people had been subjected to the Persians and were eventually swept into the Hellenistic Empire that had its origins in Alexander the Great. An incredible leader who lived only from 356 to 323 BCE, he conquered almost the whole of the known world before dying at thirty-three years of age. He believed the Greek language and culture of his time (known as Hellenism) were so significant that they should be accepted and used by the whole world. After Alexander, his generals fought over the Hellenistic Empire, and Israel passed from the Hellenistic rulers in Egypt (known as the Ptolemies) to the Hellenistic rulers in Syria (known as the Seleucids).

Especially important for the development of apocalyptic writings in Israel was the period of suffering under the Seleucid King Antiochus IV, during whose time Daniel was composed.

Greek culture, language, and religion permeated Jewish life. It is most likely that Jesus spoke Aramaic (a holdover in Judea and the surrounding region from the time of the Persian Empire) and some Greek. Indeed, Greek would have been the common language even of the Roman Empire—the language of literature, commerce, and trade. As it does in all cultures, language also provides for symbols and ways of understanding both the natural world and the potential for a supernatural reality. The Jewish people were also affected by these ideas about reality. In the Hellenistic world, the people hungered for a way to God, for salvation. They developed miracle stories and miraculous locations. Most important in this "hunger for God" was the development of the mystery religions and Gnosticism. These forms of faith had captured the hearts and minds of many. They were religions into which specially privileged and illuminated people entered, assured of salvation through contact with, or knowledge of, the gods. Such religious thinking was foreign to Judaism but very much a part of the world that saw the birth of Christianity and the writing of the New Testament.

Jesus and the people around him would also have been familiar with Hellenistic thinking about philosophy and religion. The time of Greek rule, however, had come and gone. The iron fist of the Roman Empire was now the pervasive power looming over the Jewish people.

Alexander the Great

Born in Macedonia 356 CE, Alexander was a remarkable figure who extended a form of Greek religion and culture (called Hellenism) across the whole of the Mediterranean basin, and even into northern India. He achieved stunning military victories and took non-Greek peoples into his armies and into his court. He died of an illness in 323 CE, at the age of thirty-three.

Roman Rule

After a brief period of independence, due to the victory over the Hellenistic Empire of the Seleucids in the Maccabean wars (in the second century BCE), the growth of the Roman Empire swallowed Israel. The birth and development of Christianity as a world religion owe much to the Roman Empire. Christianity came into existence during the high point of Roman rule, a period referred to as the Roman peace (the *pax Romana*). We know that in an act of violence Jesus was crucified, a Roman form of execution. But peaceful conditions that dominated the Roman system where local administrations were allowed to continue, as long as the Roman dominion was not threatened, accompanied the beginnings of a new world religion. The books of the New Testament reflect a believing community moving freely into the world beyond Judaism and the Jewish homeland of Judea.

As the Hellenistic powers faded and the Roman Empire took over, new religions emerged. This was a time when the established religions were losing their attraction. The classical Greek religions were fading, helped by the fact that the Romans did not come with new religions of their own. They tended to adapt the fading Greek religions and use them as they saw fit. Alexander the Great eventually declared himself to be a "son of God," and subsequently the Roman Emperors had themselves proclaimed as "gods" and demanded emperor worship.

These political and religious components of the Roman Empire were a constant shadow looming over the Jewish people across the world of the New

Testament. As we read the New Testament texts, we must try to take in the depth of the tension and conflict of an occupying force that at once allows for security and freedom of movement *and* is seen as the enemy who encroaches upon God-given land and liberty and who threatens their very survival as a religious people. Such is the complex world of the New Testament and the east coastal regions of the Mediterranean Sea in the first century CE. All four of the elements in this section contribute to this complexity and both to the struggle and the hope for God's intervention that we have been discussing. This is the world into which Jesus of Nazareth was born.

Jesus of Nazareth

Jesus was a Jew, and so were his first disciples. Scholars suggest the dates of his lifetime as ca. 4 BCE–30 CE. The Gospel of Matthew narrates Jesus's birth sometime before the death of Herod the Great, the puppet king of Judea and the surrounding regions, who died in 4 BCE. Further, all four Gospels as well as early Christian tradition affirm that Jesus was arrested, convicted of a capital crime, and crucified under the Roman governor Pontius Pilate. Roman records indicate that Pilate governed Judea and the surrounding regions from 26 to 36 CE. Tradition, coupled with the gospel accounts, also holds that at around age thirty Jesus took on a public ministry (Luke 3:23) that lasted some three years (see the mention of three annual Passover festivals in John 2:13; 6:4; 11:55). Scholars therefore posit that Jesus came to trial sometime in the middle of Pilate's ten-year term (ca. 30 CE).

The Gospels also indicate that Jesus grew up in Nazareth, a town that likely served as what we today might call a "suburb" of the larger city of Sepphoris in the region of Galilee. These early decades of the first century CE saw the Roman Empire at the height of its power and control of the Mediterranean, and the region of Galilee was populated by people restless in their current political and social situation. Messianic expectations were at a fever pitch. If both Jesus and his disciples grew up in Galilee, they were surrounded by these hopes. Indeed, the name Jesus Christ, so familiar to us as if it were his family name, is really a title adopted in the early Christian community, indicating the belief of his followers that Jesus of Nazareth was the expected Messiah of Israel.

Roman Emperor Worship

At least from the time of Alexander the Great (356–323 BCE), a cult developed around the figure of the emperor, giving him divine status. Often this took place after death, as authorities raised monuments in honor of the deceased emperor. However, Roman emperors, with various levels of intensity, developed cults around their person while they ruled. Initially, these cults generated unity across the empire. It does not seem likely that Christians were persecuted for not attending to their cultic obligations toward the ruling emperor during the New Testament period, although that became a problem in a later period (second and third centuries). Several authors of New Testament documents certainly have the cult of the emperor in mind when they exhort Christians to avoid all worship of false gods and to affirm the unique Lordship of Jesus Christ.

Head of Christ
by Rembrandt

It may come as a surprise to hear that we do not have a life of Jesus as we would understand the "life of" anyone. We will discuss the Gospels in more detail in the next chapter, but for now we can say that each of the four Gospels tells its story of Jesus differently. They were not written to be read as a modern biography, or "life of Jesus." It might also be a surprise to know that the man so commonly known today as "Jesus Christ" was never known by that during his life. He was known as "**Jesus of Nazareth**" (see especially Matt 2:23). He was probably also known as "Jesus, son of Joseph" (see John 1:45). These were the ways by which men were commonly identified in the ancient world. Therefore, the best we can do is trace the elements of his life by looking across the Gospels to find an outline of his story.

Jesus's story would look something like this. After his young life in Nazareth, about which we know little or nothing, he appeared on the scene at about thirty years of age. Although very different, the stories of Jesus's birth and beginnings (Matt 1–2; Luke 1–2) agree that he grew up in Galilee and began his ministry there. However, initially he was most likely a follower of John the Baptist, who may also have been related to him, as we hear in the Gospel of Luke (1:36). On some occasions, John the Baptist speaks of Jesus as one who "comes after him," probably indicating that he was his follower (see Mark 1:7; Matt 3:11; John 1:27). However, as the Baptist faded from the scene, arrested and eventually slain by Herod, Jesus began his own ministry, probably in Galilee (see John 3:22–24; Mark 1:14–15; Matt 4:12–17; Luke 4:14–15).

Jesus was a wandering teacher who brought much hope and love into a society that was oppressed by the presence of the Romans and exploited by the wealthy. As he began to teach about the coming of the reigning presence of God into the hearts and lives of all men and women, he quickly gathered many who followed him and placed their hopes in him. He was certainly seen as a prophet like the great prophets of Israel (see Mark 8:28; Matt 16:14; Luke 9:19; John 4:19, 44). He chose an inner circle of twelve to journey with him (see Mark 3:13–14; Matt 10:2–4; Luke 6:12–13; John 6:70). There was probably also a larger group of friends and disciples who followed him, including women (see Luke 8:1–3), and many people in the villages and even the towns who looked to him with hope. Indeed, he became so popular that the Romans and even

---

John the Baptist

The figure of John the Baptist appears in all four Gospels as one whose ministry precedes and points to that of Jesus. That said, the evangelists characterize the role of the Baptist somewhat differently. Interestingly, John's Gospel may preserve some of the oldest traditions about the relationship between Jesus and John the Baptist, even though John is never called "the Baptist." John speaks of Jesus as "the one who comes after me" (John 1:15, 27, 30), indicating that Jesus may once have been a follower of John the Baptist. In 3:22–26 we may have traces of a very old tradition that indicates that John and Jesus carried on parallel baptizing ministries for a time, before the imprisonment and execution of John.

Shame and Honor in the Culture of the Ancient World

Students of the NT and the ancient Mediterranean world in general must bear in mind the important place of honor and shame in these societies. Honor was universally regarded as the highest asset for human beings, while shame was the ultimate burden. Much of public life therefore revolved around ensuring one's family received honor and avoided shame. This means that, with such a high value placed on honor, humility was rarely considered virtuous. Unlike in modern society, activities such as boasting and self-promotion were esteemed, but deference and self-effacement were shameful. This makes John the Baptist's attitude toward Jesus and his mission an exceedingly important, and countercultural, witness for those around him.

Feeding of the Five Thousand; Jesus Walking on the Water (1386)

some Jewish authorities became concerned that he might cause trouble—arousing the people to rebellion (see John 11:45–54). They thought he might even be seen as the much-expected Messiah of Israel (see Mark 8:29; Matt 16:16; Luke 9:20; John 1:41).

Jesus was unhappy with any popular acclaim that he might be the expected Messiah. Throughout the Gospels he is cautious about any such acclamation. This was especially clear as he did not ride into Jerusalem on a warhorse with a sword in his hand to drive out the enemies of the true Israel (see Mark 11:1–10; Matt 21:1–9; Luke 19:28–38; John 12:12–19). If he was the hoped-for Messiah, then, his actions and teaching seemed to be redefining these standard messianic expectations. This is symbolized in the title with which he prefers to designate himself and his role, the "Son of Man" (see, e.g., Mark 2:10; Matt 8:20; Luke 5:24; John 1:51; see also Dan 7:13). Indeed, he began to speak of openness to God, to the need for unconditional love and obedience, even unto death (see Mark 8:34–9:1; Matt 16:24–28; Luke 9:23–27; John 13:1–21). And yet, Jesus made it clear to his followers that he did not see death as the end of his story. He showed trust and confidence in God, whom he dared to call "Father" (see Mark 14:36; John 5:17; 8:16, 49, 54; 10:29–30; 12:27–28; 17:1–24). God would somehow be victorious, not just in spite of but *through* Jesus's death, and vindicate his suffering (Mark 8:31; 9:31; 10:32–34). Many of the disciples, and even his inner circle of twelve, found this difficult to accept, and the Gospels tell us, in their various ways, that one of them betrayed him, another denied him, and everyone else ran away.

All the Gospels agree in what is commonly known as the Passion Narrative (Mark 14–15; Matt 26–27; Luke 22–23; John 18–19). Jesus was arrested and put through some sort of Jewish trial process, followed by a trial before the Roman governor Pilate. Ultimately, Jesus was convicted of the crime of treason—a threat to the *pax Romana*—and for this insurrection was sentenced to death by crucifixion, the Romans' preferred method of capital punishment, for its dual purpose as a public warning to others who might have similar ideas.

In the end, Jesus was crucified alone, the worst death the Romans could inflict upon anyone. After three days, women (maybe only one, Mary Magdalene [John 20:1–18]) found an empty

Crucifixion

Death by crucifixion was the most horrible process used by the Romans, reserved for the worst of criminals and those who rebelled against Roman authority. These criminals were hung on a cross of wood on the main road leading into the city to indicate that the rule of law governed the area. The uprights of the cross were often left in place to act as deterrents to all who entered the city. Victims would typically be left on the cross for days to succumb to the elements. Death would often come by suffocation as the crucified could no longer hold themselves up to inhale and their lungs would collapse.

The Temple Area

In the time of Jesus, generally called the time of the Second Temple, or even "Second Temple Judaism," the very large space occupied by the Temple in Jerusalem was made up of three discrete regions, surrounded by a large area where gentiles were permitted, called the court of the gentiles. Furthest from the sanctuary (the holy of holies) was the court of the women. Closer to the sanctuary was the court of the Israelites, strictly reserved for suitably prepared Jewish men. The final court was for the priests. It contained the altar of sacrifice and the holy of holies. It was regarded as the dwelling place of God. After the Temple's destruction in 70 CE, the rabbis remembered it as the dwelling place on earth of the "glory of God."

tomb, and more and more people had an experience of the risen Jesus (1 Cor 15:3–8). He was alive! He has been raised!

Now they began to understand that Jesus was the Messiah, but the Messiah that God wanted, not the one expected by popular culture. Now he could/should be called Jesus Christ. Many of the disciples gathered, their weakness was forgiven, they were promised they would continue his presence in the world in their meals, their prayers, their love, their hope, and in their imitation of Jesus—prepared to be faithful and obedient to God unto death, confident that God would have the last word.

The Tradition of Women at the Empty Tomb

All four Gospels report that women disciples of Jesus discovered his empty tomb. Only in the Gospel of John is Mary Magdalene alone. John singles out Mary Magdalene's journey of faith, but her presence alone at the tomb may reflect the earliest tradition. Perhaps, since the witness of one woman would not be accepted, as the tradition grew in the early church the number of witnesses increased.

The Birth of Christianity

That is how the **church** began, though it was not known by that name until much later. The English word "church" comes from the Greek word *ekklēsia*, which essentially means "gathering." Therefore, when we think of the "early church" we should not think of ornate buildings or organized hierarchies, but a relatively small gathering. The death and resurrection of Jesus created a community of fragile believers. They began to tell stories about his time among them, to celebrate a meal of thanksgiving "in memory of him," and they tried to live as he had taught them. Now deeper questions began

The Divine Passive Voice

In constructing sentences, authors use either the active or the passive voice: for example, "Peter denied Jesus" or "Jesus was denied by Peter." When authors use the divine passive voice, no agent of the action is identified. In the biblical stories, this unidentified agent is typically understood to be God; thus, the "divine passive." It appears regularly in the resurrection stories to indicate that God acted, even though God is never mentioned. See, for example, Mark 16:6:

"He has been raised." For Paul, see 1 Corinthians 15:4: "and that he was buried, and that he was raised on the third day in accordance with the scriptures." In John 20:2, the evangelist employs both the divine passive voice and irony since Mary Magdalene does not know who is the agent of the action she describes, but the audience, which has read the prologue and paid careful attention to the story thus far, is well aware that God has entered the scene.

to emerge. In the light of his death and resurrection, what was Jesus's relationship to the God of Israel whom he called "Father"? What was the gift of the Spirit he had promised would be with them? How had his death and resurrection offered a new life to humankind? It was out of all these thoughts, discussions, prayers, exhortations, and stories that what we now call **Christianity** was born.

As we discuss the claims of the first Christians, then, we would do better to think and talk in terms of a "**Jesus movement**" to really get a sense of the atmosphere of these early years. When we think of Christianity in the twenty-first century, we may think of a wide variety of ways of being "church," but we likely always think of a belief system that is well organized with a lot of resources and buildings and entrenched in the larger society. As this early Jesus movement began to gather—often in secret—to share and discuss their experiences of Jesus and their understanding of how God was working in the world, they were anything but these things. The first task of these early believers was to begin to come to a common understanding of who Jesus was and what he had accomplished through the will of God.

The members of this group within Judaism were eventually called **Christians** because of their belief that Jesus was the Christ (see Acts 11:26; 26:28; 1 Pet 4:15–16). As they affirmed their belief that Jesus was the long-awaited, long-hoped-for Messiah, however, they also had to come to terms with the fact that Jesus did not meet the common Jewish messianic expectation of God's "anointed one" who would be a geopolitical king like David and would throw off the yoke of Roman oppression. Nonetheless, Jesus's disciples were still convinced he was the Christ due to their experience of him. In their gatherings, discussions, and storytelling, they looked back into their Scriptures and began to realize that the alternative prophet-messiah who speaks the word of

---

The Name "Christian"

This name was used quite early by those who accepted that Jesus was the Christ. The origin of the name is difficult to assess. It first appears in NT documents that come from the final decades of the first century (Acts 11:26; 26:28; 1 Pet 4:16). Non-Christian references are much later, even though they refer to events from the first century. In 116 CE, the Roman historian Tacitus in his *Annals* tells of the emperor Nero's persecution of "the Christians" because of the fire of Rome in 64 CE. The Roman historian Suetonius, in his *The Twelve Caesars*, written in 121 CE, reports that the emperor Claudius banned Jewish people from Rome because of disturbances around a figure named "Chrestus." Whatever its historical origins, the early use of the word "Christian" to describe people who believed that Jesus of Nazareth was "the Christ" was appropriate.

Mary Magdalene
and the Risen Jesus.
Noli me tangere by
Jerónimo Cósida.

God and suffers, even sacrifices, on behalf of the people fit their experience
of Jesus—his life, ministry, *and* death. What really made the Jesus movement
different from other messianic movements of the first century CE, however, is
also what allowed them to survive the initial chaos of his arrest and crucifixion:
the **resurrection faith**.

The disciples' conviction that Jesus was dead, then alive again, made the
Jesus movement different than other messianic movements. Most of these early
groups would rally around a figure in which they would put their nationalis-
tic and religious hopes. When the Romans quashed their plans, often killing
the leader to set an example, the group would go into hiding and eventually
dissipate. This was the desired effect. The Gospels suggest the early Christians
experienced just such a panic at Jesus's death but overcame this early doubt
and fear as a result of their experience of the risen Jesus. Therefore, they came
to believe the resurrection to be proof that Jesus is God's Anointed One, not
bound by death. But if his role as Christ was not to put in place a new sovereign
nation like the kingdom of David, what was it?

Again, turning to their Scriptures and the long-held understandings of how God works in the world, which we discussed in the previous chapter, the Jesus movement began to recognize new covenantal activity. Paul, the most prolific early Christian theologian and author, was the first (who was preserved) to articulate that the faith and sacrifice of Jesus fulfilled the Sinai covenant stipulation of sacrifice to atone for sin. Further, the remembrance of Jesus's own preferred self-designation as the Son of Man echoed the book of Daniel's vision of one who would come from God to redeem the people. The basic belief of the developing church, then, was that God had put in place a **new covenant** through Jesus Christ. Jesus was the Messiah whose death was the sacrifice that atoned for all sin for all time and thereby fulfilled the promises of God's earlier covenants. This new covenant through Jesus was available not just to ethnic Jews, but once again to all humankind, as it was in the covenant with Adam. The determining factor for the potential receivers of God's new covenant offer was no longer being an ethnic descendent of Abraham who keeps Torah, but being anyone who believes that Jesus is the Christ, sent from God to make relationship with God available to all through his life and death. A term that we can use to encompass the entirety of this story is the **Christ Event**. This term is used as a shorthand of sorts

---

Resurrection Faith

The fundamental and founding experience of Christianity is the resurrection of Jesus. Without the encounter that the first Christians had with the risen Jesus, there would be no Christianity. This does not mean that Christianity is founded on an empty tomb. It means that Christians believe that Jesus lives on, no longer simply a good man with a powerful message. God has broken into the human story by raising Jesus from the dead and showing Jesus as the first and most perfect human being who responded unconditionally to the will of God. When Greek Christians greet one another at Easter they say: "Christ is risen!" To which the response is: "Christ is truly risen!" This encounter captures the essence of Easter faith.

The Earliest Church

In order to understand the spirit of the first Christians, we must set aside modern notions of "the church" as made up of large and well-structured organizations. The first Christians were people from various walks of life, initially Jewish, but rapidly reaching out to non-Jews, and they struggled to understand what God had done for humankind in and through Jesus Christ. Many of these struggles are reflected in the documents of the New Testament. Paul's Letters show the powerful development of a belief system that has its roots in Jewish tradition but reaches out to the whole world. Matthew's Gospel is written for a small group of Jewish Christians, struggling with their new faith and mission. Luke's Gospel and the Acts of the Apostles are directed to the gentile world. The Gospel of John is a good example of how the early church adapted its storytelling to speak to the Greco-Roman world in a way that made sense to these first recipients of the Christian message. There was no one "institutional church" as Christianity began.

to refer to the entirety of the life, ministry, death, and resurrection of Jesus as well as this developing belief that Jesus is the long-awaited Messiah who is not bound by death.

The absolute conviction in the resurrection led these early believers to articulate that since the Christ was not bound by death, neither would his followers be. Even in this they were following the recent teaching of the Jewish Scriptures (see Dan 12), and also the belief of Jesus (see Mark 12:18–27). They began to talk about right relationship with God in this world leading to eternal union with God in the heavenly realm (see 1 Cor 15). Indeed, Jesus Christ's ability to take on death and overcome it allowed for the further articulation of Jesus as the Son of God, one whose divine origins dictated that he now be understood as the risen Lord who returned to his Father and paved the way for all believers to do the same. This is the **good news** of the new covenant.

These developing beliefs, the opening of covenant relationship with God to Jews and **gentiles** (non-Jews) alike and the understanding of Jesus as divine, put the early Christians, many of whom were ethnic Jews, at odds with mainstream Judaism by the end of the first century CE. As we indicated in chapter one and again earlier in this chapter, Judaism in the early part of the century was quite diverse. Belief or, at the very least, hope that one or another was a potential messiah was somewhat commonplace. The First Jewish Revolt against Rome from 65 to 70 CE changed all this. The failure of this revolt resulted in the burning of Jerusalem and the destruction of the Temple. Judaism was once again on the brink of dissolution. Many of the groups that were so active during Jesus's life were either wiped out or dispersed in the aftermath. The Sadducees, Essenes, and Zealots were no longer unified, powerful groups. Some would have continued after the war, but they eventually disappeared. The Pharisees were reorganizing as rabbis who were attempting to reorganize Judaism by putting in place a canon of Scripture and an orthodox belief system. The early Christians, once just one more group within Judaism, could no longer be reconciled with the Jewish ethnic identity based in the Abrahamic and Sinai covenants and the continued hope for a Messiah to come. Christianity and Judaism began to diverge onto their own trajectories as distinct forms of faith. The First Jewish Revolt and this beginning separation provided the context for the writing of the Gospels and much of the New Testament.

Using historical criticism, we can reconstruct the development of the Jesus movement into the early Christian tradition to establish the historical

---

Gentiles

The term "gentile" or "gentiles" comes from the Latin *gentilis*, which means "of a family or nation, of the same clan." This term was first used in the Latin translation of the Bible, called the Vulgate, to translate the Greek word *ethnos*, or *ethnē* in the plural, meaning "nation" or "nations." The term is used in the NT to refer to anyone who is not Jewish. It is not an ethnic designation in and of itself but can be used generally of any non-Jew.

context of early Christianity and the world that facilitated the writing of
the documents that became the New Testament. This, in turn, facilitates
their exegesis. We discuss this as the stages in the development of Christian
tradition.

The Stages in the Development of the Christian Tradition

Stage 1: Palestinian Aramaic-Speaking Christianity, 30s CE

The early Jesus movement can be characterized as Aramaic-speaking and
centered in Jerusalem among ethnically Jewish disciples of Jesus who believed that he was the long-hoped-for Messiah sent by God to Israel as
promised in the covenant with David. This stage spanned the 30s of the first
century CE.

Stage 2: Jewish Christianity in the Greco-Roman Empire, 40s CE

In subsequent years, Jewish Christianity spread through Judea to Samaria and
Antioch and into the Hellenistic Roman Empire through the felt urgency of
missionary preaching. The apostles understood the risen Christ to have given
them a mission to share the good news of the new covenant to any and all
who would hear. The focus is still primarily among Jews, but the movement
into the larger empire necessitated the shift to Greek language and culture in
theological reflection and storytelling. This stage crosses the 40s of the first
century CE.

Stage 3: Christianity in the Greco-Roman World, 50s CE

In this period, Christian preaching in the Greco-Roman world began to attract larger numbers of gentiles. This new cultural milieu led to shifts in emphases to include both the Jewish roots of Jesus and his role as divine Son of God. This stage developed across the 50s and into the 60s of the first century CE primarily, but not solely, through the work of the apostle Paul and his understanding of a new covenant available to all through faith, regardless of ethnicity or social status. This, in turn, led to the widening gap between Judaism and developing Christianity. What we have just said about the role of Paul in this third stage is most likely not the whole truth, but it is the way the story of the growth of the Christian community is told in the Acts of the Apostles. There were no doubt other missionaries and even martyrs across this period, about whom we do not know. Paul is the figure whose story is told, but the rapid growth of Christianity must have been generated by others, alongside Paul.

Stage 4: The First Jewish Revolt and Its Aftermath, 60s–130s CE

The First Jewish Revolt against Rome of 65–70 CE marks the beginning of the fourth stage. The devastating loss of this war and the resulting burning of Jerusalem and destruction of the Temple was a watershed moment in the history of Judaism and development of Christianity. We discussed this era and its effects on Judaism in chapter one. By this time, the first generation of Jesus's disciples had also largely passed, many of them martyred for the profession of their newfound or newly oriented faith in Jesus as the Christ. This is the immediate context for the composition of the Gospel of Mark. The other three Gospels and Acts followed in succeeding decades. This stage crossed the turn of the century and closed with the Second Jewish Revolt against Rome (132–135 CE). This second revolt was explicitly messianic in nature, and its loss was even more devastating for the Jewish people. The Romans expelled them from Jerusalem and renamed the entire region Palestine. The year 135 CE can mark the beginning of the separation of Judaism and Christianity as distinct religious traditions.

What Have We Learned So Far? Jesus and the Good News

Christianity developed out of Judaism; therefore, we can expect similar theological worldviews in the two religious traditions. Indeed, every aspect of Christian belief finds its foundation in ancient Judaism. The hallmark of Jewish theology is monotheism, the belief in one all-powerful creator and sovereign God. This view of God and how God works in the world was countercultural, even subversive, in the Roman Empire. Christianity also maintained this strong belief system. What developed in the early Jesus movement, however, was also a Christology that was intimately connected to this theology. The common Jewish messianic expectations were somewhat diverse but understood the Messiah to be fully human. During his lifetime, Jesus set about redefining those messianic expectations. The early Christians, upon their experience of the resurrection and their reflection upon who Jesus was and what God did in and through Jesus, began to develop a further understanding of Jesus as, yes, fully human, but *also* divine. As the Christ, Jesus was the Son of Man (human) who was also the Son of God (divine). But this understanding did not take away from the oneness of God. Eventually, the early Christians also came to understand a third person in this divine relationship, which communicated the fullness of what this relationship could be in God's creation. Still using terminology from the Jewish Scriptures, Christians call this third person the Holy Spirit. Eventually the Christian communities will identify this theological understanding of God as a unity of one in three persons as **Trinity**. This intimate relationship of theology and Christology will take centuries to develop, but we can see the seeds planted across the New Testament books. As this textbook moves forward, we will also see that what the authors of the books of the New Testament say about Father, Son, and Holy Spirit sometimes creates more questions than answers. It took the church almost three hundred years of arguing, thinking, praying, and celebrating before it came to state its belief in a Triune God, commonly known as the Trinity (the Council of Nicaea in 325 CE).

> **The Second Jewish Revolt against Rome**
>
> The Second Jewish Revolt against Rome occurred from 132 to 135 CE. It was preceded by years of clashes between Jews and Romans in the area. The misrule of Rufus, the Roman governor of Judea, combined with the emperor Hadrian's intention to found a Roman colony on the site of Jerusalem and his restrictions on Jewish religious freedom and observances provoked Bar Kokhba, who claimed to be the Messiah, to lead the uprising. Although they initially gained traction and instilled hope, Bar Kokhba's forces proved no match against the methodical and ruthless tactics of the Roman military. Upon the death of Bar Kokhba, the rebellion was crushed in 135, and the Jewish people were banned from Jerusalem for a time. These consequences were possibly even more devastating than those of the First Revolt.

The Christian understanding of the new covenant bred many new developments; the aspect that is clearly recognizable around the world in the twenty-first century is ecclesiology. As we discussed in the introduction, this concept comes from the Greek word *ekklēsia*, meaning gathering, and is related to the Jewish concept of the synagogue. As we further indicated earlier in this chapter, the term *ekklēsia* comes into English as "church" and refers to the community of believers as they gather, reflect, worship, and support one another. Only eventually does this term also come to refer to buildings and the institutions of the Christian religion. What we see in the New Testament is the gathering of believers in Jesus the Christ—those who found a common theology, Christology, and worldview based on equal footing as human beings before God through Christ. This church is open and inclusive to all who believe; the cultural conditions of

Jesus, as Pantocrator
(The Church of the Holy
Savior in Chora, Istanbul)
© Guillaume Piolle

race, gender, ethnicity, and social class so pervasive in the Roman Empire no longer apply. As we explore the New Testament, we come face to face with this subversive reality and the challenges it often posed for the burgeoning tradition and still poses for Christians today.

The final components of the theological worldview that we have touched upon in this chapter are those of eschatology and soteriology. These two concepts often go hand in hand in religious traditions and are always connected in Christianity. The resurrection faith that we discussed above means that Christians believe that Jesus lived, died, and was resurrected by God to live again. After some time on earth with his disciples, the risen Christ ascended to heaven to dwell with God the Father. Many Christians believed that Jesus would return to earth one day to end the world as we know it and launch a new age of the kingdom of God on earth. This "second coming" is often referred to by its Greek term, the *parousia*. This is, broadly speaking, Christian eschatology, that at the end of days Jesus would come again to inaugurate a new reign for the faithful. Further, Jesus's victory over death also conquered death for all the faithful. What exactly this might look like, when it might happen and where and how it might manifest, vary among the New Testament authors. Again, as we saw above, the New Testament sometimes creates more questions than answers. That is fine, as the history of the church and its faith unfolds around its search for these answers. Regardless, this sort of eternal dwelling in union with God the Father and Jesus the Son and Christ is both the essence of eschatology and its intersection with soteriology, the Christian understanding of salvation.

New Testament authors write about two kinds of eschatology and soteriology. What we have discussed so far can be called **"end-time" eschatology** and looks to the future for the culmination of history and the kingdom of God. At that point, the timing of which no human can know, the faithful will be rewarded with full union with God. Those who have passed will be raised from the dead to this same eternal dwelling. Another perspective is called **realized eschatology** and focuses on the present and how salvation can be experienced now. What this means is that union with God in full relationship can be experienced the moment one accepts Jesus as the Christ and believes that God put in place a new covenant through him. This sort of "present-tense" salvation allows for a reign of God on earth in this time through the community of believers. This sort of eschatology and soteriology is beautifully expressed in the Gospel of Luke when Jesus proclaims to Zacchaeus, "Today salvation has come to this house, because he too is a son of Abraham. For the Son of Man came to seek out and save the lost" (Luke 19:9–10). Eternal life in communion with God is still promised, but that life begins now.

In the New Testament, we will find both of these kinds of belief systems fully entrenched in the developing theology, Christology, and ecclesiology of first-century Christianity. They can and do often exist together. We will therefore develop our understanding of all of these aspects of the theological worldview in more depth as we make our way through the contents of the NT.

Key Terms and Concepts

Christ Event

Christianity/Christians

church/*ekklēsia*

"end-time" eschatology

gentiles

good news

Hellenistic civilization

Jesus movement

Jesus of Nazareth

Judaism

Mediterranean culture

new covenant

parousia

realized eschatology

resurrection faith

Roman rule

symbolic worlds

Trinity

Questions for Review

1. The New Testament world was complex and diverse. With this in mind, identify and describe four major elements of this pluralistic cultural milieu.
2. Using information from the Gospels coupled with archaeological and historical evidence from the Roman Empire, scholars sketch the life and ministry of Jesus of Nazareth. How might that portrait look?
3. The birth of Christianity resulted from the early Jesus movement's conviction of the call to share the good news with the world. What exactly is this news, and why is it so good?
4. Identify and describe the steps in the movement from the life of Jesus of Nazareth to the composition of the written Gospels.
5. Discuss the stages in the development of the Christian tradition as they form the world behind the text of the Gospels.

Bibliography and Further Reading

Hurtado, Larry. *How on Earth Did Jesus Become a God? Historical Questions about Earliest Devotion to Jesus.* Grand Rapids: Eerdmans, 2005.

Johnson, Luke Timothy. *The Writings of the New Testament: An Interpretation.* 3rd ed. Minneapolis: Fortress, 2010.

Moloney, Francis J. *Reading the New Testament in the Church: A Primer for Pastors, Religious Educators, and Believers.* Grand Rapids: Baker Academic, 2015.

Nickle, Keith F. *The Synoptic Gospels: An Introduction.* Rev. and exp. ed. Louisville: Westminster John Knox, 2001.

Powell, Mark Allan. *Introducing the New Testament: A Historical, Literary, and Theological Survey.* Grand Rapids: Baker Academic, 2009.

Steggemann, Ekkehard W., and Wolfgang Steggemann. *The Jesus Movement: A Social History of Its First Century.* Translated by O. C. Dean. Minneapolis: Fortress, 1999.

White, L. Michael. *From Jesus to Christianity: How Four Generations of Visionaries and Storytellers Created the New Testament and Christian Faith.* New York: HarperOne, 2004.

The Narratives: Gospels and Acts

PURPOSE Chapter five discusses the narratives of the New Testament: the four Gospels and the Acts of the Apostles. The purpose is to provide exegetical insight into the worlds of the New Testament narratives in order to prepare students for study of the texts themselves.

For the first Christians, the memory of Jesus's life, teaching, death, and resurrection was still powerfully alive. Paul did not tell it as such, but with the passing of time and the gradual spread of the Christian communities beyond Judaism and into the larger Greco-Roman world, a question began to emerge: "Who was this man Jesus of Nazareth, whom Christians regard as the Christ, the Son of God?" Further, "how did this community come to understand itself as a church for all people?" The best way to answer that question, some believed, was to tell his story in terms of what God did for all humankind through him. In time, this telling led to the writing of what are now called gospels, as well as a narrative known as the Acts of the Apostles.

Studying the New Testament Narratives

There are four Gospels in the New Testament, all written anonymously and given the names of possible authors by Christian leaders late in the second century (Matthew, Mark, Luke, and John). These four Gospels are generally divided into two groups. Matthew, Mark, and Luke are called **Synoptic Gospels**. This expression comes from the fact that, by putting the three Gospels side by side, one can see that they closely compare with one another. They can be seen with "one look of the eye." This is what is meant by the Greek word behind "synoptic"—*syn-opsis*: "with the eye" or "seen together." This is not the case for the Gospel of John. The Synoptic Gospels all begin Jesus's ministry in Galilee and have him eventually journey to Jerusalem. After a brief but intense ministry in Jerusalem, he is arrested, tried, and executed. It is in Jerusalem that he dies and is raised. John, on the other hand, has Jesus moving in, around, and out of Jerusalem, the surrounding parts of Judea, and the region of Galilee across a two-year-plus public ministry that eventually (like the Synoptics) ends with his arrest and conviction in Jerusalem. For this reason, John is often studied separately, alongside letters contained in the NT that are identified with the same author (1, 2, and 3 John). In addition, scholars use the common nickname, the **Fourth Gospel**, to indicate its distinctive narrative. The Acts of the Apostles is studied as a genre in its own right and as the sequel to the Gospel of Luke.

Despite the overlap from the strong oral tradition that is preserved in written form, each evangelist has his own distinctive voice through which he presents his particular message for his early Christian community. To hear these voices as they stretch across the centuries and continue to teach twenty-first-century communities, we must consider once again the tools of exegesis and the art of biblical interpretation, which we have already introduced in this textbook. Therefore, we will briefly discuss the worlds behind, in, and in front of the texts of the NT narratives.

The Christian Doctrine of the Incarnation

The Christian doctrine of the incarnation was formally defined at the Council of Chalcedon in 451. The official teaching of Christianity is that Jesus Christ is at once both fully God and fully human, that his humanness does not take away from his divinity, and that his divinity does not take away from his humanity. Christianity has long called such doctrines "mysteries of the faith."

The World behind the Gospels and Acts

When biblical scholars use all the evidence available, including archaeological data, information from both in and outside the biblical text, music, art, and other artifacts of the period in order to reconstruct the world behind the text, they are seeking to establish **historical context**. We do this because we must understand as best as we can what the world looked like and what was important for the author in question. This is why we have spent two chapters on this context before we come to the literature that is preserved in the New Testament. The complex sociocultural milieu of the NT, comprised by Jewish religion, Mediterranean culture, Hellenistic civilization, and Roman rule, directly influences the perspective and content of the narratives. The life and death of the historical figure Jesus of Nazareth is the focus of the theological reflection that serves as the impetus behind the evangelists putting pen to paper. The birth of Christianity and the movement from the life of Jesus to the writing of narratives provide the historical context of the evangelists and the communities for whom they composed their narratives.

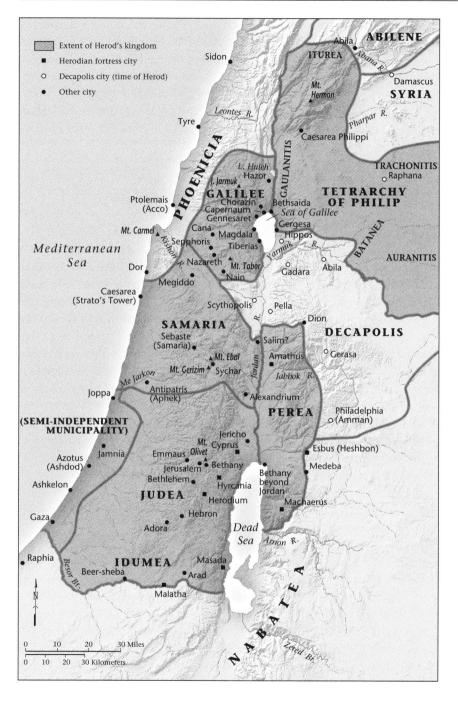

GALILEE, SAMARIA, AND JUDEA

In terms of historical criticism, then, we will trace the movement from the life of Jesus of Nazareth to the development of the New Testament narratives. Five major stages emerge: (1) the formation of the church as a community of believers; (2) the believers' teaching about their experiences; (3) the development of oral teachings (stories) about Jesus and the early church; (4) many uses of the same stories in varying contexts; and finally, (5) the crystallization of this oral tradition into the four written Gospels and Acts. Let's explore these developments in more detail.

The Formation of the Church as a Community of Believers

The community Jesus forged tells us much about the character of his ministry and even more about the strength of the bond that existed between those who believed in him as the Christ. In the previous chapter, we have already said a good deal about the early Jesus movement and the church it eventually formed. The Gospels had their beginnings in the life and teaching of Jesus of Nazareth. He was a human being, like us, who lived across the first thirty years of the Common Era. The birth of Christianity, as the Jesus movement, began as a small association of his disciples in the years that followed his death. They met, at first in secret, to reflect upon their experiences. In addition to their conviction that Jesus was the Christ who was resurrected from death, they soon came to believe that he was more than human; he was the Son of God. They then began to understand that he left them with a mission to share this good news with any and all who would hear. Across the next years, they met regularly, sharing a meal in memory of him, telling stories about him, and opening their community to all who came to share these beliefs.

The Believers' Teaching about Their Experiences

Certainly by the 40s and 50s CE, these disciples began to take it upon themselves to seek out opportunities to teach about Christ and their experiences of him. Some early Christians, like Peter and James of Jerusalem, continued their work largely in the Jewish communities, teaching in synagogues and other gatherings. Others hit the road and began to found small communities in cities across the Roman Empire. The apostle Paul eventually turned his attention exclusively to non-Jews, who are known as gentiles, and met people in the marketplace and organized small communities in the homes of believers. All the early leaders taught by sharing their stories.

The Development of Oral Teachings (Stories)
about Jesus and the Early Church

From the start, even before Jesus died, those who heard him remembered what he had said. His parables were especially memorable. They also remembered what he did and recalled the incredible authority he had over sickness and evil. They remembered that Jesus had told them that he was bringing in a new era, a time when God would reign in their hearts, minds, and lives as their king. He further indicated that this relationship with God through him is available to everyone. They remembered that, both in his teaching and in his very personality, there were clear signs that the kingdom of God was at hand. For decades, these "memories" remained unwritten. The early Christians encouraged one another in difficulty; they gathered for prayer and remembered things that Jesus had said and done. But there was no need for any "story" of Jesus. They knew it: they either had been with Jesus (the Twelve and probably some other followers, including significant women) or had at least known him (the people whose villages and homes he visited). One thing they all knew was that he had been crucified.

How did they overcome the scandal of the cross? This was the first problem that the earliest Christians had to handle. So they turned to Jesus's own teaching. Jesus had always trusted in his Father, and his Father entered the story after the crucifixion by raising Jesus from the dead. Jesus had died on a Roman cross, but the cross was now empty. The death and resurrection of Jesus might have happened at the end of Jesus's life, but they were the heart of the earliest Christian message. As Christians gathered for the celebration of a special meal, they told the story of what Jesus had said and done on the night before he died. In one of the oldest passages of the New Testament, Paul tells both this story of Jesus and how the earliest Christians began to ritualize the meal (1 Cor 11:17–34). Jesus, crucified and risen, continued to be with his followers, as they "remembered" him in a way that made him present. The "story" of Jesus's celebration of a meal, the beginning of eucharistic meals that are still the central celebration of the Christian community, must have been told often.

Another "story" that was told from the very beginnings of Christianity was the story of Jesus's passion, death, and resurrection. The fact that Jesus was crucified as a criminal was a challenge to all who followed him as the Christ and the Son of God. The narratives of Jesus's final night with his disciples, his prayer

Orality

Contemporary Gospel studies devote a great deal of attention to the obvious fact that the stories we have in the Gospels began their existence in a world in which very few people were literate. Reading is very common for us, but the Gospels began as oral (i.e., word of mouth) communication. Because this was so, it is helpful sometimes to "perform" the stories. When this is well done, we capture some of the emotional communication that can take place when a story is well told and well performed. It also takes us back to the way the Gospels began.

The Eucharist

The term "Eucharist" comes from the Greek verb that means "to give thanks." Associating giving thanks with a meal of bread and wine is based in Jesus's actions as recorded in the NT. Christian denominations have varying understandings of what happens during this ritual, which is also known as the Communion meal or the Lord's Supper. Some take part in it as a sacrament that conveys the real presence of the body and blood of Christ, while others symbolically commemorate Christ's gift of his body and blood. All Christians believe that, by participating in this meal, they are giving thanks to God for feeding and nourishing the soul.

in Gethsemane, his arrest, his trial before Jewish and Roman authorities, his crucifixion and death, the discovery of an empty tomb three days after the crucifixion, and a number of encounters between the disciples and the risen Jesus are very old. Paul also reminds the Christians in Corinth of the story he told them about Jesus's death, burial, resurrection, and appearances (1 Cor 15:1–8). Paul does not tell many stories, so this one was very important to him and to all early Christians. All four Gospels tell this particular "story" in the same sequence. This does not happen anywhere else in the Gospels. The reporting of the basic story of the passion and resurrection never changes because they were told this way *from the beginning*. The early Christians boldly told this story, along with many others, over and over again, explaining what each event and each moment meant for Jesus and for them.

Many Uses of the Same Stories in Varying Contexts

The community of believers, therefore, formed around their shared experience of Jesus and his life, death, and resurrection, and they developed their mission of sharing the good news of God's new covenant available to all through telling stories of this shared experience. This reality quickly led them outside Judea and the surrounding regions to far-flung cities of the Roman Empire and beyond. The early apostles quickly adapted to their new surroundings, absorbing new cultural practices and symbols, sometimes learning new local languages, and always finding new ways to share their stories. These new sociocultural environments facilitated a certain creativity in the early storytellers as they sought to make the truth of their stories comprehensible in these varying contexts. They became genuine authors, in the sense of "tellers of stories," as they shaped their received traditions for these new peoples and places.

We see this development in the traditions about Jesus in the final written Gospels of the New Testament, particularly in the telling of Jesus's miracle working and individual teachings. An encounter between Jesus and a Syrophoenician woman recorded in Mark's Gospel (7:24–30) becomes the story of Jesus and a Canaanite woman in Matthew's Gospel (15:21–28). One Gospel shares the story of the healing of an unidentified synagogue official's child, while another shares the name and other details about what seems to be the same event. All four Gospels share the story of Jesus miraculously feeding a multitude with a small amount of food, but the details of the scene, the crowd, and the food vary (Matt 14:13–21; Mark 6:30–44; Luke 9:10–17; John 6:1–15). Likewise, the Gospels record Jesus giving similar teachings using different symbols and metaphors. Jesus himself likely used a variety of images to suit the situation he was in, and his later storytellers also did the same. None of this mitigates the "truth" of the stories about Jesus that the early Christians shared and preserved. Indeed, it speaks to the value of the essence of these experiences and teaching that they took the steps necessary to adapt them to fresh and varying contexts so that new audiences could also benefit from their power and wisdom.

The Crystallization of This Oral Tradition into Written Gospels and Acts

We cannot be sure whether there were accounts of Jesus available in written form before the Gospel of Mark appeared in about 70 CE. There were many "stories of Jesus" alive in the early Christian communities. The parables must have rung in the ears, minds, and hearts of early listeners, and they would have been told over and over again as generations passed, but there was still no single "story of Jesus" told from beginning to end, existing in written form.

Notice that the movement thus far has all been in terms of **oral tradition**. Very few people could read or write, and what we call "oral tradition," the passing on of stories from the life and teaching of Jesus, would have been a major part of sharing faith among those first believers. They would have encouraged one another in times of difficulty, instructed their children, spoken about Jesus to their friends, and told stories to those whom they wanted to draw into their community of faith. These stories about Jesus and his teaching were shared and handed down by word of mouth in increasingly varied contexts. Over time, they began to develop into a more complete oral tradition. The Roman Empire allowed for relative freedom of movement, and natural gathering places such as markets, town squares, and theaters in the cities and villages around the empire facilitated the media for this sharing and spreading. Thus, the oral culture of the first century provided the fora for early Christian teaching and led to the development of an oral tradition about the life and ministry of Jesus.

These somewhat "fluid" oral traditions became relatively stabilized in the Christian community and were eventually "crystallized" in written form. Both

> **1 Corinthians 15:1–8**
>
> In the mid-50s CE, Paul shares with the Corinthians, "Now I would remind you, brothers and sisters, of the good news that I proclaimed to you, which you in turn received, in which also you stand, through which also you are being saved, if you hold firmly to the message that I proclaimed to you—unless you have come to believe in vain. For I handed on to you as of first importance what I in turn had received: that Christ died for our sins in accordance with the scriptures, and that he was buried, and that he was raised on the third day in accordance with the scriptures, and that he appeared to Cephas, then to the twelve. Then he appeared to more than five hundred brothers and sisters at one time, most of whom are still alive, though some have died. Then he appeared to James, then to all the apostles. Last of all, as to one untimely born, he appeared also to me."

these oral and brief written forms were used and adapted by the NT authors to tell their stories and teach their messages to the Christian community. The question that remains is, why? We noted in chapter one that, in the oral culture of the ancient world, traditions moved from oral to written form only for particular purposes, usually to capture the authority of a particular telling, as a result of specific forces, either internal, external, or both. In the case of the writing of the Gospels and Acts, the authors no doubt had their own particular reasons for putting pen to paper, but we can point to two events that had great influence in this regard. First, we note a concern internal to the developing community. By the end of the 60s CE, the first generation of apostles was all but dead, and some had been martyred for their beliefs and profession of Jesus as Christ. This situation led to a certain urgency in preserving their firsthand experiences for future generations. Second, we bring to bear an event only somewhat external to the burgeoning faith tradition. Again, by the late 60s, the Christian community was open to gentiles, that is, non-Jews, to live and worship alongside the ethnically Jewish Christians as equals in the new covenant. That said, when the Jewish rebels revolted against the Roman Empire in 65 CE, the Christians were by no means unaffected. When this First Jewish Revolt against Rome failed in the devastation of Jerusalem and destruction of the Temple in 70 CE, all the

Luke 1:1–4

Using the Greco-Roman convention of offering a dedication to his benefactor at the outset of a literary work, Luke writes, "Since many have undertaken to set down an orderly account of the events that have been fulfilled among us, just as they were handed on to us by those who from the beginning were eyewitnesses and servants of the word, I too decided, after investigating everything carefully from the very first, to write an orderly account for you, most excellent Theophilus, so that you may know the truth concerning the things about which you have been instructed."

Christians were in as much fear about what the future held as their Jewish counterparts. This too led to the acute need to solidify traditions and lay claim to the authority behind teachings of the good news of Jesus Christ and the new covenant in the written form of complete narratives that we now call Gospels and Acts.

Within the New Testament itself we find an incisive description of the stages of development that eventually led to the Gospels as we now have them. Writing to a person called Theophilus, the evangelist Luke tells him that there were eyewitnesses to the life of Jesus at the beginning who have shared their experiences, that subsequently many have written accounts about what had been accomplished, and that Luke, who has been observing this development for some time, now wants to tell his version of the story (Luke 1:1–3). He states unequivocally that he is doing this not just to tell Theophilus what happened, but to instruct him on the trustworthy basis upon which the story of Jesus has been constructed. He can be sure that his life of faith is well grounded (Luke 1:4).

Eventually, a number of narratives came to be written for use in the communities. Those who could read and write provided stories of Jesus and the early church, to be read by very few but listened to by the vast majority. To this day, we have many gospels that are not found in the New Testament, as well as several extracanonical acts. You may have heard of some of them: the Gospel of Thomas, the Gospel of Judas, the Gospel of Mary, the Acts of Paul and Thecla. By the middle of the second century, four of the many gospels were accepted, what came to be called the Gospel according to Mark (written ca. 70 CE), the Gospels according to Matthew and Luke (written ca. 85 CE), and the Gospel according to John (written ca. 100 CE); also accepted was Luke's second volume, the Acts of the Apostles (dated to ca. 85–100 CE). These narratives continued the practice of telling stories about the great figures of the past that forms a major part of the Jewish Scriptures. They were read in the churches as part of the developing Christian Scriptures.

The historical context of the Gospels and Acts is therefore one of change and turmoil, as many people, both Jew and gentile alike, attempt to understand the world around them and how God is working in it through his larger plan for history. The evangelists composed the Gospels and Acts to capture authoritative stories of the Christ Event and assist their communities of believers in negotiating this world. Source criticism comes into play as we ask questions about how the biblical authors composed the final form of the texts that we have. When we ask the question *how*, we are querying what **sources** the authors used to compose their written works. How did they develop their material? From personal experience? Oral tradition? Written sources? Some combination of all these? We will now turn our attention to these questions.

Investigating and clarifying the literary relationship between the three Synoptic Gospels has been one of the major projects of modern NT scholarship. If they varied widely in order and word choice, as John does from the other three, this would not be such an issue. Likewise, if they were largely the same, this would also not be of such concern. The questions center around how the three Gospels can have such strong similarities—sometimes verbatim overlap—and yet have such distinctive variations. This issue is known as the **Synoptic Problem**, and scholars have spent countless years at the task of "resolving" this problem. The widely accepted solution to the Synoptic Problem is known as the **two-source hypothesis** of composition. It is also called the two-document theory. The im-

---

Textual Criticism

A study of the texts of the New Testament requires that the interpreter reflect upon the most reliable texts that we have. We do not possess any of the original writings, but we have literally thousands of witnesses, some of them coming from early times. Textual criticism works with these many witnesses to reconstruct the best text possible. It is impossible to be certain, and text critics always point out that they are providing the best Greek text that can be constructed from the available manuscript evidence. This textbook does not provide a guide to textual criticism, as it is beyond its scope. Interested readers should consult the guidebook by Wasserman and Gurry listed in the bibliography. Scholars often indicate textual issues in their studies and provide readers with reasons for their choices, when these issues impact upon an interpretation.

plication is that two written sources coupled with oral sources form the tradition behind all three Gospels.

Let's look at how this works. If we line up the Gospels side by side to see how they compare and contrast, the resulting parallel is called a **synopsis**. When the entire synopsis is studied, a few basic facts stand out. Many of the same passages often appear in all three Synoptic Gospels. When this happens, these passages constitute the **triple tradition**. This designation indicates that the same words appear verbatim, or almost so, in Greek in the three Gospels, even when they appear out of order. That said, in the triple tradition, all three Gospels also often agree in the placement, or order, of the material. When all three do not agree, Mark's arrangement is typically supported by either Matthew or Luke. With regard to content, about 90 percent of Mark is also found in Matthew, and more than 50 percent is found in Luke. Further, often when either Matthew or Luke disagrees with Mark, the other agrees. It is also notable that agreement between Matthew and Luke begins where Mark begins (John the Baptist and Jesus's public ministry) and ends where Mark ends (the empty tomb). The early chapters of Matthew and Luke, which contain infancy narratives, vary widely. Likewise, the post-resurrection encounters recorded in these Gospels are entirely distinctive. These points show that, in the triple tradition, Mark is the middle term; that is, Mark is closer to both Matthew and Luke than they are to each other. All attempts to solve the Synoptic Problem must reckon with this fact. That said, there are occasions when Matthew and Luke agree in word choice, against Mark, in passages that are otherwise part of the triple tradition. Scholars call these **minor agreements**. This phenomenon is best explained by recognizing the strength of the oral traditions behind both Matthew and Luke. Therefore, after a century of exhaustive study and debate, most scholars now agree that Mark was written first and that Matthew and Luke used that narrative as their foundation and general outline. This is known as **Markan priority**.

Alternative Theories to Solve the Synoptic Problem

Long-standing Christian tradition has claimed that the Gospel of Matthew was the "first gospel." The Griesbach theory—named after the scholar who first proposed it, Johann J. Griesbach (1745–1812)—starts with that assumption, arguing for literary dependence among all three Synoptic Gospels. Matthew was used as a source for the Gospel of Luke, which appeared after Matthew. Mark, the last Gospel to appear, used both Matthew and Luke. The Gospel of Mark is a deliberate abbreviation of Matthew and Luke. Some contemporary scholars continue to endorse this hypothesis. Recently, biblical scholar Mark Goodacre has suggested that Mark was the first Gospel, but that Matthew and Luke used one another's Gospels. This suggestion helpfully eliminates a Q hypothesis.

However, Matthew and Luke have in common a good deal of material that is not in Mark, some two hundred verses. Virtually all of it is sayings material. What we mean by this is that these common verses have little to no narrative in the sense of recounting events or actions. Rather, they record the teachings of Jesus. Further, the sayings in question are some of the most famous passages, including many parables, beatitudes, and the Lord's Prayer (Matt 6:6–13; Luke 11:2–4). This material is called the **double tradition**, to designate that it is found in two of the three Gospels, specifically Matthew and Luke. The material in the double tradition is not arranged in the same way in the two Gospels, and many scholars suggest that Luke presents the more original order of the sayings. Scholars also tend to conclude that the double tradition comes from a second written source, because the material is verbatim in a second language. Jesus would have spoken Aramaic; therefore, his teachings would have been remembered in the same language: Aramaic. The Gospels are all written in Greek. These sayings of Jesus have, therefore, been translated into a second language. If individual authors were translating Jesus's sayings from Aramaic to Greek, we would expect to find some variation in their word choice and order. What we have, however, is verbatim agreement in a second language. For most scholars, this necessitates a second written source. This hypothetical collection of sayings is known as **Q**, which is short for **Quelle**, the German word for "source." So Q is a theoretical **sayings source**.

These general facts suggest that Matthew and Luke had access to two sources of material and utilized them independently to construct their own Gospels. Strict advocates of the two-source hypothesis believe that these sources, Mark and the sayings source (Q), were both written. Lack of proof of Q's existence is its acknowledged weakness, but it remains the prevailing solution to the so-called Synoptic Problem. In addition to the material provided by the two documents, both Matthew and Luke had access to other information

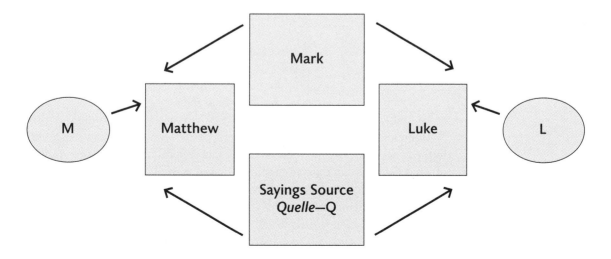

not available to, or at least not used by, the other. This information is often the contextual detail, the word choice, and the imagery and symbolism that reflect their specific traditions. It is unnecessary to understand this material as written; in fact, it makes better sense to understand it as the oral tradition specifically preserved by the communities of the individual evangelists. We can refer to these traditions as **M material** and **L material**, respectively.

Throughout the history of Christianity, scholars have argued about the question of John's dependence upon the Synoptic Gospels. Some of the very early leaders of the church (especially Augustine) suggested that John provided his Gospel to "fill in" many of the details that Mark, Matthew, and Luke left out. This will not do. We can take for granted that, as a gifted author and storyteller, John molded and shaped the oral traditions that came to him—through his own experience or through the experience of his community—into a narrative whole. It is clear from a single reading of John that this Gospel is quite distinctive. Differences from the Synoptic Gospels include setting much of Jesus's public ministry in Jerusalem and Judea instead of Galilee, a significant absence of the "kingdom of God" motif, Jesus's teaching style in long discourses and dialogues instead of parables, and the presentation of Jesus's miraculous activity in seven distinctive signs, including three episodes unique to this Gospel. Yet there are also important similarities with the Synoptic Gospels, especially at the beginning of Jesus's public ministry, with John the Baptist, and in the concluding passion and empty-tomb narratives.

> **Jews and Christians in the Gospel of John**
>
> The well-known problem of John's primarily negative use of the expression "the Jews" has been accurately and sensitively described by a significant Johannine scholar, John Ashton. On encountering this problem, he suggests, one must "recognize in these hot-tempered exchanges the type of family row in which the participants face one another across the room of a house which all have shared and all call home" (*Understanding the Fourth Gospel*, 151).

Some argue for a direct source relationship with the Synoptics, particularly Luke, but no definitive reliance can be proven. Others argue for additional sources known only to John, most often a distinctive "signs source" that contains the seven or eight specific miracle stories found in the Gospel, and possibly an account of the passion and resurrection. Many scholars today set this theory aside due to lack of clear evidence for an independent written tradition. Nowadays there is increasing agreement that John was certainly aware of the Synoptic Gospels, especially Mark and Luke. However, he does not use them as a source in the way that Matthew and Luke used Mark. John reflects creatively on traditions also found in the Synoptics, retelling them in a way that reflects his own understanding of what God has done for humankind in and through Jesus Christ. Using a French word that is easy to understand in English, scholars now talk of John's *réédition* (reedition) of passages from the Synoptic Gospels. Therefore, we can say that the independent traditions that came down through the Fourth Evangelist had circulated long enough alongside the Synoptic traditions that the evangelist assumes basic knowledge of the events of Jesus's public ministry and life and that he arranges a few choice events in the narrative for dramatic effect, to highlight the nature and mission of Jesus as Christ and Son of God.

The World in the Gospels and Acts

As we approach the world in the text of the Gospels and Acts, we begin with broad literary criticism. Therefore, our first task is to ask a question about **genre**. The term "genre" comes to us from French and refers to a category of artistic endeavor that has a particular form, technique, or content. In literature, genre refers to the type of writing an author chooses to use as the medium for the message. The evangelists chose to share in narrative form their understandings of the good news of the Christ Event. Interpreters must respect that form. Narratives have characters, settings, and plots with beginnings, middles, and ends, among other characteristics. Narratives, even "true" stories of historical figures, are also developed, shaped, and told by authors, through their points of view, to tell the stories that they believe their audiences need to hear. This does not make the stories any less "true." All humans have perspectives, and all potential audiences have needs.

Take an example from our own lives. Often when we answer questions, we tell stories to make a point. The simplest question, "how was your day?" can elicit very different responses from us depending upon who the questioner is. Employers need certain data, while parents or grandparents need other information. Children—nieces, nephews, younger brothers and sisters—need still different material. We speak to our friends and other intimates in still different tones, with distinct areas of emphasis. Our responses to each and every one of these questioners will be different, and yet every story about "how our day was" can be true. We are forthright and sincere with each of these stories that we tell, although we may begin and end in different places, use very different language (it is rarely advisable to speak to grandparents and buddies with the same slang), and focus on entirely different events. Our NT storytellers, by necessity, do the same thing. This is why, with all the overlap in the four Gospels, each has its own unique voice.

Once we settle on the notion of stories and storytellers, we must determine what kinds of narratives we have. Christian church tradition has long called these narratives "gospels" and "acts." A **gospel** is the literary form of Christian narratives about Jesus. The term is a translation of the Greek noun *euangelion*, which means **good news**, as it is derived from the verb form that means "to announce or proclaim something good." The term has also come to mean the Christian message in general. Thus, for Paul, the first in the New Testament to use the word "gospel" for the message of the Christ Event, the word referred to good news of the saving effect of Jesus's death and resurrection. The Gospel of

The Etymology of *Euangelion* to Gospel

The Greek word for "gospel" is *euangelion*. The expression has a long history, as both a noun and a verb in the LXX and the Letters of Paul, as indicating "good news." Beginning with Mark, it is used to describe the literary form of a story of the life of Jesus. When the expression was used in Old English, a direct translation of "good news" was "god" (i.e., "good") + "spel" (i.e., "news"). Eventually, the Old English "godspel" became the well-known English word "gospel."

Burridge and the *Bios*

Scholars have long wondered why Mark chose to communicate his message about the person, teaching, death, and resurrection of Jesus by telling a story of his life, beginning with the witness of John the Baptist and his baptism and ending with the women at an empty tomb. Richard Burridge (*What Are the Gospels? A Comparison with Greco-Roman Biography*) has gained widespread support by means of close comparison of the literary shape and the rhetorical purpose of gospels and Greco-Roman biographies, called by the name *bioi*, which means "lives." It is likely that the gospels are a Christian use of that form of literature.

Mark is the first to apply it to his story of Jesus as good news (Mark 1:1). The writer of a gospel is, thus, an **evangelist**, from the same Greek root. In modern times, this term has also taken on the meaning of one who preaches this good news, but we will use both terms in their narrower senses to refer to the early Christian literary genre and its authors. Indeed, this literary genre as we know it today was in some sense invented by the early Christians as an adaptation of the ancient Greco-Roman genre called the ***bios***. Gospels are narratives—stories—that share the good news of the Christ Event. As we have just mentioned, the evangelist Mark, writing about 70 CE, first used this term to identify this type of writing. Notice, however, that this is some forty years after the life of Jesus. As we introduced in chapter one, it was some time before the early Christians saw the need to start telling the story of Jesus's life, teaching, death, and resurrection.

An **acts** is a literary form, common in the ancient Greek world, that is a narrative account of the heroic deeds of famous historical or mythological figures. The term is a translation of the Greek ***praxeis***, and the titles of such narratives typically also denote the subject(s) at hand. The NT contains one example of this genre, entitled the Acts of the Apostles. Further, Luke-Acts is the conventional abbreviation for the two volumes known individually as the Gospel of Luke and the Acts of the Apostles. Such a title calls attention to a conviction that the two volumes form a single literary project. No ancient manuscripts have been preserved in which they appear joined, and the early church leaders always treat them separately, but they also always assume common authorship. Volume one (Luke) fits well with the other Gospels, while volume two (Acts) provides the introduction to the early church and thereby an introduction to Paul's Letters. The apostles in question seem to be Peter, across the first half of the narrative, and Paul, across the second. Acts ends with Paul in Rome, while the collection of Paul's Letters traditionally begins with his Letter to the Romans. The portrait of Paul in Acts emphasizes his place within the larger mission of the church led by Peter and the other apostles. The literary unity of the two volumes is indicated by the dedications in each volume, which also provide a window into the author's intentions (Luke 1:1–4; Acts 1:1–5). Although the traditional title of the Acts of the Apostles suggests that it is the *praxeis* that focus on heroic deeds and their consequences for the masses, some scholars suggest that the genre of **historiography** of a people is a better fit for the text Luke provides. By this, they indicate that Luke's second volume is a written history based on critical examination of sources, culminating in the synthesis of the formative events for the development of the church community.

In one sense, gospels and acts are like biographies in that they tell stories of people who really lived in our world like us. However, gospels and acts are not biographies in the modern sense. They share little to nothing about the protagonists' formative years, associations, education, and in no way attempt to present complete lives or to explain the social, cultural, historical, or political forces that could have influenced who they came to be. They simply relate certain material they deem crucial to the witness of the "good news" and development of the church. Therefore, in the sense that gospels and acts tell life stories, they are ancient biographies that focus on the events in the lives of the protagonists that are key for understanding the *meaning* of these lives. Ancient biographers could not always check facts and did not necessarily have access to verbatim records of their heroes' speeches. They were comfortable in describing the types of things that happened and the sorts of things that would have been said in order to share their messages. Therefore, when it comes to gospels and acts, we are best served by moving away from the idea of the modern biography and toward a new genre created by the earliest evangelists that was related to the ancient biography but focused on sharing the good news of the Christ Event and the formation of the early church.

The pervasive characteristics of the evangelists' literary style, coupled with the underlying themes they weave through their writing, provide the substance from which they shape their narrative to tell the story they believe their audiences need to hear. This shaping results in an overarching outline and narrative flow to their plots and messages. The term **structure** refers to a composition and its parts and to the organization of something. In literature, the structure of a text is the organization of its parts composed as a whole. As we introduced in chapter two on exegeting biblical texts, by establishing a broad outline, or structure, of the narrative we are respecting the fact that the authors chose a particular genre through which to share their particular message. In this case,

---

Biography as Proclamation

Perhaps the greatest challenge a twenty-first-century reader of a gospel faces is to recognize that the gospel story is not primarily a collection of "stories about the life of Jesus." However much actual history might lie behind them, they are written to **proclaim the great truths** about Jesus and how we should respond to him. As John tells his readers, these things are written "that you may go on believing, and that through believing you may have life in his name" (John 20:31). A gospel has the form of a biography but should not be confused with a modern biography, as its purpose is to proclaim the truth about what the author thinks God has done and continues to do.

for example, they chose to write a story as opposed to a letter, a sermon, or any other genre of literature. Stories unfold in certain manners, and knowing where we are in the story helps us exegete any particular passage. Thereafter, we can explore and exegete the text along this structure. In this way, we can make sense of what happens when. It may be helpful, therefore, to understand structures as guides or roadmaps for entering the narrative worlds of the biblical authors. In order to arrive at these roadmaps that guide exegesis, we look for textual markers that serve as signposts along the way. This is called establishing **literary context**.

As we indicate in chapter two, form criticism is a further step in literary criticism, as it seeks to specify the literary form or sub-form of a given biblical passage. We begin to ask questions about the different literary forms an evangelist uses to flesh out his larger narrative, be it a gospel or an acts. The NT narratives include a number of common forms, each of which have conventional structures and purposes. The Synoptic Gospels include Jesus teaching with a number of parables, while the Gospel of John prefers to share Jesus's teaching in extended dialogues and discourses. Both the Gospels and Acts include miracle stories, pronouncement stories, and historical accounts. Understanding these different forms on their own terms allows interpreters to further draw out the authors' intended meanings as they unfold their larger plots and relate their messages of good news for their early Christian communities.

Literary Forms in the NT

Like the OT, the NT contains numerous literary forms. Indeed, a number of the forms are found across the Scriptures and are not limited to one testament or the other.

Parable: typically, brief stories that offer a comparison that teaches a lesson. The term comes from the Greek verb that means "to go around," such that a parable offers a roundabout way to evoke an insight resulting in a more profound impact than a direct response.

Pronouncement story: a brief narrative that culminates in a significant saying or pronouncement, on the part of Jesus. They are typically structured in three parts: setting, action, and resulting pronouncement.

Miracle story: as the name suggests, these are narrative episodes that include the performance of a miracle or, to use John's term, a sign. The basic structure of these stories, although they can be quite lengthy, is: the description of a need, the miraculous act itself, followed by the consequences of the miracle.

Dominical sayings: these "sayings of the Lord" are often independent proclamations that have no clear setting or strong narrative framework. These were preserved in the oral tradition and are often clustered together in the final form of the Gospels.

Apocalyptic episodes: exotic language and descriptions that point to a dramatic final entry of God into the human story in Christianity, associated with the second coming of Christ and appearing in the Gospels (e.g., Mark 13:1–38) and the book of Revelation.

When we discussed source criticism in the previous section, we noticed that each Gospel contains material that is unique to that author's perspective on the Christ Event and the voice he uses to express the good news. This material that is distinctive to each evangelist may come from variations in the oral traditions they received or may simply be subject to their larger literary projects. Recognizing and analyzing the Gospels' unique offerings, even when they result in discrepancies and inconsistencies in the "story of Jesus," can reveal much about their writers' intentions and individual perceptions of Jesus and his significance. This, as we also introduced in chapter two, is called redaction criticism. We ask questions about how the authors edited and shaped the traditions they received in order to tell their stories in particular ways, for particular effects. The NT authors have particular agendas: they are overtly evangelistic. What we mean by this is that they do not want their audiences to finish hearing or reading their stories and go home or put them away and say, "That was nice; I think I'll take a nap." Rather, they desire their stories to change lives. The goal would be for their audiences to believe that Jesus is the long-awaited Messiah and to change their lives—even risk their lives—accordingly. Every plotline, character development, and symbol is shaped toward this end. Therefore, it is crucial to understand that each evangelist, just like every storyteller in history, makes these important choices.

The Use of Synopses in Gospel Studies

One of the most useful tools, even for a beginning student of the Gospels, is a book called a "synopsis." The texts of the Gospels are placed side by side in three columns, usually with Mark in the center. With a "glance of the eye" (synopsis) the student can see what each evangelist has done in reporting the same event. For example, Mark 8:27–30 tells of Peter's confession of Jesus as "the Christ" at Caesarea Philippi, followed by Jesus's warning not to spread this about. A glance at the synopsis will show the student that Matthew 16:13–20 adds to Peter's longer confession ("You are the Christ, the Son of God"), during which Jesus blesses him and tells him that the church will be built upon him and this confession of faith. Luke 9:18–21 is much briefer. There is no setting at Caesarea Philippi, but Jesus asks his disciples who they think he is, while he is praying. Peter makes the correct confession of faith, "the Christ of God," and Jesus goes on to predict his suffering and death. Without reference to commentaries, any student can glean some idea of what each evangelist is trying to do as he tells the same story differently. This example can be repeated for many Gospel passages, where Matthew and Luke have used Mark, or where Matthew and Luke both use a different source, but at a different place in the story and in different words.

The World in Front of the Gospels and Acts

As we also indicated above, the early Christian community produced many gospel narratives about Jesus or collections of his sayings, but the four we commonly refer to as Matthew, Mark, Luke, and John are those recognized as authoritative for Christianity. It is appropriate to note here that the evangelists never identify themselves by name anywhere in their writing. The titles, for example, "according to Mark," "according to John," "Acts of the Apostles" etc., are added late in the second century CE in order to differentiate them from one another as the Christian leaders participated in debates about the canon. These leaders identified the evangelists through their strong oral traditions from the first generation of apostles. Even careful study, however, cannot verify these traditional attributions. Nonetheless, we will continue to refer to the Gospels and Acts by their traditional authors.

As we have noted, each evangelist has his own unique perspective on the Christ Event, and each Gospel presents a distinctive portrait of Jesus and his life and ministry. This means that, try as we might, we cannot reconcile the chronologies and details of each Gospel into one seamless story. The fact that the primitive Christian community did not compose or adopt one official version free from these contradictions is itself significant. Perhaps the early church leaders saw that Jesus and the Christ Event could not be reduced to a single perspective. Jesus elicited widely divergent responses in people, so the formers of the canon retained these for the community of faith. The manner in which these distinctive portraits of the good news affected audiences and the responses they elicited is the focus of the world in front of the text.

As we discussed in the previous section, the evangelists desired their audiences to respond by believing that Jesus was the Christ and to change their lives accordingly. The questions we must ask each evangelist include what, according to their understanding of the good news and their communities' needs, that believing entails and how exactly they expect lives to change. Here we must reiterate that the belief that Jesus is the Christ and Son of God necessitated paradigm shifts for both Jews and gentiles. Ethnically Jewish believers had to redefine their messianic expectations from a military king, like David, who would establish a sovereign nation to a suffering and vindicated Son of Man who gave himself unconditionally to God's will, even unto death. God's acceptance of Jesus's obedient and loving way of life and sacrificial death put in place a new covenant open to all humankind. Gentile believers had to let go of their Greco-Roman ideals of gods and heroes to

---

Gospels in the Early Church

Preserving the distinctive perspectives of the Gospels was certainly the mindset of the church leaders late in the second century, when the names Mark, Matthew, Luke, and John were attached to the four Gospels of the New Testament. They faced the danger that the four different stories would be collapsed into one coherent story. At that time, a person called Tatian developed a document called the Diatessaron, which did exactly that. Names were thus given to each of the Gospels so that their uniqueness would be recognized and respected.

embrace a savior who was a peasant executed as a common criminal. The apostle Paul described this reality in this way: "For Jews demand signs and Greeks desire wisdom, but we proclaim Christ crucified, a stumbling block to Jews and foolishness to Gentiles" (1 Cor 1:22–23). Paul goes on to say, however, "but to those who are called, both Jews and Greeks, Christ the power of God and the wisdom of God" (1 Cor 1:24). This power and wisdom are what each evangelist sought to instill and inspire in their audiences to meet their needs and speak to their contexts. Now, some two thousand years later, audiences are still asking questions in order to interpret these messages and apply their power and wisdom to their own lives.

The Gospels and Acts

Because this textbook is an introduction to interpreting the New Testament, our task is to prepare its readers for the task of exegeting the NT, not exegeting for them. Therefore, what we will provide in the final section of these chapters is, for lack of a better term, a basic diagram of the worlds of each text.

We begin with the world behind the text and what can be understood as the basic questions: Who? What? Where? When? Why? How? Asking the question *who*, we are really asking a question about authorship. This is a complicated question when it comes to the Gospels and Acts. They, like many texts in the ancient world, were all written anonymously. Issues such as "intellectual property" and "bylines" are concerns of our world, not theirs. The message of the text was what primarily mattered. Writers of the biblical books are true authors in the sense that they are more than just editors of received oral traditions. Rather, they composed, developed, and shaped their material to share the message their audiences needed to hear. That said, self-interest and notoriety were not part of their perceived mission. What did matter, however, was credibility. For their message to be received and responded to as they hoped, their compositions had to carry the weight of authority. For the early Christian communities, the apostles—the first generation of disciples that Jesus sent out to spread the good news—had this authority. These were the authors whose messages they held dear. Asking the question *what* is really asking a question about what type of literature we have. This is a question of genre. Asking the question *where* is asking a question about the origins of these texts. We are concerned with the location of the author and the writing com-

> **Ecumenical Councils and Christian Doctrine**
>
> Christianity and its Scriptures burst onto the religious scene of the Mediterranean world, making extraordinary claims about God, God's revelation in and through Jesus, and the gift of the Spirit Paraclete. It took the Christian church centuries to debate and state what this all meant. The great Christian doctrines were the result of meetings of bishops and Christian leaders, generally at the request of the emperor, called ecumenical councils. The most important early councils were Nicaea (325 CE: the Trinity), Constantinople I (351 CE: Christology), Ephesus (451 CE: the role of Mary as Mother of God), Chalcedon (451 CE: Christology), and Constantinople II (553 CE: Christology).

**Papal Apology to the Jewish
People for the Roman Catholic
Church's Role in the Holocaust**

Pope John Paul II was born Karol Wojtyla on May 18, 1920, in Poland. Growing up, he had Jewish friends and neighbors and witnessed the Holocaust firsthand. Once he became Pope in 1978, he devoted himself to condemning anti-Semitism and improving Jewish-Christian relations, calling for mutual understanding and respect. In 1994, he established full diplomatic ties between the Vatican and Israel and was instrumental in the 1998 document "We Remember: A Reflection on the Shoah," which expressed deep sorrow for the failures of the church. In 2000, he visited Israel and publicly apologized for the persecution of Jews by Catholics over the centuries. John Paul II died on April 2, 2005.

munity. If we can suggest where the author and intended audience reside, we can couple information in the text with archaeological and other written evidence from that region to learn more about what was going on in that community, what images and symbols might be important to them, and how the community might be faring in their larger society and culture. When we ask the question *when*, we are trying to determine the date of composition for the literature. Sometimes this questioning is focused on when texts reached their final form, but some scholars also try to determine when earlier drafts were composed and how the text may have shifted before the text was finalized. Asking the question *why* is questioning the purpose for the writing. In earlier chapters, we discussed the predominantly oral culture of the ancient world. Therefore, why did this author take on the arduous task of putting pen to paper (or quill to papyrus, as it were) in this context? All authors have agendas, reasons for writing; so what is the purpose behind each evangelist's writing project? Asking the question *how*, we are querying what sources the author may have used to compose his written works. In this case, how did the evangelists write their Gospels and Acts?

We proceed to the world in the text. Interpreters study the final composition of a biblical author and try to glean what the original outline would have been if the author had written one. Because we do this after the fact and we cannot ask the authors about their structuring techniques, we can never be certain about this process. Nonetheless, this is done in order to get a big picture of the author's flow of thought in writing, which, in turn, aids in exegeting, or drawing out, the intention in writing. This does mean, however, that responsible biblical scholars can devise different structures to given passages that do not agree with each other. These varying structures can sometimes affect interpretations, but exegetes must simply do the best they can and work in dialogue with one another and the larger tradition. Therefore, in these diagrams of the NT narratives, we give "suggested structures," acknowledging that the work of other good scholars may well vary from our own.

The world in front of the text is a widely variegated phenomenon. Therefore, to offer food for thought in terms of how these texts would have been received by the first audiences, as well as how they may affect audiences thereafter and into our time, we offer several major literary and theological themes for each NT narrative.

The Four Evangelists
from *The Book of Kells*

Icon of St. Mark
the Evangelist by
Emmanuel Tzanes
(seventeenth century)

The Gospel according to Mark

Who: The Gospel: Anonymous.

Tradition: "Mark" identified in 1 Pet 5:13 as Peter's "son" (i.e., his disciple); fourth-century church historian Eusebius quotes second-century leader Papias: "Mark, having become the interpreter of Peter, wrote down accurately, though not indeed in order, whatsoever he remembered of the things done or said by Christ. For he neither heard the Lord nor followed him, but afterward . . . he followed Peter, who adapted his teaching to the needs of his hearers. . . ."

What: A gospel (a narrative of the good news) and adaptation of the Greco-Roman *bios*.

Where: Gentile or Hellenistic Jewish Christian community traditionally in Rome, but possibly closer to the events at hand, such as southern Syria.

When: 65–75 CE, during the First Jewish Revolt against Rome or shortly thereafter.

Why: To strengthen the faith of those in danger due to the war or persecution (see Mark 13), as well as to lay claim to tradition and openness to gentiles.

How: Oral tradition and possible briefer written accounts.

Suggested Structure:

1:1–13   Prologue: The Beginning
1:14–8:30   Who Is Jesus?
    1:14–3:6   Jesus and the Leaders of Israel
    3:7–6:6a   Jesus and His New Family
    6:6b–8:30   Jesus and the Disciples
8:31–15:47   The Suffering and Vindicated Son of Man: Christ and Son of God
    8:31–10:52   On the Way from Blindness to Sight
    11:1–13:37   The Symbolic End of Israel and the World
    14:1–15:47   The Crucifixion of the Son of Man, Christ, and Son of God
16:1–8 [9–20]   Epilogue: A New Beginning

Prevailing Themes:

- The kingdom/reign of God
  - Jesus teaches more about the "kingdom of God" than any other subject, a term that is better translated as "reign of God" to signify its verbal action: the phenomenon of God reigning, which is an active reality that transcends space and time.
- Jesus as the Messiah who is Son of Man and Son of God
  - Mark's Christology is expressed through the so-called "messianic secret" as Jesus, across the Gospel, silences those who would proclaim him Messiah. As the plot unfolds, Mark redefines the role of Messiah as the Son of Man and Son of God. Jesus is not the Messiah because he is a powerful king like David, but because he is the suffering Son of Man who is understood to be the Son of God through his crucifixion.
- Discipleship through the cross
  - The disciples are characterized as misunderstanding the messianic mission, despite Jesus's teaching, understanding only afterward, based on the hope of the empty tomb.

Icon of St. Matthew
the Evangelist
(nineteenth century)

The Gospel according to Matthew

Who: The Gospel: Anonymous.

Tradition: Matthew, one of Jesus's twelve disciples and former tax collector (see 9:9–13); fourth-century church historian Eusebius quotes second-century leader Papias, "So then Matthew wrote the oracles in the Hebrew language, and everyone interpreted them as he was able."

What: A gospel (a narrative of the good news) and adaptation of the Greco-Roman *bios*.

Where: An ethnically Jewish Christian community in a prosperous urban environment; many scholars, along with church tradition, suggest Antioch, in the Roman province of Syria.

When: 80–90 CE.

Why: To extend Mark's Gospel by providing a history of salvation and doctrine of the church (an ecclesiology, see 16:13–20).

How: Oral tradition (M); possible written sources include Mark and a sayings source (Q).

Suggested Structure:

1:1–4:16 Prologue: The Coming of the Messiah
    1:1–2:23 The Infancy Narrative
    3:1–17 John the Baptist and Jesus
    4:1–16 Preparation for the Messiah's Ministry
4:17–11:1 The Messiah's Ministry to Israel of Preaching, Teaching, and Healing
    4:17–25 The Beginning of Jesus's Ministry
    5:1–7:29 Jesus's Sermon on the Mount
    8:1–11:1 Jesus and the Twelve Disciples in a Ministry of Word and Deed
11:2–16:12 The Crisis in the Messiah's Ministry
    11:2–12:50 Jesus Encounters Opposition to Being God's Commissioned Agent
    13:1–58 Jesus Teaches the Parables of the Kingdom
    14:1–16:12 The Progressive Crisis of the Messiah's Ministry
16:13–20:34 The Messiah's Journey to Jerusalem
    16:13–23 Peter's Confession of the Messiah and the Turn toward Jerusalem
    16:24–18:35 The Transfiguration and the Call to Discipleship
    19:1–20:34 The Journey to Jerusalem and the Teaching on the Kingdom
21:1–28:15 The Messiah's Death and Resurrection
    21:1–27 The Turning Point in the Messiah's Ministry
    21:28–25:46 The Final Teaching of the Messiah's Public Ministry
    26:1–28:15 The Passion Narrative and the Empty Tomb: Victory over Death
28:16–20 Epilogue: The Great Commission

Prevailing Themes:

- The abiding presence of God in the world
- The seamless flow from Jewish law to Christian faith in God's plan
- The universal scope of the good news in terms of God's plan for the history of salvation to incorporate all humankind

Icon of St. Luke the
Evangelist (eighteenth
century)

The Gospel according to Luke

Who: The Gospel: Anonymous.

Tradition: Fourth-century church historian Eusebius writes, "But Luke, who was of Antiochian parentage and a physician by profession, and who was especially intimate with Paul and well acquainted with the rest of the apostles, has left us, in two inspired books, proofs of that spiritual healing art which he learned from them. One of these books is the Gospel, which he testifies that he wrote as those who were from the beginning eye-witnesses and ministers of the word delivered unto him, all of whom, as he says, he followed accurately from the first"; see Phlm 23–24; Col 4:14; 2 Tim 4:9–11.

What: A gospel (a narrative of the good news) and adaptation of the Greco-Roman *bios*.

Where: Some say Rome or Achaea, but it is widely accepted that provenance is less important for understanding Luke's appeal to a broad Hellenistic Christian audience.

When: 80–90 CE.

Why: To provide an orderly account (see 1:1–4) appropriate for the Greco-Roman world.

How: Oral tradition (L); possible written sources include Mark and a Sayings Source (Q).

Suggested Structure:

1:1–4   The Dedication to Theophilus

1:5–4:13   Prologue

     1:5–2:52   The Infancy Narrative

     3:1–22   John the Baptist's Ministry

     3:23–4:13   Jesus Prepares for Ministry

4:14–9:50   Jesus's Ministry in Galilee

     4:14–6:11   The Mission Begins

     6:12–9:6   The Apostolic Community Is Gathered and Instructed

     9:7–50   Christological Turning Point and End of the Galilean Ministry

9:51–19:44   Jesus and the Disciples Journey to Jerusalem

     9:51–14:35   The Prophet on His Way to Jerusalem I

     15:1–32   The Search for the Lost One—Limitless Compassion

     16:1–19:44   The Prophet on His Way to Jerusalem II

19:45–21:38   Jesus in Jerusalem

     19:45–21:4   Jesus, the Temple, and Conflict with Israel's Religious Leaders

     21:5–38   Jesus's Discourse: Future of the Temple, Jerusalem, and the World

22:1–24:35   Jesus's Passion, Death, and Resurrection

24:36–53   Epilogue: The Ascension

Prevailing Themes:

- Various models for understanding Jesus
  - Jewish models: Messiah, Son of Man, Prophet like Moses, Elijah, Suffering Servant
  - Hellenistic models: Philosopher, Immortal, Benefactor/Savior
- Salvation happens now, throughout the lifetime of Jesus and into today
  - Jesus claims that the reason he has come is to "seek out and to save" (19:10) and that this salvation happens today, at the moment of acceptance.
- The continual, progressive success, growth, and triumph of the Christian mission

Apostles Peter and Paul
by El Greco

The Acts of the Apostles

Who: Acts: Anonymous

Tradition: Fourth-century church historian Eusebius states, "But Luke, who was of Antiochian parentage and a physician by profession, and who was especially intimate with Paul and well acquainted with the rest of the apostles, has left us, in two inspired books, proofs of that spiritual healing art which he learned from them. . . . The other book is the Acts of the Apostles which he composed not from the accounts of others, but from what he had seen himself" (see also the "we" sections of Acts 16:10–17; 20:5–21:18; 27:1–28:16).

What: The title suggests an acts, a genre common in the ancient Greek world, which is a narrative account of the heroic deeds of famous historical or mythological figures, in this case, the "Apostles"; some scholars prefer the genre of historiography of a people.

Where: Some say Rome or Achaea, but it is widely accepted that provenance is less important for understanding Luke's appeal to a broad Hellenistic Christian audience.

When: 90–100 CE, after the writing of the Gospel of Luke (see Luke 1:1–4; Acts 1:1–5).

Why: To show how Jesus's followers carried out his commission to bring the church to the "end of the earth" (1:8) through the guidance of the Holy Spirit; it further shows the continuation and connection from Judaism to Christianity that advocates for Christianity as an acceptable religion in the Roman Empire.

How: Oral tradition; brief written accounts of the early church; some suggest the "we" sections cited above indicate Luke's personal experience and composition.

Suggested Structure:

1:1–5 Dedication

1:6–2:13 Introduction: Jesus's Ascension and the Formation of the Church through the Gift of the Holy Spirit

2:14–8:1 Peter and the Early Church

8:2–12:25 Peter, Paul, and the Expansion of the Early Church

13:1–14:28 Paul's First Missionary Journey

15:1–35 Jerusalem Decree about the Gentile Mission

15:36–18:22 Paul's Second Missionary Journey

18:23–21:14 Paul's Third Missionary Journey

21:15–28:16 Paul's Imprisonment in Jerusalem and Journey to Rome

28:17–31 Conclusion: The Church Reaches the Ends of the Earth in Rome and Beyond

Prevailing Themes:

- The Holy Spirit is the primary actor in the formation of the church. The spread from Jerusalem to Rome indicates the Spirit-filled progress "to the ends of the earth" (1:8).
- God's plan for the salvation of the world was offered to Jewish people first, then extended through the gentiles to all humankind.
- The true Israel is, therefore, believing Jews and gentiles together.

The Beloved Disciple,
Scenes from the Life
of St. John the Divine
by Andreas Ritzos

The Gospel according to John

Who: The Gospel: The Beloved Disciple (13:23; 18:15–16; 19:26–27, 35; 20:4, 8; 21:7, 21–25)
Church Tradition: Late second-century church leader Irenaeus quotes early second-century leaders Papias and Polycarp who claim the Beloved Disciple is John the son of Zebedee, one of Jesus's twelve disciples.

What: A gospel (a narrative of the good news) and adaptation of the Greco-Roman *bios*.

Where: Ephesus, a prominent port city of the Roman Empire in Asia (modern Turkey).

When: 90–100 CE.

Why: "Now Jesus did many other signs in the presence of his disciples, which are not written in this book. But these are written so that you may believe that Jesus is the Messiah, the Son of God, and that through believing you may have life in his name" (20:30–31); the developing separation of Christianity from Judaism also necessitated a telling of the story that explained how the one who died for being the Jewish Messiah became known as Messiah to a wider group of Jewish and gentile Christians instead.

How: Oral traditions and possible familiarity with the Synoptic Gospels and perhaps a reedition of them.

Suggested Structure:

1:1–18   The Prologue
1:19–12:50   The Book of Signs
    1:19–51   The First Days of the Revelation of Jesus
    2:1–4:54   From Cana to Cana: Journey of Faith
    5:1–10:42   Jesus and the Feasts of Judaism
    11:1–12:50   Moving to Glory
13:1–20:31   The Book of Glory
    13:1–17:26   The Last Discourse
    18:1–19:42   Jesus's Passion and Death
    20:1–29   The Resurrection and Gift of the Holy Spirit
    20:30–31   The First Conclusion to the Gospel
21:1–25   The Epilogue

Prevailing Themes:

- Jesus as fully God and fully human
- Jesus as the true revelation of God through his incarnation, ministry, death, and resurrection
- The new covenant put in place by the Christ Event has two new commandments:
  1. Receive and believe in Jesus as Christ and Son of God
  2. Love one another and remain in Christ as a community
- The community formed is made up of those from all humankind, empowered to be "children of God," based in this believing and loving (see 1:12; 11:51–52)

What Have We Learned So Far? The Good News of the Gospels and Acts

Given that this chapter has focused upon the genres of gospels and acts in the New Testament, it follows that what we have focused upon is Christology and ecclesiology. All four Gospels in the New Testament in some part ask and answer the question, "Who is Jesus?" His followers quickly identified him with the long-hoped-for Messiah, God's Anointed One, but his later evangelists had to make sense of how that could be, given that he did not turn out to be the commonly expected anointed king in the Davidic line, nor did he ever seem to claim such. As we have discussed in earlier chapters, Christology is the study of what it means to be the Messiah/Christ and what effect that might have. The Christian teaching of Jesus Christ came to understand him as both fully human and fully divine, but there is a great deal of range in this doctrine. Scholars, therefore, often distinguish Christology on a continuum of "low" to "high." A low or lower Christology presents Jesus in terms that do not necessarily include or focus on divinity; while a high or higher Christology presents Jesus in terms that include, or even focus on, aspects of divinity. At least part of the task of each evangelist, then, is to present their understanding of how Jesus came to be called the Messiah and what that designation means in God's plan.

> **Anti-Semitic Abuses of the Gospel of John**
>
> Because of its manner of identifying the opponents to Jesus's mission as "the Jews," the Gospel of John has long been a favorite tool of those Christians with anti-Semitic intentions. From Nazi passion plays to misguided homilies, the Gospel has been abused through the centuries. The exegete's duty is to draw the complex and nuanced terminology of the evangelist, who was living and writing in a tense historical situation.

The Gospel according to Mark, the first of the Gospels to appear, established the essential elements of the plot followed in the other two Synoptic Gospels: John the Baptist announces Jesus, his ministry in Galilee, a journey to Jerusalem, a ministry in Jerusalem, the final night, arrest, Jewish and Roman trials, crucifixion, death, and resurrection. Mark's account is brief, but this should not lead us to think that it lacks depth and subtlety. Mark's Gospel appeared about 70 CE and focuses strongly upon Jesus's vindication as Son of Man and Son of God through suffering. Its Christology is relatively low. He also portrays the disciples as good people who struggle to comprehend Jesus's teaching and way of life. Mark's brief but powerful account of Jesus's life and teaching is full of twists, turns, and surprises. Above all, it is a word of encouragement to disciples of all ages. It was written for an early Christian community suffering for the faith, but also because of their experience of failure to live up to the demands of discipleship. They hear a story of Jesus, whose death makes sense out of suffering and whose presence to failing disciples never falters. He is always going before them to Galilee. There they will see him.

The Gospel according to Matthew depends heavily upon the Gospel of Mark. It most likely appeared in the 80s of the first century, somewhere in the Roman province of Syria, where Jewish Christians were establishing their identity in a new world. Even at first glance, one can see that Matthew has stories about the conception and birth of Jesus (Matt 1–2) and an account of the appearance of the risen Jesus to women and to the disciples (28:1–20). Most of the Gospel of Mark appears in Matthew's story, but it is told in a different way. As well as the Markan material, Matthew presents Jesus as the perfection of the promises to Israel, and his "church" as the true Israel (Matthew is the only Gospel that uses this term, in 16:18 and 18:15). He instructs his disciples to bring the good news to all the nations. We see the beginnings of an explicit ecclesiology as well as a higher Christology. Written and received in a largely Jewish-Christian community, Matthew shows that Jesus fulfills the hopes of Israel as the Son of David and reaches out to all nations as the Son of Abraham (see 1:1). Matthew looks back to the past and forward into the future, describing himself as a scribe "who brings out of his treasure what is new and what is old" (13:52). Jesus fulfills and perfects the promises made to Israel (5:17–18), establishing a new people of God missioned by the risen Jesus to go out to all the nations (28:16–20). The death and resurrection form a turning point in God's everlasting presence to his people. Earlier Jesus and the disciples went to the lost sheep of Israel (10:6; 15:24). The crucified and risen Jesus commands them to make disciples of all nations in the one God (28:19).

The Markan story is also very formative of the Gospel according to Luke, but this author is far more creative. Written across the 80s and 90s of the first century, Luke's work is made up of two volumes (the Gospel and the Acts of the Apostles), directed to the gentile churches. Universal and compassionate, especially for the marginalized in society, Luke also makes radical demands on those who would be disciples of Jesus. Over the two volumes, Luke's narrative covers some sixty years of the Christ Event and the development of the Christian church through the apostolic missions. Luke portrays a still higher Christology and presents the foundational ecclesiological narrative upon which all future understandings of church are built. Luke's decisive contribution to the development of early Christian literature, then, is in his telling one story about God's fulfilling his promises to Israel through both the life, death, and resurrection of Jesus and the birth and spread of the church.

The Gospel of John is very different. Jesus is regularly in Jerusalem, especially for the celebrations of the great feasts (Passover [John 2], Sabbath [John 5], Passover [John 6], Tabernacles [7:1–10:21] and Dedication [10:22–42], Passover [11:55–19:42]). Written at the end of the first century (about 100 CE)—after more reflection, life in the Spirit, and prayer—the understanding of Jesus as the Christ and the Son of God has developed even further. Though some of the stories from the Synoptic Gospels reappear (e.g., the multiplication of the loaves and fishes, the confession of Peter, the passion narrative), the Jesus of the Gospel of John is also different. He is presented as the preexistent *Logos* (John 1:1–18). He knows all things and leads believers—both the disciples in the story and the audiences of the story—into an ever-greater commitment of faith, so that everyone might believe more deeply that Jesus is the Christ, the Son of God, and have life because of this belief (see 20:30–31). John presents the highest Christology of the New Testament narratives.

Although most of Paul's Letters are written prior to the composition of the Gospels and Acts, these narratives provide the story upon which all the apostolic missions are embedded. They give New Testament readers a context through which to understand the canonical letters.

Key Terms and Concepts

bios
double tradition
euangelion/good news
evangelist
Fourth Gospel
genre
gospel
historical context
historiograph
literary context
L material
M material
Markan priority

minor agreements
oral tradition
praxeis/acts
Quelle/Q/Sayings
réédition/reedition
sources
structure
synopsis
Synoptic Gospels
Synoptic Problem
triple tradition
two-source hypothesis

Questions for Review

1. Define what gospels and acts are as genres of literature. Identify several key issues one must bear in mind when studying them.

2. What precipitated the movement from oral tradition to written narratives about Jesus and the early church? Discuss the five-step process presented in this chapter.

3. What is the Synoptic Problem? What is the prevailing theory of its solution? Articulate the different written and oral traditions and what sources scholars suggest may account for them.

4. What do scholars mean by the "structures" of the biblical books? How does mapping a structure of a text aid in exegeting it?

5. What might be an abbreviated way of discussing the varying Christologies of the four evangelists?

Bibliography and Further Reading

Aland, Kurt. *Synopsis of the Four Gospels: Greek-English Edition of the Synopsis Quattuor Evangeliorum.* 10th ed. Swindon: United Bible Societies, 1993.

Ashton, John. *Understanding the Fourth Gospel.* Oxford: Clarendon, 1991.

Brown, Raymond E., SS. *An Introduction to New Testament Christology.* New York: Paulist, 1994.

Brown, Sherri, and Francis J. Moloney. *Interpreting the Gospel of John: An Introduction.* Grand Rapids: Eerdmans, 2017.

Burridge, Richard. *What Are the Gospels? A Comparison with Graeco-Roman Biography.* The Biblical Resource Series. 2nd ed. Grand Rapids: Eerdmans, 2004.

Eusebius. *The Church History.* Translated by Paul L. Maier. Grand Rapids: Kregel Academic & Professional, 2007.

Goodacre, Mark. *The Synoptic Problem. A Way through the Maze.* Understanding the Bible and Its World. New York: T&T Clark, 2004.

Johnson, Luke Timothy. *The Writings of the New Testament: An Interpretation.* 3rd ed. Minneapolis: Fortress, 2010.

Kloppenborg, John S. *Q, the Earliest Gospel: An Introduction to the Original Stories and Sayings of Jesus.* Louisville: Westminster John Knox, 2008.

Moloney, Francis J., SDB. *The Living Voice of the Gospels: The Gospels Today.* Grand Rapids: Baker Academic, 2007.

———. *Reading the New Testament in the Church: A Primer for Pastors, Religious Educators, and Believers.* Grand Rapids: Baker Academic, 2015.

Nickle, Keith F. *The Synoptic Gospels: An Introduction.* Rev. and exp. ed. Louisville: Westminster John Knox, 2001.

Powell, Mark Allan. *Fortress Introduction to the Gospels.* Minneapolis: Fortress, 1998.

———. *Introducing the New Testament: A Historical, Literary, and Theological Survey.* Grand Rapids: Baker Academic, 2009.

Sanders, E. P., and Margaret Davies. *Studying the Synoptic Gospels.* Salem, OR: Trinity International, 1990.

Schneiders, Sandra M. *Written That You May Believe: Encountering Jesus in the Fourth Gospel.* New York: Crossroad, 1999.

Skinner, Christopher W. *Reading John.* Eugene, OR: Cascade, 2015.

Skinner, Matthew L. *Intrusive God, Disruptive Gospel: Encountering the Divine in the Book of Acts.* Grand Rapids: Brazos, 2015.

Throckmorton, Burton H., Jr. *Gospel Parallels, NRSV Edition: A Comparison of the Synoptic Gospels.* 5th ed. Nashville: Thomas Nelson, 1992.

Wasserman, Tommy, and Peter J. Gurry. *A New Approach to Textual Criticism: An Introduction to the Coherence-based Genealogical Method.* Atlanta: SBL Press; Stuttgart: Deutsche Bibelgesellschaft, 2017.

Paul and His Letters

PURPOSE Chapter six outlines the story of the apostle Paul and introduces his letters. The purpose is to provide exegetical insight into the worlds of Paul's letters in order to prepare students for study of the texts themselves.

As we introduced in chapter one, the largest category of literature in the New Testament canon is the **letters**. By letter, we are referring to pieces of written communication that may include a variety of literary forms sent from one person or group to another for particular purposes. These letters are also sometimes called by the cognate of the original Greek term *epistolē*, in English, **epistle**. The early church leaders who formed the New Testament canonized twenty-one letters, fourteen of which were attributed to the apostle Paul, while seven were attributed to other apostolic leaders from the first generation of the church. Our attention in this chapter will focus on Paul and the letters attributed to him. These letters are, in canonical order, Romans, 1 and 2 Corinthians, Galatians, Ephesians, Philippians, Colossians, 1 and 2 Thessalonians, 1 and 2 Timothy, Titus, Philemon, and Hebrews. Hebrews, however, which does not claim to be written by Paul, poses a particular challenge for scholars who, in the end, have largely determined that it does not belong to Paul's heritage. We will, therefore, discuss it in more detail in the next chapter, alongside the Catholic Epistles. After some introductory remarks, we will proceed through the rest of the worlds of these texts to prepare readers for a more systematic interpretation.

One of the later letters of the New Testament, 2 Peter, refers to Paul's writings, sometimes called the **Pauline corpus** (Paul's name as an adjective coupled with the Latin term for

Hebrews and Its Role in the Canon

The Letter to the Hebrews has long been associated with Paul, but this has been an unfortunate association because it was regarded as a letter. It is not a letter but a theological tract. It was written in the most eloquent Greek in the New Testament, most likely by a well-educated Hellenistic Jew in the 80s CE. Urging the superiority of Christ over all other possible approaches to God and urging Christians to loyalty and faithfulness, it is better studied with the later documents of the Christian canon.

"body"), as a difficult group of Scriptures that can be easily misunderstood and even distorted. Of all the books in the New Testament, only the Letters of Paul are referred to so directly as a complex body of teaching that we must approach with care. Indeed, difficulties in interpreting Paul arose even before the writing of 2 Peter. Paul himself had to correct the understanding of an early letter to the church in Corinth (1 Cor 5:9–13). Indeed, the history of the interpretation of Paul is a history of conflict. This conflict became especially acute during the sixteenth century as the reformers questioned the way the Catholic tradition had understood Paul. In other words, Paul is one who regularly evokes strong opinions, to say the least. We can be sure that, had Paul been everyone's favorite apostle, we would not have the depth and breadth of the writings that the early church preserved, nor would he have become the dominant voice in the New Testament.

The World behind Paul's Letters

The goal of a generally historical approach to Paul and his letters is to describe and explain as accurately and impartially as possible just who Paul was, what he stood for, and what he achieved. We will begin with a discussion of source criticism as this will set boundaries for our analysis of the rest of the material traditionally attributed to the apostle Paul. We must first identify and evaluate the sources we have for study. These sources are generally divided into two or three categories, depending upon the scholar's position on the authenticity of each letter. The New Testament contains thirteen letters addressed to various churches and individuals that are formally identified as composed and sent by Paul. As indicated

> **2 Peter 3:14–18**
>
> Therefore, beloved, while you are waiting for these things, strive to be found by him at peace, without spot or blemish; and regard the patience of our Lord as salvation. So also our beloved brother Paul wrote to you according to the wisdom given him, speaking of this as he does in all his letters. There are some things in them hard to understand, which the ignorant and unstable twist to their own destruction, as they do the other scriptures. You therefore, beloved, since you are forewarned, beware that you are not carried away with the error of the lawless and lose your own stability. But grow in the grace and knowledge of our Lord and Savior Jesus Christ. To him be the glory both now and to the day of eternity. Amen.

> **1 Corinthians 5:9–13**
>
> I wrote to you in my letter not to associate with sexually immoral persons—not at all meaning the immoral of this world, or the greedy and robbers, or idolaters, since you would then need to go out of the world. But now I am writing to you not to associate with anyone who bears the name of brother or sister who is sexually immoral or greedy, or is an idolater, reviler, drunkard, or robber. Do not even eat with such a one. For what have I to do with judging those outside? Is it not those who are inside that you are to judge? God will judge those outside.

above, at various times in church history, the so-called epistle to the Hebrews has also been counted among the Pauline Letters. It does not, however, itself make this claim, and its style and content indicate that it is a theological treatise composed by another later Christian writer. Of the thirteen letters, there is general scholarly agreement that at least seven were authentically written by Paul himself. These **undisputed letters** are, in canonical order, Romans, 1 and 2 Corinthians, Galatians, Philippians, 1 Thessalonians, and Philemon. These are, therefore, **primary sources** for studying Paul, his life, theology, and teaching. By primary sources, we are indicating that they are "first-person" accounts of the material that scholars need to reconstruct the life and thought of Paul of Tarsus.

Scholars differ on the remaining six letters, some or all of which, though bearing Paul's name, may have been written after the apostle's time to achieve the authority that name would render. These so-called **disputed letters** are: 2 Thessalonians, Colossians, Ephesians, 1 and 2 Timothy, and Titus. If scholars dispute that a letter is authentically written by the historical figure Paul, they refer to them by various appellations, including **post-Pauline**, **pseudo-Pauline**, or **deutero-Pauline**. The term *post* indicates "after," while the terms *pseudo* and *deuteron* are Greek for "false" and "second," respectively. All these terms indicate that the scholars that use them understand these letters to be **secondary sources** for studying Paul. This indicates that they are "secondhand" sources for understanding the person and work of the historical figure. If these letters are not written by Paul, they would have come from authors who wished to continue the Pauline tradition into a later religious and sociocultural setting. It is important to understand that this means they would not have regarded themselves as being disloyal to Paul. Scholars who do not dispute authenticity understand all the Pauline Letters to constitute a single category of primary sources. Scholars who dispute one or another of them, but not all six, have further varying understandings of what constitutes primary and secondary sources. Of the six letters, Colossians and 2 Thessalonians are often regarded as authentic, while Ephesians and the so-called Pastoral Epistles (1 and 2 Timothy, Titus) are more often understood to be post-Pauline.

The scholar's third major source for the life and teaching of Paul is the canonical Acts of the Apostles, which, despite its title, focuses not on all the apostles equally, but first on Peter, then on Paul. Paul first appears in Acts 7:58 and then is mentioned again in 8:1–3. His encounter with the risen Christ is recounted in 9:1–31, and the

Scholarly Terminology

Scholars use the expressions "primary" and "undisputed" to refer to those letters in the New Testament that were certainly written by Paul (e.g., 1 Thessalonians, Romans, Philippians). Others, which may or may not have come from Paul himself, are generally called "secondary" or "disputed" letters of Paul (e.g., 2 Thessalonians, 1 and 2 Timothy, Ephesians). "Primary" refers to information that comes firsthand, and "secondary" indicates secondhand information.

The Acts of the Apostles

Acts is the sequel to the Gospel in a two-volume work traditionally understood to be composed by the evangelist Luke. Chapter five gives more detail on what scholars refer to as Luke-Acts. For the purposes of the current chapter, we focus on the details Acts provides on the person and ministry of Paul.

beginnings of his ministry are narrated in 11:25–30. Then, the entire second half of the narrative (13:1–28:31) is presented as a travelogue of Paul's life and mission to the gentiles. If it was indeed written by the Luke to whom Paul referred as "one of his fellow workers" in his Letter to Philemon (23–24) and "the beloved physician" in the Letter to the Colossians (4:14), then Acts would have special value as an account written by an eyewitness to some of the events. Indeed, several passages in the travelogue portion of Acts switch to the first-person plural ("we"; 16:10–17; 20:5–21:18; 27:1–28:16). There are, however, many discrepancies between Luke's account and Paul's own retelling of events in his letters. It seems that, while Luke relied upon certain traditions about Paul that are historically valuable, these have been conformed to his own purposes, one of which is to portray the apostolic age as a time when the message about Jesus was spreading relentlessly and rapidly, when believers were completely unified and empowered by the Holy Spirit. Thus, Acts is also considered a secondary source by scholars, even though some important contemporary scholars continue to use it to form the narrative background to Paul's life.

These sources help scholars use historical criticism to reconstruct the life and ministry of the apostle Paul. What follows is a brief suggested summary of this material.

The Life of the Apostle Paul

Name

In his letters, the apostle calls himself "Paul," the Greek, *Paulos*. This name is also the one given in 2 Pet 3:15 and from Acts 13:9 forward. Prior to Acts 13, he is called "Saul," in Greek, *Saulos*, the Greek form of the Hebrew name *Shaūl*. The spelling *Saoul* is found in Paul's accounts of his encounter with the risen Christ (9:4, 17; 22:7, 13; 26:14) and is a direct transliteration of that Hebrew name, Saul, the name of the first king of ancient Israel. Acts 13:9 marks the transition from calling him Saul to calling him Paul, except for the form *Saoul* used in recounting his encounter with the risen Christ (22:7, 13; 26:14).

The name *Paulos* is the Greek form of the common Roman family name, *Paulus*. We can only speculate how Paul got such a name. It is possible that he was called both Saul and Paul from birth, with Saul used in Jewish circles and Paul used in Greek circles. Indeed, many Jews of the day had two names, one Semitic and the other Greek or Roman, for intercourse in the larger empire. The names were often chosen for the similarity in sound. There is no evidence that there was a name change that occurred at Paul's encounter with the risen Christ, even though popular adage would have us believe so. Indeed, the name "Saul" is used after that event until 13:9. The change could be due to a change in Luke's sources. Most likely, however, it is a purposeful change

Peter and Paul
by José de Ribera

that reflects Luke's theological agenda and Paul's own mission—from Jew to gentile—since it reflects the account recorded in Acts 13:6–12, where the Saul-Paul name identification is first recorded. In this account, Paul experiences his first conversion of a **gentile**, a non-Jew, to **the Way** (Acts 9:2; 18:25–26; 19:9; 22:4; 24:14, 22), the Jesus movement. This gentile was the Roman proconsul in Paphos on the island of Cyprus who carried the family name Paulus. This Roman official of some wealth and means accepted Paul's teaching of the good news and seems to have become the model for Paul's mission to the gentiles. In the ancient Roman Empire, well-connected benefactors often gave their names to those whom they chose, or "adopted," to reap the benefits of their wealth in their particular philosophical, social, or theological missions. This is a likely scenario for Paul finding both his new name and his new identity as the **apostle to the gentiles**.

Paul's Youth and Early Career

The date of Paul's birth is unknown. In the custom of the day, someone would be considered an "elder" or "old man" once he reached his 50s. A "youth" or "young man" would fall between the ages of twenty and forty. Paul refers to himself as an "old man" in Philemon 9, and Luke refers to him as a "young man" at the account of the lynching of Stephen. The account of Stephen's martyrdom, in Acts 7:54–8:1, states that Saul was present and approved of his execution (7:58; 8:1), which is best dated at around 35 CE. This would place Paul's birth sometime in the first decade of the first century. Paul does not say where he was born, but his name connects him with a Roman township in some way. He does boast of his Jewish background and traces his lineage to the tribe of Benjamin. He was a "Hebrew born of Hebrews . . . as to the law a Pharisee" (Phil 3:5–6) who was "extremely zealous for the traditions of my fathers" and excelled his peers "in Judaism" (Gal 1:14). In calling himself a Hebrew, he may have been indicating that he was a Greek-speaking Jew who could also read the Scriptures in the original Hebrew. Further, his letters reveal that he knew Greek well and addressed the gentile churches by quoting Jewish Scriptures from the LXX. Traces of Stoic diatribe found throughout his letters also show that he had a Greek rhetorical education. Luke presents Paul as a "Jew" and a "Pharisee" born in Tarsus, a Hellenistic town of Cilicia (Acts 22:3, 21:39), as having a sister (23:16), and as a Roman citizen from birth. This information is consistent with what we glean from Paul's letters and, if correct, explains much of his background and worldview.

In Pompey's reorganization of Asia Minor in 66 BCE, Tarsus became the capital of the province of Cilicia. Later, freedom, immunity, and citizenship were granted to the town by Mark Antony and confirmed by Augustus. This historical setting explains Paul's Roman connections. Tarsus was a well-known center of culture, philosophy, and education. The surpassing reputation of its schools and cultural status is mentioned often by the political and philosophical literati of the day. Thus, the Lukan Paul can boast that he is a "citizen of an important city" (Acts 21:39). The Lukan Paul also boasts of being "brought up in this city [Jerusalem] and educated at the feet of Gamaliel" (Acts 22:3)—that is, Rabbi Gamaliel I, the Elder, whose renown in Jerusalem flourished around 20–50 CE. This too contributes to Paul's Semitic training and mode of thought, but Paul strangely

Rabbi Gamaliel I

This prominent Jewish leader, as early Christianity emerged, was the grandson of a famous rabbi, Hillel. Gamaliel features in Acts 5:33–40, where he urges the Sanhedrin to show moderation to the disciples. The Acts story of Paul claims that he was Paul's teacher (Acts 22:3). While it is possible that the zealous Paul (see Gal 1:14) would have sought out the best Jewish teacher, there is some dissonance between the moderation of Gamaliel and the fervent Saul/Paul. Even Paul's later passion for his gospel is somewhat at odds with the Gamaliel known to us only from the Acts of the Apostles. We cannot be sure of the historical relationship between Gamaliel I and Paul, but behind the account of Acts is Paul's commitment to traditional Judaism.

THE ROMAN EMPIRE FOCUSING ON TARSUS

never mentions this feature of his youth in his letters. It is also odd that, while Gamaliel is regarded as a wise and more broad-minded interpreter of Torah (see Acts 5:33–39), this is not reflected in Paul's pre-Christian attitude to the new religion. Regardless, by the time of his encounter with the risen Christ, Paul must have been not merely a rabbinical disciple, but a recognized teacher with the right to make binding decisions with regard to the law. Such authority is presupposed in his going to Damascus to arrest Christians and in his voting against Christians as a member of the Sanhedrin.

The Turning Point in Paul's Life

Paul wrote of the crucial turn in his life in Gal 1:16, following upon his career in Judaism and zealous persecution of the burgeoning church. After his revelation, he withdrew to Arabia and then returned to Damascus. Three years later, he went to Jerusalem. Thus, sometime around 36 CE, the Pharisee became a Christ-believer and eventually an apostle to the gentiles. Paul regarded the experience near Damascus as the turning point in his life. We must be careful about calling this experience a "conversion," however, as in our contemporary environment, a "conversion" suggests a shift from one religion to another. This is not so for Paul. It was for him an encounter with the risen Lord that he never forgot and that he understood as the basis for his apostolate, but he always understood himself to be Jewish. As a result of that revelation of Jesus as the Christ, Paul became a servant of Christ with a compulsion to preach the gospel of that Christ.

Paul was a man who always had a passion for God. His adhesion to God never changes. He is never "converted" from that. What changes is his unconditional commitment away from Torah (which he does not abandon) to an equally zealous belief in the saving death and resurrection of Jesus, as the new paradigm for how God relates to creation. Luke carefully associates Paul's conversion with his persecution of the church as he pursued the scattering Christians. Thus, what he had understood to be heresy became, in fact, his truth.

> ### Paul's Encounter with the Risen Christ
>
> According to Luke Timothy Johnson (*The Writings of the New Testament: An Interpretation*), of all the early Christian leaders, Paul was most aware of the problems a crucified Messiah posed for Judaism. Nonetheless, as a result of his encounter with the risen Christ, Paul's zeal for Torah was transformed in light of his conviction concerning Jesus as the Christ. He began to understand Jesus as the fulfillment of all that he had previously valued—a fundamental paradigm shift from a relationship with God achieved through Torah to one through faith. Thus, he began to believe that God fulfilled the old covenant and put in place a new covenant. In light of all this, we must take care when we call this turning point a conversion on Paul's part, as his belief system remained within Judaism.

He began to understand Jesus as the fulfillment of all that he had previously valued—a fundamental paradigm shift: from relationship with God achieved through Torah to relationship with God through faith. Thus, Paul began to believe that God fulfilled the old covenant and put in place a new covenant. Therefore, we must take care when we call this turning point a "conversion" on Paul's part. His passionate faith in the God of Israel, whom he eventually sees as the Father of Jesus Christ, the Son of God, never changes. He understood his role now to be to spread this good news, particularly to non-Jews, or gentiles. Once God's design was freed from a strict adherence to Torah, then God's saving care for the gentiles was a logical next step for Paul.

Paul's Mission

Acts organizes Paul's missionary activity into three segments, which we often refer to as his **missionary journeys**. There is some correlation between the Pauline and Lukan data for these missionary journeys. They cover ca. 46–58 CE, the most active years of Paul's apostolic career, as he evangelized in Asia Minor and Greece. The first missionary journey may have lasted ca. 46–49 CE. It is recounted solely in Acts (13:3–14:28) and is confined to the bare essentials. Paul himself gives no details

Conversion in Contemporary Conversation

Today's use of the expression "conversion" indicates a total change of direction. Applying the term to religious experiences, someone might be "converted" from Christianity to Islam or from Buddhism to atheism. In commercial language, we "convert" one currency into another. Even in the New Testament, the word "conversion" indicates a "turning back" from one's mistaken ways to find God's way, often rendered as "repent" (see Mark 1:15). It implies a total change of direction, religiously, politically, or even financially. As we have indicated, this word, so often used of Paul's transition from passionate Judaism to being a dedicated follower of Christ, is not really applicable. Paul maintained his passionate commitment to the God of Israel. But he accepted that the crucified and risen Jesus is God's Messiah.

of his missionary activity in the fourteen years prior to the so-called Jerusalem Council. One of the issues raised in this first mission is the relation of the new faith to Judaism, and more specifically the relationship of gentile Christians to ethnically Jewish Christians. Are these gentiles to be circumcised and required to observe the Mosaic law? At the end of his first mission, while Paul is in Antioch, Jewish Christians from Judea arrive and begin to insist on just such requirements. When this leads to a full-fledged dispute, the Antiochene church sends Paul, Barnabas, and others up to Jerusalem to consult the apostles and elders about the status of Gentile converts. This visit results in the Jerusalem Council recounted in Acts 15.

In Galatians 2:1–10, Paul tells of this same visit. He speaks of the gospel that he had been preaching to the gentiles in terms of a "revelation" that he laid before "those of repute" in Jerusalem. In his words, "they added nothing to it." James, Cephas (the Aramaic version of Peter's name that Paul uses), and John realize the grace given to Paul and Barnabas and extend to them the hand of fellowship. The issues settled on this occasion involve circumcision and food: the former is not obligatory, and gentiles are not required to adhere to the full rigor of Jewish laws regarding the latter. The Jerusalem Council thus frees the nascent church to open itself to the world apostolate then confronting it. Paul's position is vindicated.

The second missionary journey occurs ca. 50–52 CE and is recounted across Acts 15:36–18:22. Paul chooses Silas for his companion, and they set out from Antioch to make their way through Syria and Cilicia and back through the towns of southern Galatia and eventually to Lystra, where Paul takes Timothy on. From there they pass through Phrygia into northern Galatia and found new churches before eventually returning to Antioch.

The third missionary journey falls ca. 54–58 and is narrated in Acts 18:23–21:16. Leaving Antioch, Paul travels once again through northern Galatia and comes to Ephesus. This center of the province of Asia becomes the home of his missionary work for the next three years. By the end of this time Paul is considering a return to Jerusalem with a collection from his gentile churches in response to an injunction at the Jerusalem Council to remember the poor and needy. He seems to want the delivery of this collection to mark the end of his evangelization of the eastern Mediterranean (see Rom 15:30–33). Thereafter, according to Romans 1:11–15 and 15:22–29, he wants to visit Rome and travel to Spain and the West. When spring arrives, Paul sets sail from Corinth (Acts 20:3).

PAUL'S MISSIONARY JOURNEYS

For the rest of Paul's career, we are dependent solely upon Luke's information in Acts 21:17–28:31. This account covers several years after ca. 58 CE in which Paul endures a long imprisonment. Arriving in Jerusalem, Paul and his companions pay their respects to James in the presence of the elders of the church. James tries to avoid any disturbance Paul's presence might cause among the Jewish Christians in Jerusalem but fails. Some Jews from Asia see Paul in the Temple precincts, accuse him of advocating violation of Jewish law, and set upon him to kill him. He is saved by the tribune of the Roman cohort, who puts him under protective arrest. He is eventually brought before the Sanhedrin, then sent to the procurator of Judea, Antonius Felix. Expecting a bribe for his release, Felix keeps Paul in prison for two years. When the new procurator, Porcius Festus, arrives, Paul appeals to Caesar and requests a trial in Rome. By virtue of Paul's Roman citizenship, Festus must grant his request. Escorted by a Roman centurion, and probably accompanied by Luke, they set sail and are ultimately shipwrecked off the coast of Malta. After wintering there, they set sail again and finally reach the capital of the empire. For two more years Paul is kept under house arrest with a soldier to guard him. This does not deter his evangelization and prolific ministry: "He lived there two whole years at his own expense and welcomed all who came to him, proclaiming the kingdom of God and teaching about the Lord Jesus Christ with all boldness and without hindrance" (Acts 28:30–31).

The End of Paul's Life

Paul's arrival in Rome and unhindered preaching of the gospel there form the climax of Luke's story of the spread of the Word of God from Jerusalem to the capital of the civilized world, i.e., "the ends of the earth" symbolized in Acts 1:8. The mention of "two whole years" does not imply that he died immediately thereafter, regardless of the enigmatic ending of Acts. Those who regard the Pastoral Letters as genuine writings of Paul consider them to have been composed by him after this Roman house arrest. They suggest he visited the East again and set up Timothy as the head of the church in Ephesus and Titus as the head of the church in Crete. Second Timothy is composed as Paul's last will and testament, written as he was facing death. The letter suggests he was arrested at Troas and brought to Rome again.

For other details about the end of Paul's life we are dependent upon later ecclesiastical traditions, which are heavily laced with legend. For example, did Paul ever visit Spain? In Clement of Rome's first letter to the Corinthians, written around 95 CE, Clement suggests just this visit to Spain, another trial, and Paul's martyrdom. Eusebius is the first to mention Paul's second imprisonment in Rome and his martyrdom under Nero, according to Tertullian, by beheading. The persecution under Nero lasted from the summer of 64 until Nero's death on June 9, 68 CE, so it is hard to pinpoint a year for Paul's martyrdom, but the preferred year is 67 CE. Paul is said to have been buried in Italy on the Via Ostiensis, near the site of the modern basilica of San Paolo fuori le Mura (Saint Paul's outside the Walls).

In Acts and Paul's own letters, only a handful of events can be dated extrabiblically, which is necessary for a time frame that can be deduced according to our modern calendar. Paul's career time line is therefore impossible to determine with certainty. Synthesis of internal data from his letters and external data from Acts and public records provides a rough framework and dates. The diagram that follows presents an overview of that information.

Clement of Rome on the End of Paul's Life

"[Paul] taught the whole world uprightness and traveled to the extreme west [Spain?]. And after he had borne witness before the authorities, he was taken from this world and went to the holy place, having proved himself the greatest model of endurance" (ca. 95 CE).

Eusebius on the End of Paul's Life

"After defending himself, [Paul] was again sent on the ministry of preaching, and coming a second time to the same city suffered martyrdom under Nero. During this imprisonment he wrote the second epistle to Timothy, indicating at the same time that his first defense had taken place and that his martyrdom was at hand" (ca. 325 CE).

Suggested Chronology of Paul's Ministry

Early 30s: Activity as a rabbi and eventual persecutor of the Jesus movement (Acts 7–8; Phil 3:4–11)

Mid 30s: Encounter with the risen Jesus Christ and beginnings of life in Christ (Acts 9; Gal 1:11–14)

Late 30s: First visit to Jerusalem (Acts 9; Gal 2)

Late 40s–Early 50s: Beginning of missionary activities in Asia Minor (see Acts 13–17). Paul gives no details of activity in the fourteen years prior to the Jerusalem Council of 49 CE.

- **The First Missionary Journey** (ca. 46 to 49 CE; see Acts 13–14). An issue raised in this first mission is the relation of the new faith to Judaism, particularly the relationship of gentile Christians to older Jewish converts.
- **The Jerusalem Council** (see Acts 15; Gal 2). The result frees the early church from strictly Jewish roots, opening it to the broader Greco-Roman world. Paul's role in bringing gentiles into the new covenant is vindicated.
- **The Antioch Incident** (see Acts 15; Gal 2). The question of Jewish dietary law for gentile converts was raised again with Peter.
- **Jerusalem Decree on Dietary Matters** (see Acts 15). James of Jerusalem convenes the elders; their decision is sent as a letter to local churches.
- **The Second Missionary Journey** (ca. 50 to 52 CE; see Acts 15–18). Paul chooses Silas for a companion; they set out from Antioch and take on Timothy and Luke.

Mid–Late 50s: Residence in Ephesus; conclusion of missionary work in Asia Minor (see Acts 18–26)

- **The Third Missionary Journey** (ca. 54 to 58 CE; see Acts 18–20). Paul's preaching the new Christian "Way" in Ephesus prompts travel through the winter of 57–58. He planned a return to Jerusalem with a collection from gentile churches to mark the conclusion of his spread of the "good news" in the eastern Mediterranean.

Late 50s–Mid 60s: Jerusalem to Rome and Beyond (see Acts 27–28 and later church writings)

- **Last Visit to Jerusalem and Arrest** (ca. 58–60 CE; see Acts 21–26). Paul and companions arrive in Jerusalem to pay respects to James and the church elders. He is saved from riots by the Roman tribune and put under protective arrest (ca. 58–60).
- **Appeal to Caesar and Journey to Rome** (ca. 60 CE; see Acts 27–28). After trial and testimony, Paul appeals to his Roman citizenship and is sent to Rome.
- **The End of Paul's Life** (ca. 61–67 CE). Paul was imprisoned in Rome for two years (ca. 61–63; see Acts 28). Church tradition claims he continued west, was imprisoned again in Rome, and martyred under Nero (ca. 63–67 CE).

The World in Paul's Letters

We can now turn our attention to Paul's letters themselves. The world in Paul's texts reveals a complex person who was both a passionate pastor and powerfully intellectual theologian. These letters also tell us a great deal about early Christianity. Understanding Paul's life and ministry in his own terms and interpreting his letters (and his thought) in light of his life experiences and relationships is the primary concern for those asking questions about the world in his texts. So, what can we say about Paul's ministry and his letters?

The Ministry Paul's Letters Reveal

The Christian movement found its first and most vivid voice in the letters of Paul. These letters reveal a character forceful yet with great complexity. For

---

Paul's Associates

Paul worked with a large team of men and women of varying ethnicities and socioeconomic statuses, including, but not limited to:

Apollos	Acts 18:24; 19:1; 1 Corinthians 1:12; 3:4–6, 22; 4:6; 16:12; Titus 3:13	Silas/Silvanus	Acts 15:22, 27, 32, 40; 16:19, 25, 29; 17:1, 4, 5, 10, 14, 15; 18:5; 2 Corinthians 1:19; 1 Thessalonians 1:1; 2 Thessalonians 1:1; 1 Peter 5:12
Aristarchus	Acts 19:29; 20:4; 27:2; Colossians 4:10; Philemon 24		
Barnabas	Acts 4:36; 9:27; 11:22, 25, 30; 12:25; 13:1, 2, 7, 42, 43, 46, 50; 14:1, 12, 14, 20; 15:2, 12, 22, 25, 35, 36, 37, 39; 1 Corinthians 9:6; Galatians 2:1, 9, 13; 4:10	Tertius	Romans 16:22
		Timothy	Acts 16:1, 3; 17:14, 15; 18:5; 19:22; 20:4; Romans 16:21; 1 Corinthians 4:17; 16:10; 2 Corinthians 1:1, 19; Philippians 1:1; 2:19; Colossians 1:1; 1 Thessalonians 1:1; 3:2, 6; 2 Thessalonians 1:1; 1 Timothy 1:2, 18; 6:20; 2 Timothy 1:2; Philemon 1
Erastus	Acts 19:22; Romans 16:23; 2 Timothy 4:20		
Gaius	Acts 19:29; 20:4; Romans 16:23; 1 Corinthians 1:14		
		Titus	2 Corinthians 2:13; 7:6, 13, 14; 8:6, 16, 23; 12:18; Galatians 2:1, 3; 2 Timothy 4:10; Titus 1:4
Luke	Colossians 4:14; 2 Timothy 4:11; Philemon 24		
Onesimus	Colossians 4:9; Philemon 10	Tychicus	Acts 20:4; Ephesians 6:21; Colossians 4:7; 2 Timothy 4:12; Titus 3:12
Phoebe	Romans 16:1		
Priscilla/Prisca and Aquila	Acts 18:2, 18, 26; Romans 16:3; 1 Corinthians 16:19; 2 Timothy 4:19		

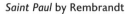

many, coming to grips with Christianity means coming to grips with Paul. His personality is strong and full of contradiction. He had a remarkable organizing ability and worked side by side with missionaries of both genders and all ethnicities. His modes of thought are equally difficult to pinpoint. He is fond of the either/or. He develops antitheses such as death/life, sin/righteousness, flesh/spirit, law/grace, works/faith, wisdom/folly, and power/weakness. At the same time, more than anyone else, he seeks to reconcile opposites: God/world, Jew/Greek, female/male, slave/free, and rich/poor.

Crucial to the process of understanding Paul's ministry is the personal experience that distinguishes Paul among all the first witnesses: He was a persecutor of the church who was then called by the risen Lord to be an apostle. Paul is paradigmatic for understanding the way a religious experience can re-create a symbolic world. Acts emphasizes that Paul's call was a personal encounter with Jesus, the result not of a logical deduction but of an unexpected, shattering collision that reversed Paul literally in mid-stride. Both the Acts narrative and the letters understand this experience as a radical turning point issuing in a command to be the apostle to the gentiles.

Reconstructing the full account of Paul's ministry is a difficult task. Acts is more concerned with patterns of preaching and with Paul's direction to gentiles. Likewise, the letters are written to communities already established, and thus much of his ministry and foundational practices are tacitly assumed. The sources, however, do agree on some important patterns in his ministry. Paul's mission was almost entirely an urban one. Paul worked with his hands to support himself, but his mission required considerable financial assistance. Travel was expensive. Paul did not work alone but as the head of a team.

The Pauline mission must have involved at least forty people—male and female from all levels of society. His ability to organize and mobilize these coworkers must have been considerable. Beyond this, the evidence is lacking. Likewise, it is difficult to trace a development in Paul's thought within the corpus of his extant letters. The first letter was written some twelve years after he began his missionary work. We cannot date the remaining letters with certainty. Nevertheless, the rhetoric of each letter, the issues faced, and the names of the communities to which they were sent enable us to develop a speculative order in which they appeared. We can say that the customs and traditions of the churches themselves were important to him. Paul chose organization and structure over spontaneity and freewheeling administration. In addition, the larger social setting within which all these sources originated must be borne in mind: both the developing Christian community and the Greco-Roman culture.

Hallmarks for Studying Paul's Letters

Analysis of the sources results in four hallmarks with which to approach Paul and his letters.

- The undisputed letters are written to communities, not individuals, and as such were likely intended to be read aloud in public. Even what we call Philemon is ultimately addressed to his entire house church.
- Paul's letters are situation specific and particularly related to the matters at hand for the community addressed.

- While each letter had its own occasion and purpose, all serve the general purpose of providing an "apostolic presence" even when the apostle is physically absent.
- The letters are organized and composed with care, using a professional scribe. Paul adapts the conventional Hellenistic letter format to serve his apostolic function.

The Character of Paul's Letters

Paul's correspondence was carried out in a cultural setting that both valued and highly developed the art of writing letters: posterity was in mind as much as correspondence. In the ancient world, letters were composed for a variety of purposes: for instruction, propaganda, as well as to commend travelers between communities. The one universal function, however, was to make the one absent present: the letter was understood to bear the presence of the sender. The nature of Paul's letters is marked by great variety. Philemon is essentially a personal note. First and Second Timothy and Titus are letters to delegates in the field. Ephesians is very public, an encyclical of sorts. Romans and Colossians are written to churches founded by others and are more formal, while Philippians is gentle and nurturing, written to Paul's dearest community. Galatians is full of harsh rebuke and polemic. They are all, however, occasional, i.e., written for specific purposes to specific people. Paul always writes as the apostle, intending that his letters be read aloud to the congregation; and he always writes out of a sense of need, not as a hobby or diversion. Since writing on parchment or papyrus was specialized and even tedious, the job was often taken by an **amanuensis**, or specially trained secretary. Many of Paul's letters were also cosponsored.

Paul's style is highly dialogical, with significant use of the oral-diatribe form—associated with both preaching and the pedagogical setting of the classroom. He also uses extensive traditional materials and his own commentary on the Hebrew Scriptures. The **Hellenistic letter** had a simple structure: it began with an address: from A to B, greetings; the body followed; concluded by a short farewell, usually including a health or good-fortune wish. Paul adapts this basic structure and expands it for his particular needs. In **Paul's letter structure**, he alters the "greetings" to "**grace**," adds the Jewish greeting "**peace**," and often characterizes both the recipients and the

---

Paul's Coauthors

Timothy	2 Corinthians 1:1; Philippians 1:1; Colossians 1:1; 1 Thessalonians 1:1; 2 Thessalonians 1:1; Philemon 1
Silas	1 Thessalonians 1:1; 2 Thessalonians 1:1
Sosthenes	1 Corinthians 1:1
Brethren with him	Galatians 1:2

Greco-Roman Letters

There are many documents in the New Testament that we call "letters," but very few of them are typical first-century letters. Like contemporary letters (beginning with "Dear" greetings, body of the letter, conclusion, and signing off with "Sincerely" or the like), Greco-Roman letters also had a fixed form. The best examples of such letters in the New Testament are 2–3 John. They are both about the same length, fitting on a single piece of papyrus, and they have the following format:

Opening Formula: Sender to recipient, greetings.

Body of the Letter: The issues that the writer wishes to discuss, his concerns, and his desire to be with them again.

Conclusion: Final wishes for peace, prosperity, and/or good health.

role he will be taking in the letter. He follows the greeting with a prayer that typically takes the form of a **thanksgiving**, with considerable variation to suit the situation. The **body of the letter** addresses the specific needs of the community and develops his argument, often in terms of both teaching and the ethical consequences of that teaching. The body then eases into the **final greetings and farewell**, which are often fairly extensive as he takes the opportunity to maintain connections and relationships across distances.

Based upon this discussion, the diagrams that follow offer suggested historical contexts and structures of the letters attributed to Paul. As we have indicated in previous chapters, these serve as roadmaps of our best determination of the external evidence and internal logic of the letters. Further exegesis may proceed along these or similar outlines.

Paul's Typical Letter Structure

Paul adapts the Hellenistic format for his apostolic need:

Greeting: alters "greetings" to "grace" and adds the Jewish greeting "peace"

Thanksgiving: follows the greeting as a prayer, with variation to suit the situation and praise the recipients

Body of the letter: addresses specific community needs, often developing the argument in terms of teaching and ethical encouragement

Farewell: eases gradually into final greetings and farewell, which are often fairly extensive

---

Paul's Self-Characterizations

servant/slave of Jesus Christ (Rom 1:1)

servant/slave of Christ Jesus (Phil 1:1)

apostle of Christ Jesus (1 Cor 1:1; 2 Cor 1:1)

apostle "sent neither by human commission nor from human authorities, but through Jesus Christ and God the Father, who raised him from the dead" (Gal 1:1)

apostle of Christ Jesus "by the will of God" (Eph 1:1; Col 1:1)

apostle of Christ Jesus "by the command of God our Savior and of Christ Jesus our hope" (1 Tim 1:1)

apostle of Christ Jesus "by the will of God, for the sake of the promise of life that is in Christ Jesus" (2 Tim 1:1)

servant/slave of God and an apostle of Jesus Christ "for the sake of the faith of God's elect and the knowledge of the truth that is in accordance with godliness" (Tit 1:1)

prisoner of Christ Jesus (Phlm 1)

The Undisputed Letters Attributed to Paul

The first group of letters are undisputed: those that biblical scholars regard as being composed by the apostle Paul.

The First Letter to the Thessalonians

When: ca. 50–52 CE.
Why: To respond to concerns about the end time and provide comfort and consolation.

Suggested Structure:

1:1   The Address
1:2–10   The Thanksgiving
2:1–5:22   The Body of the Letter
    2:1–3:13   Paul's Teaching
        2:1–12   Defense of Paul's Ministry
        2:13–16   Thanksgiving in the Bond of Suffering
        2:17–3:13   Concern and Reassurance
    4:1–5:22   Ethical Appeals
        4:1–8   The Call to Holiness
        4:9–12   Communal Relationships
        4:13–5:11   Death, Eschatological Hope, and the Need for Vigilance
        5:12–22   Church Order
5:23–28   Final Greeting

The First Letter to the Corinthians

When: ca. 55–56 CE.
Why: To respond to concerns and queries, both practical and theological (1:11; 7:1).

Suggested Structure:

1:1–3   The Address
1:4–9   The Thanksgiving
1:10–15:58   The Body of the Letter
    1:10–6:20   Responses to Reported Scandals
        1:10–4:21   Divisions and the Word of the Cross in the Community
        5:1–6:20   Moral Abuses
    7:1–15:58   Responses to Corinthian Queries on Moral and Liturgical Issues
        7:1–40   Marriage and Celibacy
        8:1–11:1   Freedom and Knowledge vs. Charity
        11:2–34   Liturgy and Worship
            11:2–16   Dress and Decorum at Liturgies
            11:17–34   Celebration of the Eucharist
        12:1–14:40   The Gifts of the Spirit
        15:1–58   The Christian Confession and the Resurrection
16:1–24   Final Greetings

The Letter to the Galatians

When: ca. 55–56 CE.
Why: To respond to the Galatian Christians' "forsaking the gospel" (1:6) and provide a theology of justification by faith (2:15–21).

Suggested Structure:

1:1–5   The Address
    The Thanksgiving?
1:6–6:10   The Body of the Letter
    1:6–4:31   Paul's Teaching
        1:6–2:21   Defense of Paul's Gospel of Christ and Authority
        3:1–4:31   Faith, Freedom, and the Fulfillment of the Scriptures in Christ
    5:1–6:10   Ethical Appeals
        5:1–26   True Freedom and Walking in the Spirit
        6:1–10   Christ in the Life of the Community
6:11–18   Final Greetings

The Second Letter to the Corinthians

When: ca. 57 CE.
Why: To respond to and reconcile his strained relationship with the Christians in Corinth.

Suggested Structure:

1:1–2   The Address
1:3–11   The Thanksgiving
1:12–13:10   The Body of the Letter
    1:12–7:16   Paul's Relationship with the Corinthians
        1:12–2:13   Past Relationships
        2:14–7:4   Paul's Ministry
        7:5–16   Resolution of the Crisis
    8:1–9:15   The Collection for Jerusalem
    10:1–13:10   Paul's Defense of His Ministry
13:11–13   Final Greetings

The Letter to Philemon

When: ca. 60–62 CE.
Why: A witty, carefully crafted entreaty to Philemon on behalf of Onesimus, a slave.

Suggested Structure:

1–3   The Address
4–6   The Thanksgiving
7–22   The Body of the Letter
    7–16   Paul's Teaching: A Plea for Onesimus
    17–22   Ethical Appeal
23–25   Final Greetings

The Letter to the Romans

When: ca. 58 CE.

Why: A profound theological reflection on justification and salvation through faith in the crucified and risen Christ and letter of self-introduction with plans to visit and base a ministry to Spain there (1:11–15; 15:22–33).

Suggested Structure:

1:1–7   The Address
1:8–15   The Thanksgiving
1:16–15:13   The Body of the Letter
    1:16–11:36   Paul's Fundamental Teaching
        1:16–17   The Thesis: Justification by Faith
        1:18–3:20   The Antithesis: Universal Sin
        3:21–31   The Thesis Restated: Universal Faith
        4:1–25   Demonstration of the Thesis by Example: Abraham, Model of Faith
        5:1–21   Exposition of the Thesis: Justification Given in Christ
        6:1–11:33   Objections and Responses to the Thesis (Efficacy)
            6:1–23   Implications of the Gift
            7:1–25   The Role of the Law
            8:1–39   The Fruit of Righteousness: Life in the Spirit
            9:1–11:36   The Salvation of Israel and the Justice of God
    12:1–15:13   Ethical Conclusions
        12:1–13:14   The Church and the World
        14:1–15:13   Divisions and Unity
15:14–16:27   Conclusion and Final Greetings

The Letter to the Philippians

When: ca. 60–62 CE.

Why: A warm letter of fellowship written from prison to encourage continued community and ministry (1:12–19; 2:1; 3:10; 4:15).

Suggested Structure:

1:1–2   The Address
1:3–11   The Thanksgiving
1:12–4:20   The Body of the Letter
    1:12–2:30   Paul's Teaching
        1:12–30   The Progress of the Gospel
        2:1–11   Imitating Christ
        2:12–30   Life in Community
    3:1–4:9   Ethical Appeals
        3:1–11   The Life of Faith
        3:12–4:1   The Life of Hope
        4:2–9   Joy and Peace
    4:10–20   Paul's Fellowship with the Philippians
4:21–23   Final Greetings

The Disputed Letters Attributed to Paul

This second group of letters are disputed, those that many biblical scholars doubt as being composed by the apostle Paul.

The Letter to the Colossians

When: ca. 62–64 CE if authentic; ca. late 60s if by disciple; ca. 80s if post-Pauline.
Why: To show the supremacy, sufficiency, and divinity of Christ, as well as how Christians are to live in the world and before God (see Col 3).

Suggested Structure:

1:1–2   The Address
1:3–14   The Thanksgiving
1:15–4:6   The Body of the Letter
    1:15–2:23   Paul's Teaching
        1:15–23   Christological Hymn and Implications
        1:24–2:5   Paul's Ministry and Example
        2:6–23   Warnings about False Teachings
    3:1–4:6   Ethical Appeals
        3:1–17   New Life in Christ
        3:18–4:1   Household Relationships
        4:2–6   General Exhortations
4:7–18   Conclusion and Final Greetings

The Letter to the Ephesians

When: ca. 62–64 CE if authentic; ca. 70s–80s if post-Pauline.
Why: To affirm the transforming significance of Jesus's death and resurrection into a later era and establish the church as the body of Christ; likely composed based upon the Letter to the Colossians.

Suggested Structure:

1:1–2   The Address
1:3–14   The Thanksgiving
1:15–6:20   The Body of the Letter
    1:15–4:24   Paul's Teaching
        1:15–2:22   Unity of the Church—Jew and Gentile in Christ
        3:1–4:24   God's Plan and the Universal Mission of the Church
    4:25–6:20   Ethical Appeals
        4:25–5:14   Speech and Action
        5:15–6:9   Community Life
        6:10–20   Spiritual Warfare
6:21–24   Final Greetings

The Second Letter to the Thessalonians

When: ca. 50–52 CE if authentic; ca. 80s if post-Pauline.
Why: To follow the first letter to quell panic about end times and encourage community.

Suggested Structure:

1:1–2　The Address
1:3–12　The Thanksgiving
2:1–3:15　The Body of the Letter
    2:1–17　Paul's Teaching
        2:1–12　Warning about the Parousia
        2:13–17　Thanksgiving and Prayer
    3:1–15　Ethical Appeals
        3:1–5　Prayer
        3:6–15　Apostolic Example and Warning Against Idleness
3:16–18　Final Greeting

The First Letter to Timothy

When: ca. 64–67 CE if authentic; late first or early second century if post-Pauline.
Why: For Timothy, as head of the Ephesian church, with guidance for God's household.

Suggested Structure:

1:1–2　The Address
1:12–17　The Thanksgiving
1:3–11; 1:18–6:19　The Body of the Letter
    1:3–11; 1:18–4:16　Paul's Message to Timothy on Teaching
        1:3–11　False Teaching
        1:18–4:16　Ministry and the Mystery of the Gospel
    5:1–6:19　Paul's Message to Timothy Regarding Ethical Duties
6:20–21　Final Recommendation and Greeting

The Second Letter to Timothy

When: ca. 64–67 CE if authentic; late first or early second century if post-Pauline.
Why: To present Timothy, his closest confidant, a final testament.

Suggested Structure:

1:1–2　The Address
1:3–5　The Thanksgiving
1:6–4:8　The Body of the Letter
    1:6–18　Exhortations to Timothy
    2:1–26　Images of Timothy as Pastor
    3:1–4:8　False Teaching and Steadfastness
4:9–22　Personal Requests and Final Greetings

The Letter to Titus

When: ca. 64–67 CE if authentic; late first or early second century if post-Pauline.
Why: For Titus as head of the Cretan church with instruction for church order.

Suggested Structure:

1:1–4　The Address
1:5–3:11　The Thanksgiving and the Body of the Letter
    1:5–16　Pastoral Charge
    2:1–3:11　Paul's Message to Titus: Teaching the Christian Life
        2:1–10　Christian Behavior
        2:11–3:11　Transformation of Life
3:12–15　Conclusion and Final Greetings

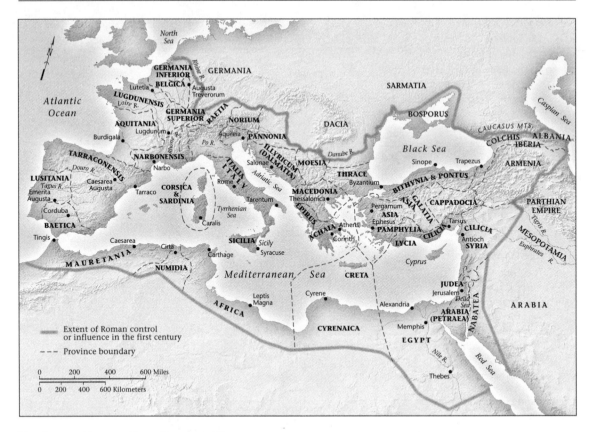

THE ROMAN EMPIRE, FIRST CENTURY CE

The World in Front of Paul's Letters

One of the apostle Paul's many distinctions is that he can be understood as the first
Christian theologian. He provides our earliest record of written contemplation of
God and God's work in creation from a specifically Christian viewpoint, that is,
from the perspective of the **Christ Event**. Again, the term "Christ Event" is a shorthand way of referring to the multifaceted complexity of decisive moments of the
earthly and risen life of Jesus Christ. Paul often focuses on the passion and death
of Jesus, but these moments taken together form only one component of the Christ
Event. Paul also often depends upon the resurrection and exaltation of Christ in
re-forming his theology. Although many have noted how little interest Paul shows
in Jesus's life prior to the passion, we suggest that the life and teaching of Jesus are
also foundational to Paul's understanding of the Christ Event and therefore to
the response in action he advocates to his churches. The Christ Event, therefore,
includes, at the very least, the three decisive moments of the life and teaching of
Jesus, the passion and death of Jesus, and the resurrection of Jesus the Christ.

Detail of Saint Paul
from *Saint Peter and
Saint Paul* by El Greco

In terms of the world in front of the text, we are primarily concerned with
how Paul's messages impacted his first audiences, in this case, the recipients
of his letters, and then how they may impact audiences today. As we have indicated, Paul's letters are largely situation specific. Therefore, we will focus on
his more sweeping theological developments to allow for a more complete understanding of how Paul understands God's action in history, through Israel,
and turning on the Christ Event. The difficult part of this task has always been
that Paul is not a literary evangelist. He has not written a gospel that lays out
his understanding in a narrative form. He is a pastor and practical theologian,
and his literary offerings come in the form of letters. Nonetheless, his theology
and self-understanding as apostle and pastor are rooted in the story of Israel

and how the God of Israel has acted in consistent covenant relationship through the Christ Event. But what do we mean by theology here? As he did not write theological treatises but letters in response to pastoral concern and congregational occasion, Paul's theology is focused on his attempts to understand who God is and how God is acting in the world. Thus, Paul's letters always have in their backdrop the gospel that he received, so what he writes about the gospel is his theology. Thus, his theology is not found in carefully crafted theological concepts but in the manner in which these letters interpret what happened, is happening, and will happen in the good news, as he received it by revelation. This theology manifests in the concrete ways in which he writes. Therefore, this theological narrative, as Paul understands it, can be gleaned from his letters with the theological concerns of God's integrity, fidelity, and actions in history. So, Paul is not a systematic theologian but a concrete practical theologian who proclaims the salvation provided by Jesus Christ when he responds to, pastors, and comforts his flock.

Paul understands God's action in history as the story of the salvation of humankind, so his theology must be identified with a narrative of salvation history (Rom 11:12, 25–26; 15:7–13). Further, Paul was immersed in the Jewish writings prevalent in his time and working out of a **Jewish apocalyptic worldview** that focused on the revelatory activity of God in the unfolding of God's plan in and for history. Apocalypticism appears in times of persecution, rejection, and severe hardship. It arose in Judaism in the second century BCE in response to an erosion of values from within and an attack on those values from outside and found its classic expression in the Jewish Scriptures, during the Maccabean period, in the book of Daniel (ca. 165 BCE). Thus, it is essentially crisis literature. Despite its elaborate symbolism, the apocalyptic worldview typically presents a rather straightforward interpretation and resulting picture of history: even when all appearances are to the contrary, God is in command of the world. Therefore, even if God's people suffer trials and tribulation, God will ultimately intervene decisively on behalf of the faithful and the oppressed and bring history to its final goal: the communion of God with humankind and all God's creation. Thus, the function and emphasis are always focused on encouragement and comfort. The main objective of Jewish apocalyptic literature is to give suffering people hope and consolation in the face of affliction, but also to demand fidelity and steadfastness in the face of persecution. Paul viewed God's action in creation and history from a Jew-

Apocalypse and Apocalypticism

Early Christianity emerged at a time when the people of Israel were wondering about their failures and the destruction of their nation and city by pagans in 70 CE. Where was God in what had happened? Developing a literary form that had already responded to that question during earlier destruction and failure (especially in the book of Daniel), Jewish thinkers responded with what we call "apocalypticism." Given the importance of this issue and the New Testament book that uses the same literary form (the book of Revelation), we have devoted chapter eight to the apocalypses and the nature of apocalypticism.

ish apocalyptic perspective. Particularly in his Letter to the Galatians, Paul's theology is founded in an apocalyptic narrative about the end of the old age and the beginning of a new one. Therefore, Paul's theology is best understood in terms of a narrative that provides a turning point in the revelation of salvation history, coupled with a gospel that in turn reveals a participatory and indwelling soteriology in God's plan to bring creation to its goal.

Paul's Jewish apocalyptic worldview understood time linearly: history had a beginning, is ongoing, and will ultimately have an end. But this beginning and the culminating end were, and are, the same: the glory of God. Before God broke into the abyss and created, God's glory was all that was (2 Cor 4:6). This is likewise the goal of the world God created: to dwell with God in glory, and once the world reaches its end, the glory of God will abide. The goal of the individual is to dwell, now and forever, in the glory of God (1 Thess 2:12). Therefore, although we speak of this as linear, its goal is to come "full circle," so to speak. Thus, history should not be envisioned along a horizontal continuum, but somehow with the beginning and end in the same substantive space. Since Paul also understands the Christ Event as a turning point in history, a circle is also not the most accurate pictograph. The best way to diagram this vision of history might be the chiasm. Although the literary structure of the chiasm is an imperfect analogy that cannot be "proven" as the structure of Paul's story, this image of a beginning and end on the same vertical plane (i.e., in the same substantive space), with the Christ Event as the crucial turning point (Rom 3:22–23) that turns history back toward God and the promise of God's glory (Rom 15:7), is a helpful visual aid.

As Paul attempts to reconcile his revelatory encounter with the risen Christ (Acts 9:1–9; 22:6–21; 26:12–18; 1 Cor 15:3–8; Gal 1:11–16) and the gospel he has received with his embedded Jewish apocalyptic worldview, he looks back on history as revealed in the Scriptures and develops a covenantal narrative of salvation history. God broke into space and time and acted through the word of creation, and thus came the world as we know it and humankind as we know it in Adam (Gen 1–3). The character of this word is one of **covenant**. As we laid out in chapter three, the metaphor of covenant is the primary means by which the biblical authors in the Jewish Scriptures express the special relationship between God and God's creation in general, and God's chosen people Israel in particular. Both the texts that narrate the story of Israel and its relationship with God, on the one hand, and the prophetic literature that communicates God's will and summons Israel to live rightly in this relationship, on the other, are replete with accounts of and references to God's covenantal activity in the world. In addition to detailed recounting of covenant-making and covenant-renewing rituals and ceremonies, this literature preserves the broader themes and symbolism of the covenant metaphor. These storytellers and prophets integrate this language into their larger works in order to share their message of life in unique relationship with God, even when the term "covenant" does not

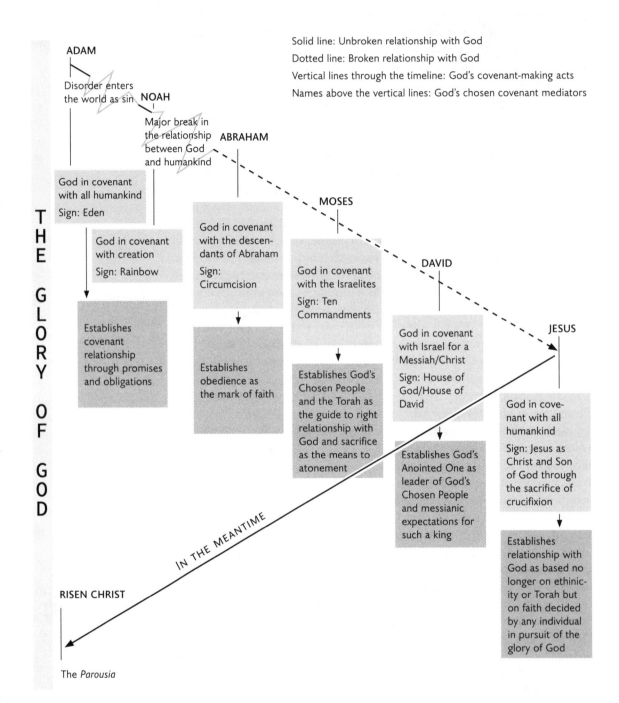

Solid line: Unbroken relationship with God

Dotted line: Broken relationship with God

Vertical lines through the timeline: God's covenant-making acts

Names above the vertical lines: God's chosen covenant mediators

ADAM

Disorder enters the world as sin

NOAH

Major break in the relationship between God and humankind

ABRAHAM

God in covenant with all humankind

Sign: Eden

God in covenant with creation

Sign: Rainbow

MOSES

God in covenant with the descendants of Abraham

Sign: Circumcision

God in covenant with the Israelites

Sign: Ten Commandments

DAVID

Establishes covenant relationship through promises and obligations

Establishes obedience as the mark of faith

God in covenant with Israel for a Messiah/Christ

Sign: House of God/House of David

JESUS

Establishes God's Chosen People and the Torah as the guide to right relationship with God and sacrifice as the means to atonement

Establishes God's Anointed One as leader of God's Chosen People and messianic expectations for such a king

God in covenant with all humankind

Sign: Jesus as Christ and Son of God through the sacrifice of crucifixion

T H E   G L O R Y   O F   G O D

IN THE MEANTIME

RISEN CHRIST

The *Parousia*

Establishes relationship with God as based no longer on ethinicity or Torah but on faith decided by any individual in pursuit of the glory of God appear. This story of covenantal relationship that began with the inbreaking of God is, of course, also Paul's story of history.

Genesis 1–3 recounts the incursion of God into space and time in the word of creation, which suggests that the foundation of the covenantal relationship with God is communication. God makes an implicit covenant with Adam and all creation by way of this creative act (1 Cor 15:45–49). God created the world, and humankind, to be in a perfect relationship of union with him. Unmediated relationship with God gave freedom by way of obedience. Paul would say that this cosmology and anthropology suggest that humankind is truly free, most fully human, when obedient to God (Rom 6:15–23). This covenantal relationship, full of the promises of intimate relationship with God and care of creation, as well as the obligation of obedience in refraining from eating from the tree, is marked by the dwelling place of Eden, where humankind can commune with God "in the evening breeze" (Gen 3:8). Early on, however, there was a breakdown for which Adam bears the burden through his act of disobedience (Rom 5:19), which led to a fundamental disordering of the intended order of creation. Sin and death enter the world through disobedience (Rom 5:12–18; 1 Cor 15:22) and quickly spread as humankind grows (Gen 4:1–6:8). God begins to rectify this relationship with creation by offering a covenant through Noah (Gen 6–9). Noah's obedience makes possible God's covenant with creation (Gen 9:8–17). For humankind's part, however, sin spread through disobedience to the covenantal relationship (Rom 11:30–32). This disorder reaches a climax in these early chapters with the story of the Tower of Babel (Gen 11:1–9). This etiological story of the origins of differing languages and the spread of humankind over the earth also provides a symbolic narrative of the scattering of humankind, which was created to be in union with God. There is a significant break in the narrative here by way of genealogy (Gen 11:10–32), after which something distinctive begins, though it is still consistently covenantal.

God broke in and acted again through the word of covenant with humankind. This time, however, God chose to work through one man and his descendants (Gen 12:1–4). The mediator of this covenant was Abraham, and Abraham's obedience resulted in the next step in the covenantal union with God. God promises Abraham a blessing, descendants, and land, as well as the extension of this covenantal relationship to Abraham's descendants, through Abraham's faithful obedience (Rom 4:13, 18–22). The sign of this covenantal activity is circumcision (Gen 17:1–14). Eventually, God's covenant with Abraham results in the birth of a people, the twelve tribes of Israel, who, marked by circumcision, are likewise the descendants of God. Abraham thus becomes Paul's go-to model for righteousness before God, apart from Torah (Romans 4; Gal 3:1–4:8). However, Paul is quick to point out that, although circumcision becomes the mark of this covenant, God reckoned Abraham's faith to him as righteousness prior to the command for circumcision (Gen 15:6; Rom 4:9–12). Circumcision was given as a seal of the righteousness of faith already lived

(Rom 4:11). Thus, Abraham is the ancestor to all who would believe, which in turn allows this same righteousness to be reckoned upon them. "For this reason, those who believe are blessed with Abraham who believed" (Gal 3:6–9; see also Rom 4:16–17). This was God's plan all along, Paul would say, but initially God worked through this one man and his descendants to provide a model for righteousness for all humankind.

In the following centuries, God remembers his covenant with Abraham through the exodus (Exod 1–15)—a formative event in the history of Israel. The will of God's chosen people Israel results in the formation of the Sinai covenant, as mediated by Moses and marked by the giving of the Ten Commandments (Exod 19–20). God perfected this obedience through the giving of the full Torah, the gift that guides God's people to righteousness due to the presence of transgression (Gal 3:19). Through Torah, the Israelites were able to atone for sin and attempt to reconcile themselves with God in a new way: through the discipline of the law and the act of sacrifice to God (Gal 3:24; Phil 4:18; see Exod 20:24; Lev 7; 19; 22). Paul understood this gift itself, however, as imperfect, in the sense that it reunited humankind with God, but it did not save; it did not justify (Rom 8:3; Gal 3:19–20). Nonetheless, the Torah is by no means opposed to the promises of God through Abraham (Gal 3:21). Rather, the law is good and both shines a light on sin and provides a path for righteousness (Rom 7).

Eventually, this chosen people of Israel formed a nation with a king. The king that epitomizes a unified Israel in union with God is David. In recognition of this, God makes a covenant with David, the mark of which is a house—a house for God in the Temple and a house for David in his dynasty (2 Sam 7). The hope for a messiah and messianic expectations grew out of this covenant. Paul speaks little of the Davidic covenant in his story of the gospel and salvation history, but he does look to David as one who speaks of blessedness for all who are righteous irrespective of works of the law (Rom 4:6–8). Further, his sheer focus on Jesus as the Christ and descended from David (Rom 1:2) bespeaks his commitment to and incorporation of this covenant into his story of God's work in the world.

And history moves forward. The kingdom divides, and both nations eventually fall, leading once again to a physical scattering of the people through the Babylonian exile. The prophets are united in understanding this fall of the nation and scattering of the people to be the result of Israel's breach of covenant with God. Eventually, the Israelites return and rebuild, but when Roman rule takes over in the first century BCE and the extreme hardship of foreign rule leads to the spread of the apocalyptic worldview, the people of Judea are ripe for a revelation, and hopes for God's promised messiah to come and bring in God's kingdom reach a fever pitch.

God responds with a new act of obedience that brings on a new creation. Paul most clearly elucidates this act in the "Christ hymn" of Phil 2:6–11. The story of this hymn is the story that underlies all else in Paul's understanding of the good news. God breaks into space and time in a new act of covenant that is consistent with all previous covenantal activity in God's story with Israel. For Paul, fidelity on God's part in this relationship is also fundamental; therefore, determining the justice of God in this story is likewise essential (Rom 9–11). However, this covenantal act is also distinctive and unique. For Jesus is not only the human mediator of God's covenant, as was Abraham, Moses, and the others before him, he is the divine Son of God who also *is* the covenant gift itself. The preexistent Christ Jesus, in the form of God, empties himself into human form, "becoming obedient to death, even death on a cross" (Phil 2:6–8). The paradox is that this scandalous death from the human perspective is in truth God's gift of expiation, a sacrifice that brings about the atonement that fulfills all God's earlier covenantal activity and puts in place a new covenant whereby justification to any and all is made possible by the faithful obedience of Christ (Rom 3:21–26; Gal 2:16, 20; 3:22; Phil 3:9).

Just as right relationship with God was ruptured by the disobedience of the one man, Adam, the new act of faithful obedience of the one man, Jesus, is the grace that brings justification (Rom 5:1–21; 1 Cor 15:20–28). Representing humanity before God, therefore, Christ effected a "divine interchange" whereby humanity becomes the righteousness of God (2 Cor 5:21), is freed from the law (Gal 3:13), and fulfills its just requirements in Christ (Rom 8:3). Through the life and ministry, death, and resurrection of Jesus Christ, all of God's prior covenantal activity is brought to fulfillment (1 Cor 15:3–4). Jesus is the new Adam whose faithful obedience (following the Abrahamic covenant) leads him to be the sacrifice that atones for the sin of all humankind (following the Sinai covenant) and exalts him as the Christ who redeems God's people (following the Davidic covenant) and reconciles the ruptured relationship between God and humankind. Christ is indeed the climax of Israel's story. But Christ is also the turning point in God's salvation history with all humankind. As the one ultimate redeeming sacrifice, the Christ Event brings about an acquittal and new relationship between God and creation in a new covenantal relationship—open to all humankind.

This opening of unmediated relationship with God brings about a state whereby humankind can live in glory now, though Paul is not so naïve to think that it is just glory now. Humankind is making its way back to the glory that is full dwelling with God. Again, this is a Jewish worldview, a rereading of a Jewish apocalyptic schema. It is the end of history that will bring God's plan to fruition. In his early letters to the Thessalonians, Paul focuses on the *parousia* as this final incursion of God into creation that brings salvation in terms of life together with Christ for the faithful (1 Thess 4:13–5:11). Later, Paul focuses on the resurrection of Christ as the firstfruits of resurrected life with Christ in the glory of God (1 Cor 15:1–28; Rom 6:5–11).

This understanding of **salvation history** is all rooted in God's ongoing covenantal relationship with creation and humankind as the apex of that creation. The Christ Event, according to Paul, is the turning point of history and God's salvific work in creation with humankind. If the life and ministry of Jesus shows God's faithfulness to confirm the promises to the patriarchs, as well as God's mercy and glory to the gentiles (Rom 15:8–9), and the crucifixion puts in place the new covenant through which Jew and gentile alike are justified by the faith of Christ (Gal 3:24–29; Rom 3:21–31; 5:12–21), then the resurrection is for Paul the proof of the possibility of this new hope and life in the Spirit (Rom 8). Humankind still has the choice to accept this gift of covenant relationship or not. The gift is free and available to all. And this is the theology that Paul gives to the world in front of his letters.

What Have We Learned So Far? Paul and His Mission

Participation in the gospel provides life in the new community of the faithful. This is also how Christianity makes sense in terms of its Jewish history, and how it was born and began to spread among first the Jewish people and then also to the gentiles through the vocation of Paul and his developing theology of salvation history. The primary actor of this story is God, who is Father; the agent of salvation is Jesus Christ, who is Son and Lord; and the beneficiaries are all people who choose to inhabit the faithfulness of Christ in the hope of salvation in the glory of God. From his turning point, Paul devoted his life to spreading this good news to all who would hear it. Paul's anthropology, therefore, radical as it was for the first-century Roman Empire, was that all were equal and equally gifted before God through Christ. Indeed, every person has the power to accept or reject God's offer of covenant relationship (Paul's theology) through faith in Christ (Paul's Christology), which both spans this life and goes beyond it in right relationship with God (Paul's eschatology and soteriology).

Key Terms and Concepts

amanuensis

apostle to the gentiles

body of the letter

Christ Event

covenant

disputed letters

epistolē/epistle

final greetings and farewell

gentile

grace and peace

Hellenistic letter

Jewish apocalyptic worldview

letters

missionary journeys

Pauline corpus

Paul's letter structure

post-/pseudo-/deutero-Pauline

primary sources

undisputed letters

salvation history

secondary sources

thanksgiving

the Way

Questions for Review

1. What does it mean to discuss primary and secondary sources for studying Paul? Identify texts from each group and how they are categorized as such.
2. Sketch Paul's background as a Jewish man, leader, and rabbi of the first century. How did this influence his first interaction with the Jesus movement?
3. What is the basic format of a Greco-Roman letter? How does Paul adapt this format to meet his apostolic and theological needs?
4. In what respect can we say that Paul looks to Jewish apocalyptic ideas in developing his understanding of what God has done for humankind in and through Jesus Christ?
5. What is Paul's theology of salvation history? What does this mean, and what are scholars discussing when they attempt to construct Paul's theology in this manner?

Bibliography and Further Reading

Beker, J. Christiaan. *Paul's Apocalyptic Gospel: The Coming Triumph of God.* Philadelphia: Fortress, 1982.

Brown, Sherri. "Faith, Christ, and Paul's Theology of Salvation History." In *Unity and Diversity in the Gospels and Paul: Essays in Honor of Frank J. Matera*, edited by Christopher W. Skinner and Kelly R. Iverson, 249–71. Early Christianity and Its Literature 7. Atlanta: Society of Biblical Literature, 2012.

Collins, Raymond F. *Letters That Paul Did Not Write: The Epistle to the Hebrews and the Pauline Pseudepigrapha.* Eugene, OR: Wipf & Stock, 1988.

Fitzmyer, Joseph A. *Paul and His Theology: A Brief Sketch.* 2nd ed. Englewood Cliffs, NJ: Prentice Hall, 1989.

Gorman, Michael J. *The Apostle of the Crucified Lord: A Theological Introduction to Paul and His Letters.* 2nd ed. Grand Rapids: Eerdmans, 2016.

———. *Reading Paul.* Eugene, OR: Cascade, 2008.

Hays, Richard. *The Faith of Jesus Christ: The Narrative Substructure of Galatians 3:1–4:11.* 2nd ed. Grand Rapids: Eerdmans, 2002.

Horrell, David G. *An Introduction to the Study of Paul.* 2nd ed. T&T Clark Approaches to Biblical Studies. London: T&T Clark, 2006.

Johnson, Luke Timothy. *The Writings of the New Testament: An Interpretation.* 3rd ed. Minneapolis: Fortress, 2010.

Martyn, J. Louis. "Apocalyptic Antinomies in Paul's Letter to the Galatians." *New Testament Studies* 31 (1985): 410–24.

Matera, Frank J. *God's Saving Grace: A Pauline Theology.* Grand Rapids: Eerdmans, 2012.

———. *New Testament Christology.* Louisville: Westminster John Knox, 1999.

Moloney, Francis J. *Reading the New Testament in the Church: A Primer for Pastors, Religious Educators, and Believers.* Grand Rapids: Baker Academic, 2015.

Tatum, Gregory, OP. *New Chapters in the Life of Paul: The Relative Chronology of His Career.* Catholic Biblical Quarterly Monograph Series 41. Washington, DC: Catholic Biblical Association of America, 2006.

Wright, N. T. *Paul: A Biography.* San Francisco: HarperOne, 2018.

Hebrews and the Catholic Epistles

PURPOSE Chapter seven explores the later documents of the New Testament, known as Hebrews and the Catholic Epistles. These texts present a variety of understandings of and responses to both the Christ Event and the challenge of faith for a community in a complex world.

The previous chapter discussed the group of letters in the New Testament known as the Pauline corpus. Our focus will now turn to tracing the emergence and content of the remaining seven letters known as the Catholic Epistles or, in some Christian traditions, the General Letters. We can discuss what led to the inclusion of these seven documents, some of which are not particularly weighty, over against other more substantial documents from the same period (e.g., the Didache, the Letter of Clement, or the Shepherd of Hermas). In the context of the worlds of each letter, we will examine their reception as part of the NT Scripture. First, however, we must turn our attention to Hebrews, an anonymous tract often connected to the apostle Paul. At one time or another, all eight of these texts were identified as letters, but we will show that identifying

---

Early Christian Extracanonical Documents

Understandably, as the Christian communities grew in strength and number, early Christian authors wrote documents for the encouragement and instruction of believers. Some of them were very important and were regularly found in the earliest collections of Christian books but eventually were not included in the Christian canon. For example, the Didache offers important instruction on the early Christian mission and the celebration of the Eucharist. The Letter of Clement to the Corinthians is a passionate insistence on the importance of love and unity in a Christian community. And the Shepherd of Hermas, among other things, considers the critical problem of post-baptismal sin. All three of these documents, among many others, probably appeared at the turn of the first and second centuries CE.

their genres is somewhat complex, and this will aid in interpreting them and understanding their role in the canon. Each text has its own story, and, because of their complexity, we will spend a bit more time on them individually than we have on the previous NT texts.

Hebrews

Hebrews is regarded as one of the most elegant and passionate documents in the Bible, if not *the* most. In the New Testament, it is also unique in genre, style, and both Christological and ecclesiological presentation. This distinctive text from the early Christian tradition merits some extended attention.

The World behind Hebrews

Although included in the canon as part of the collection of Paul's Letters, contemporary interpreters are all but unanimous in accepting that Hebrews was not written by Paul. These doubts have been present since the earliest times. Indeed, the fourth-century church historian Eusebius quotes Origen, an important third-century church leader, as concluding that "only God knows" who wrote Hebrews (*Church History* 6.25.14). Therefore, much about the date and place of the origin of Hebrews, and its original author, cannot be determined. There is very little reference to people, places, and time in the document itself. The mention of Timothy and Italy in 13:23–24 is the only exception. A working hypothesis is that Hebrews was written by a cultivated Jew during the 80s CE. The author was familiar with philosophical currents of the day (especially Philo, a Jewish philosopher working in Alexandria who was influenced by Plato) but was ultimately dependent upon the Jewish Scriptures for inspiration. It was written, in the most eloquent Greek in the New Testament, to Christians in Rome (see 13:23–24), to affirm the superiority of Jesus Christ subsequent to the trials they have experienced under Nero (see 10:32–34) and prior to those that might lie ahead, exhorting them to accept suffering, as Jesus did (see 12:3–4). Hebrews most likely appeared before the time of the Roman emperor Domitian in the 90s.

Philo of Alexandria

Although there is no evidence of any contact between early Christian writers and the famous Hellenistic Jewish scholar Philo of Alexandria (25 BCE–50 CE), he wrote many significant works as Christianity was born. Deeply immersed in Greek philosophy, especially the philosophy of Plato, he studied the Jewish Bible (especially the Torah) and interpreted it, largely through the use of allegory, in a way that was acceptable and understandable to the many Jewish communities that flourished in the Greek-speaking cultures of northern Egypt. The Letter to the Hebrews and the Gospel of John, which are later Christian books, do not reflect any dependence upon Philo's work, but it can be said that they often use his same methods of interpreting Judaism through Greek philosophical lenses.

The World in Hebrews

It is difficult to identify the precise literary form of Hebrews, as it contains exhortation to faithfulness and perseverance, as well as a passionate **theological treatise** that argues for the superiority of Christ, but it also bears some signs of a letter, especially in the instructions and the conclusion in 13:1–25. It may, therefore, be best to discuss the genre as a written treatise or homily with an epistolary ending. Through this form, Hebrews gracefully argues that all God's former institutions and means of communication with humankind have been perfected in Jesus Christ. The author does this by arguing for the superiority of Christ in a careful and elegant manner, which can be structured as follows:

1:1–4   Introduction: The Definitive and Unique Revelation Spoken by God through His Son
1:5–13:19   The Body of the Treatise
    1:5–2:18   The Superiority of the Son to the Angels
    3:1–5:10   Jesus Christ the Faithful and Compassionate High Priest
    5:11–10:39   The Eternal Priesthood and Saving Sacrifice of Jesus Christ
    11:1–12:13   The Life of the New Community through Models of Faith
    12:14–13:19   Final Exhortations to Peace and Fidelity
13:20–25   Conclusion: Epistolary Blessing and Greetings

This "structure" must not be regarded as a straitjacket within which Hebrews should be interpreted. The theological, Christological, and ecclesial instructions outlined above run back and forth across the whole document. As the preexistent Son of God, the Christ is superior to Wisdom. As Son, he is superior to the angels, having experienced both lowliness and exaltation. There can be no exaltation without suffering, and Jesus, who has been made perfect through his suffering, is the pioneer of salvation. Perhaps more than any other document in the New Testament, the unconditionally human status of Jesus Christ is stated (see 2:14–18; 4:14–5:10), beautifully summed up by two memorable passages: "For we have not a high priest who is unable to sympathize with our weaknesses, but one who in every respect has been tempted as we are, yet without sin" (4:15); and "In the days of his flesh, Jesus offered up prayers and supplications, with loud cries and tears, to him who was able to save him from death, and he was heard for his godly fear. Although he was a Son, he learned obedience through what he suffered" (5:7–8). The law of Moses foreshadowed the new covenant, which came to reality in the person and work of Jesus. Jesus is thus superior to Moses (3:1–4:13). The superiority of the word of the Son perfects all that has gone before (1:1–4). Unlike the law, "the word of God is living and active, sharper than any two-edged sword, piercing to the division of soul and spirit, of joints and marrow, and discerning the thoughts and intentions of the heart" (4:12).

Codex Freerianus
(Hebrews and 2 Timothy)

Only in Hebrews do we see the theme of the priesthood of Jesus as Christ developed. Across the treatise, the author wants to show that the mediation and the atoning sacrifice of Jesus's death and resurrection are superior to the sacrificial ministry of the former priesthood exercised in the Jerusalem temple. This is again rooted in his human condition (see 5:1–10). There is now only one sacrifice, offered once and for all in Jesus's death (10:11–12). The effects of this sacrifice last forever (7:23–25, 26–27). Further, Jesus's sacrifice establishes a heavenly tabernacle and creates a new and eternal covenant between God and the believer (8:1–10:18).

Hebrews also exhorts believers who have been through recent suffering to faith and endurance (10:19–12:29). They are to look to the remarkable witnesses with which they are surrounded (12:1–2), but courage and commitment to their own discipleship is called for (12:3–13), and there are warnings about the consequences that flow from a rejection of "him who warns from heaven" (12:25). The work closes with early Christian recommendations on ethical matters: hospitality, care for prisoners, marriage, possessions, obedience to authorities, and mutual care. But moral exhortation is based upon the theological/Christological argument of Hebrews: "For Jesus also suffered outside the gate in order to sanctify the people through his own blood" (13:12). Before ending with a traditional letter-like formula (13:20–25), another memorable word from Hebrews draws the document to closure: "Here we have no lasting city, but we seek the city which is to come" (v. 14).

The World in Front of Hebrews

Within the literary confines of the introduction (1:1–4) and the letter-like conclusion (13:20–25), there appears to be a deliberate unfolding of the themes of Jesus Christ as the end-time judge (1:5–2:18), the new community (3:1–5:10), the sacrificial role of Jesus Christ in bringing eternal salvation (5:11–10:39), a way of life for the new community (11:1–12:13), and a return to Jesus Christ as the end-time judge of a community of peace, justice, and love (12:14–13:19). Hebrews is bold in its presentation of the uniqueness and superiority of Jesus, over against every other institution. Yet Jesus Christ has shared unconditionally in every human experience, even temptation; but he never sinned (4:15). His crucial role as the one who saves humankind by means of the "once and for all" sacrifice of himself depends upon his oneness with humankind.

The Catholic Epistles

The role of 1 John seems to have led to the development of a group of **Catholic Epistles**. These seven books located toward the end of the New Testament are sometimes called the **General Letters**. These two terms are synonyms: the former is derived from original Greek words, while the latter provides a more common English translation. Therefore, both terms can be used interchangeably. The application of the expression "catholic," meaning "universal" or, as above, "general," has its own history in the tradition. Toward the end of the second century CE, the term "catholic" was first used to describe an individual letter when Clement, Bishop of Alexandria (who died in 215 CE), called the letter arising from the so-called Jerusalem Council, mentioned in Acts 15:22–29, a "catholic epistle." With this identification, he was indicating that it was written by all the apostles to the church in general. The prominent church leader Origen, writing in the first half of the third century, seemed to be the initiator of a trend to call 1 John the "catholic epistle." He also refers to 1 Peter by the same term.

Thus, it seems that the term began to be used to identify certain formal letters that were written to the universal church, as distinct from those addressed to a local congregation. In other words, they were written to a wider, more general audience. Thus, the term was originally used to designate the encyclical nature of a letter, rather than its canonical or authoritative status.

By the fourth century, the expression "Catholic Epistles" was used to identify seven NT documents as a collection: James, 1 and 2 Peter, 1, 2, and 3 John, and Jude. A number of letters had already been gathered in the name of Paul, and they were always identified in terms of their destination, that is, their audience. These remaining letters cannot be identified by their audiences, so each one is known by its author. The general nature of these letters was a determining factor leading to the collection as they addressed the various **community conflicts** arising as the newly developing Christian churches settled in the Greco-Roman world. However, the expression "catholic" may also have been given to these seven letters to finalize the debates that still swirled around their authority and canonical status at the time the church historian Eusebius was writing in the first half of the fourth century. Ultimately, in a letter written in 367 CE, Athanasius, the influential and often controversial bishop of Alexandria, includes the list of books he deems to be the canon of the New Testament. He includes, by name, what he identifies as the "seven epistles called catholic." This Thirty-Ninth Festal Letter was very influential in the formation of the final New Testament canon.

Again, it was the role of 1 John that led to the development of a tradition of a group of "Catholic Epistles." The association of 2 John with 1 John, and then the association of 3 John with 2 John, eventually led to the canonical 1, 2, and 3 John. The same causal sequence led to the inclusion of Jude, once 1 and 2 Peter were accepted. First Peter held a prominent role in the scriptural tradition from the early stages. Second Peter was eventually associated with 1 Peter, and the dependence of 2 Peter upon the Letter of Jude led to the inclusion of Jude in the canon. Apostolic authority had—as we indicated in chapter one on canonical origins—an influential role. The apostle James, or James the "brother of the Lord" and head of the church in Jerusalem (Acts 12:17; 15:13; 21:18; 1 Cor 15:7; Gal 1:19; 2:9, 12), was understood to be the author of the Letter of James (Jas 1:1).

Athanasius and His Thirty-Ninth Festal Letter

Throughout this book, we have indicated the processes that eventually led to the acceptance of certain books into the Christian canon and the exclusion of others. This process was already under way in the second century, as we know from the Muratorian Canon (see above, pp. 26–27). Throughout the third century, the question of the canon inspired great debate, with Origen and Eusebius as the main protagonists. The growing unanimity in the East and the West can be found in the thirty-ninth Easter Letter of Athanasius, bishop of Alexandria (296–373 CE). He listed the twenty-seven books regarded as the inspired Scriptures of the Christian church in 367. From that time onward, all Christendom accepts these books into its canon of sacred Scripture.

The apostle Peter was taken to be behind 1 and 2 Peter, and Jude was drawn into the collection because of 2 Peter and Jude's potential identity as the brother of Jesus (Jude 1). The apostle John, the son of Zebedee, was traced to 1, 2, and 3 John, alongside their connection to the Gospel of John. We will discuss these implications in further detail below. These early identifications of authorship are disputed by many contemporary scholars, who suggest the documents are **pseudepigraphical**, or bear false inscriptions, and the identified authors are **pseudonyms** to give later disciples the authority of the tradition of the apostles.

A final feature that determined the group of "seven epistles called catholic" may have been the search for "seven." There were fourteen recognized Pauline letters (two sets of seven, including, as was believed at the time, the "Letter to the" Hebrews), as well as seven letters to the churches in Revelation (Rev 2:1–3:22; more will be said about this in chapter eight). The group of seven Catholic Epistles continues to present the perfect number "seven" in the New Testament canon.

In addition, as a group of letters with more general addressees, they seem to be addressing various **heresies**, or sects that were developing as the Christian movement spread. This was exceedingly important as the tradition developed. The weightiest matter, however, which led to the cohesion of these seven letters was the apostolic authority credited to 1 John and 1 Peter. As already mentioned, 2 John was attached to 1 John early on, and 3 John followed. The strong claims of the author in 2 Peter led to its inclusion alongside Jude. The Letter of James, despite its slow canonical progress, had authority as the letter of "the brother of the Lord." Due to the troubled history of the authority of these letters, compared to the early acceptance of the four Gospels and Paul, their place in editions of the NT is not fixed. Eusebius lists 1 John and 1 Peter, then Revelation. He then lists the "disputed books" James, Jude, 2 Peter, 2 John, and 3 John (*Church History* 3.25.2–3). Athanasius lists the Gospels and Acts, then the Catholic Epistles be-

---

The Symbolism of Seven

Across the Bible, and especially in the book of Revelation, the number seven is associated with completeness. It does not necessarily indicate perfection, but it means that a series (of events, days, etc.) is complete. Already in the book of Genesis, the seven days of creation, reflected in the seven-day week, mark a period of completion. Seven is also the combination of the divine (three) and the earth (four). In the final compilation of the Christian canon, series of seven completed the Pauline literature (two times seven) and the Catholic Epistles (seven). The book could be regarded as "completed" with a collection highlighted by sevens.

The Muratorian Canon Fragment and the Later Documents of the NT

We have already noted the existence of the fragment discovered by Muratori in the Ambrosian Library in Milan, which may be the oldest witness to a collection of authoritative Christian Scriptures (see above, pp. 26–27). It contains most of the books of the New Testament but does not mention Hebrews, James, 1 and 2 Peter, and 3 John. Other Christian works (e.g., the Shepherd of Hermas) are mentioned and regarded as orthodox, but they are too late to be included in the list as part of Christianity's sacred Scripture.

Facsimile of the
Muratorian Canon

```
uesce pLine scificaresunt pertikeriaona
Lauoecenses aLianaLscanorinos paulino
minefincte adhesem marcionis eraliaplu
raquae Inchatholicam eclesiam recepinon
potest felenim cummelle misceri noncon
cruit epistolasanelude etsuperscricto
Iohannisduas Incatholica habentur cisapi
entia abamicissalomonis Inhonoriipsius
scripta apocalapse etiamIohanis erpe
tritantum recipemus quamquidam exnos
tris Legi Ineclesianolunt pastorem uero
nuperrim ettemporibus nostris Inurbe
roma hermaconcripsit sedente cache
tra urbis romae aeclesiae pio eps frater
eius etideoLegieumquide Oportetsepu
plicareuero Ineclesia populo Nequelinter
profetas conpletumnumero Nequelinter
apostolos Infine temporumpotest.
Arsinoi autem seu ualentini.uel mitiadey
Nihilintotum recipemus. Quietiam Nouu
psalmorum Librum marcioniconscripse
runt Unacumbasilide assianom catafry
cum contituturem
```

fore the Letters of Paul. This order was widely followed in the early manuscript tradition and is still followed in the Greek Orthodox tradition. The Western tradition places them after the Letters of Paul, due to their being placed there by Jerome, in the Latin Vulgate (see chapter one for detail). Almost all the Greek manuscripts have the sequence James, 1 and 2 Peter, 1, 2, and 3 John, and Jude. This is the order found in most Bibles, both in Greek and the various modern translations.

The Worlds of the Catholic Epistles

As a result of the canonical and literary connections we have been discussing, the Catholic Epistles are often discussed in smaller groups. James is sometimes discussed on its own and sometimes with 1 Peter. Likewise, 1 Peter is sometimes discussed on its own, with James, or with 2 Peter and Jude. The three epistles associated with John are always discussed together, sometimes with the Gospel of John and sometimes on their own. We will discuss James, then the Letters of Peter and Jude, and conclude with the Letters of John.

The Letter of James

Scholars have traced echoes of the Letter of James in Christian documents as early as 1 Clement and the Shepherd of Hermas (possibly as early as late in the first century CE). Despite the possibility of early dating, and that it was known and used at the turn of the first Christian century, we have already seen that it does not appear in the earliest list of the Christian NT, the Muratorian Fragment. The first certain traces of **James** appear in the third century in the writings of Origen. He cites it as Scripture but gives the impression that it was disputed—but not by him. Eusebius continues this impression but is the first to say that the Lord's brother, James, is regarded by many as the letter's author. In the East, however, it was widely recognized, culminating in the list provided by Athanasius in 367 CE. In the Latin church, there are doubters, especially Jerome. It is upon Jerome's hesitations that first Erasmus and then Luther based their polemic against its place in the canon.

The World behind James

In the NT, five people are named *Jakōbos*: James, the son of Zebedee (Mark 1:19; 3:17; Acts 12:2); James, the son of Alphaeus (Mark 3:18); James, the brother of Jesus (Mark 6:3; 1 Cor 15:7; Gal 1:19; 2:9, 12; Acts 12:17; 15:13; 21:18; Jude 1); James the younger (Mark 15:40); and James, the father of the apostle Judas (not Judas Iscariot: Luke 6:16; Acts 1:13). In the epistle, the author does not identify himself but simply writes: "James, a servant of God and of the Lord Jesus Christ, to the twelve tribes in the Dispersion: greeting" (Jas 1:1). Yet the very brevity of this introduction suggests that the author "James" was well known by those to whom he wrote and that he wrote in the belief that his views would be re-

---

Luther and James

The critical turning point in Martin Luther's (1483–1546) journey toward his separation from the Roman Catholic Church was his insight, after long and passionate reading of the Letters of Paul, especially Romans, that a human being is not saved by what she or he does ("works") but by the free and gracious act of God, and—despite weakness and failure on the part of the believer—the believer's response in faith. As this was fundamental to his understanding of Christianity, he had little regard for the Letter of James, which insists that faith must be manifested in works: "Show me your faith apart from your works, and I by my works will show you my faith" (Jas 2:18). That he may have misunderstood James's point is an issue that lies beyond the scope of this textbook. He accepted the Christian tradition's judgment, however, and included the Letter of James in his German translation of the New Testament.

James the Brother of the Lord by Tzangarolas Stephanos

spected. He writes with perhaps more authority even than Paul, who develops a far subtler rhetoric throughout his corpus. If the "James" who authored this letter was an apostolic figure, only James, the son of Zebedee, and James, the brother of the Lord, can be considered. As the former was executed ca. 44 CE, under Herod Agrippa I (Acts 12:2), he cannot be a contender. The presence of communities addressed as "in the Dispersion" and the issues discussed by the letter presuppose a later situation in early Christianity. That leaves only James, the brother of the Lord, long regarded by Christian tradition (although not without problems) as the author of the Letter of James.

Is this identification possible? The answer must be "yes," although not without its difficulties. This James, who joined the Christian community after the death and resurrection of Jesus, was not an original disciple or one of the Twelve (see Mark 3:21, 31–35; John 7:5), but his influence in the earliest church understandably grew steadily. Paul met with him as early as his first visit to Jerusalem (Gal 1:19), and with the persecution of Agrippa I and Peter's flight from Jerusalem, he seems to have assumed leadership of that community in the period around 43–48 CE. In Gal 2:9, James, the brother of the Lord, stands as first among the "pillars," which probably indicates that he leads the community in Jerusalem at that time. There are many traditions surrounding the death of James, but it is reasonably well established that in 62, along with other unnamed Christians, he was condemned to be stoned to death by the high priest Annas the Younger, on the charge of violating the Torah (see Josephus, *Jewish Antiquities* 20.199–203).

If James, the brother of the Lord, is the author of the Letter of James, it is the product of a strongly Jewish-Christian community situated in Jerusalem and written before 62 CE. There is much in the letter that could be linked to that time, especially the insistence upon the unity of faith and Jewish-Christian traditions that show a very close link with early Jesus traditions. Of course, there are numerous arguments against this identification as well. Most have to do with the lack of Christology and direct mention of Jesus in the letter, as well as the interpretation of the content as anti-Pauline. These arguments lead to a date late in the first century, which further leads to unknown authorship. These arguments, however, should be resisted in favor of the potential for an early composition with apostolic authorship from Judea and intended for burgeoning Jewish Christianity.

The World in James

The Epistle of James has long captivated and frustrated scholars, as both its structure and content are difficult to grasp. Although the unity of the letter has not been seriously questioned, the author's rapid shift from one topic to the next, with no explicit strategy or conclusion, has led some to assert that there is no internal logic to the text. With regard to content, Martin Luther has famously dismissed this piece of Scripture as the "epistle of straw," due to the author's strong focus on faith coupled with works, along with Luther's own inability to read the text apart from his narrow interpretation of the letters of Paul. More recently, however, James has spurred renewed interest as scholars begin to allow James "to be James" and to render his own exhortation of the gospel message. These scholars explore the work as a literary whole with quite an intricate form and an underlying framework as an epistle. In his opening verse, James claims to be writing a "letter." In this same address, however, it becomes clear that he is putting forth a literary epistle, a tract intended for publication and wide circulation, as distinct from an actual letter in the vein of Paul's correspondence to specific communities or people. By placing James's correspondence within the genre of the literary epistle, we can approach its structure and content from a more holistic perspective.

A close reading of the epistle as a whole reveals that all the topics taken up in the body of the letter are mentioned in chapter 1. After the greeting in v. 1, the rapid shifts in vv. 2–27 give basic overviews of the issues at hand, setting the tone and context for the message to come. James 1:2–27 thus serves as an *epitomē*, providing a formal introduction to the body of the letter.

Luke Timothy Johnson's Observations on the Authorship of James

In arguing for the early dating of the epistle, and attributing it to James of Jerusalem, Johnson (*The Writings of the New Testament*, 449–59) observes:

1. James lacks any of the classical signs of late pseudonymous authorship, according to the criteria used by scholars. For example, there is no fictional elaboration of the author's identity or authority, such as is found in many pseudonymous works.

2. James reflects social realities and outlooks appropriate to a community in the early stages of its life. It is concerned with morals rather than the manners of the dominant culture, and its system of values challenges that dominant culture. It reflects a sense of oppression and persecution, accompanied by an active sense of imminent judgment.

3. James has been noted for its proximity to Jesus's teaching and its use of Jesus's sayings. The link between these sayings and those in the Synoptic sayings tradition strengthens the argument for the Palestinian provenance and early dating of James.

4. James most resembles the writings of Paul. To account for the combination of similarity and difference in their language is to view them as first-generation Jewish Christians deeply affected by Greco-Roman moral traditions yet fundamentally defined by allegiance to the symbols and story of Torah.

5. James contains incidental details that could be taken as evidence for a Palestinian provenance, in sharp contrast to a writing like Protoevangelium of James, which purports to be early and to come from Palestine yet betrays ignorance of local realities.

6. If 1 Clement knew and used James, then that appropriation by an author dated from Rome around 96 CE argues in favor of a composition of James at a substantially earlier date.

The themes of this introductory chapter are:

- steadfastness in trial and prayer (vv. 2–8)
- reversal of the situation of the rich and the poor (vv. 9–11)
- friendship with the world versus friendship with God (vv. 12–18)
- the use of the tongue (vv. 19–21)
- the need to act out of religious conviction (vv. 22–27)

This introduction provides both the unifying theme and the guiding theological principles that unfold throughout the epistle. The tone set is one of **paraenesis**, an imperative instruction, as James exhorts his readers by command, all the while identifying with his beloved brethren (1:2, 9, 16).

The movement from topic to topic is marked by these imperatives. The five major blocks of material in the body of the epistle take up the themes presented in the introduction in reverse order. A helpful structure, therefore, looks like this:

1:1   Greeting
1:2–27   *Epitomē*: Presentation of the Themes of the Epistle
2:1–5:18   Body of the Epistle
    2:1–26   Faith and Works: Acting out of Religious Conviction
    3:1–12   The Work of the Community and Proper Speech
    3:13–4:10   Friendship with the World versus Friendship with God
    4:11–5:6   Improper Speech and the Work of the Rich
    5:7–18   Steadfastness in Trial and Prayer: Enduring in Religious Conviction
5:19–20   *Conclusio*: Summary of the Consequences of Living the Epistle

James presents a series of exhortations that cross the spectrum of life situations that his audiences will encounter as they settle into community together. Throughout this instruction, a foundational moral code is presupposed through which the author constructs the required worldview. James speaks to this community through the full authority of *the name of the Lord* and understands himself as both servant and teacher in this new life in light of the coming of that Lord (1:1; 3:1; 5:7–9).

Epitomē

This Greek expression roughly indicates what we would nowadays describe as the "table of contents" of a book. However, in the Greek literary tradition, the *epitomē* was also part of the book itself, introducing the audience to the themes that are developed at greater length across the book, a rhetorical strategy that would arouse the interest of its audience. Contemporary study of the Letter of James recognizes that 1:2–27 serves as an *epitomē*, outlining themes that are then dealt with, in reverse order, in the body of the letter.

The World in Front of James

The Epistle of James, a servant of God and of the Lord Jesus Christ (1:1), provides a window into a messianic movement that is beginning to develop into a community of faithful in the midst of a larger Hellenistic sociocultural environment. Whether one dates the epistle early or late, the author's perspective rings true. By addressing his epistle to the "twelve tribes of the Dispersion," the author is both acknowledging this larger Hellenistic environment and situating his community *in* it though not *of* it. His understanding of the particularly theological and eschatological nature of his community over against this environment is implicit in this identification, is made explicit through the substance of his correspondence, and is brought full circle in its conclusion. The formation of the community engenders a new action arising from the "implanted word" that produces the "first fruits" of God's creatures who lead the way of salvation (1:18, 21; 5:19–20). In addition, the repetition of "my brothers and sisters" and key terms both within and across topics leads the audience along. James uses this technique to striking effect as he eases his brethren into more and more profound paraenesis. The cumulative effect of this pattern hooks the audience as it prepares for the substance of his message. James's goal in this epistle is life-altering, if taken to its fruition. He calls the community, even as he has been called, to live in communion in the fullness of faith, and this is the profoundly eschatological saving action that will ultimately bring about redemption and restoration.

The Letters of Peter and Jude

In 1 Pet 5:13, we read: "She who is the fellow elect one in Babylon greets you, along with Mark my son." Through the Middle Ages, this was taken as a reference to Rome and was a firm indication that the letter was an authentic letter of the apostle **Peter**. A majority of scholars still hold Rome as the likely place of origin of this letter, but Petrine authorship is more difficult to maintain.

Paraenesis

This Greek term is used to describe a form of writing (or speaking) that is different from narrative or theological discussions often found in NT letters. Generally (although not always) toward the end of a letter, the author turns his attention directly to his audience, stops "informing" them or "teaching" them, and begins to command or exhort them to strive for higher moral achievement. It can be positive, in which the author exhorts the pursuit of certain forms of behavior, or negative, exhorting the audience to abstain from other forms of behavior.

Interestingly, it is not widely known or used by early witnesses in the West and is missing from the Muratorian Canon. It is, however, cited by church leaders in the second century. It is also used in the East early in the second century. On this evidence, the current tendency to date the letter in the second century should be resisted, and its early place in the accepted tradition (both Origen and Eusebius include it among those that are certain) is assured.

For a number of internal reasons, Jude appears to be closely related to 2 Peter and has served the author of the latter in his longer treatment of the same issues. The two letters deal with parallel difficulties within early Christian communities. The author of 2 Peter used the Letter of Jude to compose his attack on errors that were creeping in. Whereas Jude is a more general letter, denouncing opponents without giving many hints of the situation of the Christians receiving the document, 2 Peter is carefully descriptive of a specific attack on the Christian understanding of God as the Lord of all history, and more attention is given to the uniqueness of the Christian message and the Christian vocation. Second Peter is not mentioned in the second century, despite its heavy insistence upon Petrine authorship (1:1; 3:1). Neither the early church leaders nor the Muratorian Fragment mentions it or cites it. Origen is the first to do so in association with the Christian canon but regards it as "contested." From then on, it appears but never with great authority. Even into the fourth century, it is in doubt, but the authority of Athanasius in the East, along with important church leaders in the West, eventually assure its place in the canon.

We can now give a brief overview of the worlds of each of these epistles.

The First Letter of Peter

The early association with the figure of Peter—and the perennial significance of its powerful message—no doubt assured 1 Peter a place in the canon in both the East and the West. Although we cannot be certain that the apostle Peter was the author of the letter, the profound Christology, especially the association between Jesus and the figure of the Suffering Servant from Isaiah, creates the impression of an author with a deep understanding of what God has done for humankind in and through Jesus Christ.

The World behind 1 Peter

Is "Peter an apostle of Jesus Christ" Simon Peter of Galilee? Several considerations have led contemporary scholars to doubt this traditional identification. The language of 1 Peter is among the best prose of the NT; it has its own polish and dignity. Many have questioned the role of Silvanus (1 Pet 5:12), asking whether he was the letter's bearer or its amanuensis. If the latter, this responds to the issue of language, but this is highly speculative. Some note how odd it is that there are so few reminiscences of the life of Jesus. The connection between this letter and the rest of the NT all comes down to common oral tradition, not necessarily direct literary links. Thus, it is difficult to claim that Simon Peter actually penned this letter. Pseudonymity is very possible in an effort to foster the good of the recipients. There was a desire to render the letter "apostolic," whether or not the author was ultimately interested in Peter. If the letter did come from a leader in the Christian community of Rome, and this group looked to Peter for authority, then Peter is the natural choice. If the letter is authentically written by the apostle Peter, it would be dated to ca. 64–68 CE. If it is pseudepigraphical, this would push its authorship to later in the first century CE.

The World in 1 Peter

The author's strong focus upon the person of Jesus Christ as someone who innocently suffered and went patiently to death in order to change the situation of the audience leads to a general acceptance that the audience needs to be encouraged through instruction. God has transformed their situation and will continue to do so. The first transformation results from their once being "homeless" (2:11), but God has given believers their "home" (2:5; 4:17). They now possess something that they never had before. However, all is not smooth sailing in that new home. They appear to be undergoing some form of suffering (see 1:6; 3:13–17; 4:12–19). Most likely this does not indicate a world in

---

The Suffering Servant

Four so-called songs of the suffering servant appear across the final section of the book of Isaiah (Isa 42:1–4; 49:1–6; 50:4–9; 52:13–53:12). The servant is humiliated, suffers grievously, but is finally vindicated. It is difficult to know who is indicated. Many argue, especially in light of the explicit mention of "Israel" in 49:3, that the servant is the suffering nation. Others suggest that "Israel" in 49:3 is an explanatory gloss added to the text and understand the servant as a suffering prophet. As the early church reflected upon the suffering and vindication of Jesus of Nazareth, they turned to Isaiah's servant and began to read the songs as prophecy about a suffering Messiah. This may be present, for example, in Mark 10:45: "For the Son of Man came not to be served but to serve, and to give his life a ransom for many." The use of suffering-servant language from Isaiah 53 to refer to the sufferings of Jesus Christ is most developed in 1 Peter: "He committed no sin, and no deceit was found in his mouth" (1 Pet 2:22; see Isa 53:9); "He himself bore our sins in his body" (1 Pet 2:24; see Isa 53:4); "By His wounds you have been healed. For you were going astray like sheep" (1 Pet 2:24–25; see Isa 53:5–6).

Icon of the Apostle Peter
(fourteenth century)

which believers are being systematically persecuted for their faith. It probably reflects an earlier period when Christian believers were beginning to experience a certain hostility and mistrust. The "newness" of Christianity led to a different form of social interaction. Belief in a new life generated by the death and resurrection of Jesus was regarded as odd in the Greco-Roman society of the time. Such beliefs created a general hostility, but not necessarily persecution. Peter addresses this situation with instructions to the leadership of the community (5:1–2), to their blessedness in loving Jesus Christ, even though they have never seen him (1:8). He warns them of dangers (5:8) but assures them that, because of God's love for them, shown in the self-sacrificing death and resurrection of Jesus, "who bore our sins in his body" (2:24–25; see Isa 53:5–6), they are now "a chosen race, a royal priesthood, a holy nation, God's own people" (2:9).

The letter addresses, instructs, encourages, and exhorts believers living in that world in the following fashion:

1:1–2   Epistolary Introduction
1:3–2:10   The Dignity and Responsibilities of the Christian Vocation
    1:3–12   Salvation from the Father through the Son, Revealed by the Spirit
    1:13–2:10   Holiness That Requires the Responsibilities of a Life in a New Household
2:11–12   Living in a Pagan World
2:13–3:12   The Community in the Larger World
    2:13–17   Behavior toward Civil Authority
    2:18–3:7   Behavior in the Family
    3:8–12   Love and Humility
3:13–4:11   The Community in the Face of Suffering
    3:13–17   Confidence in Christ as Lord
    3:18–4:6   Based upon the Person of Jesus Christ
    4:7–11   Looking toward the End of Time
4:12–5:11   Behavior in the Midst of Rejection and Suffering
    4:12–19   A Share in Christ's Suffering
    5:1–11   Community and Leadership in a Time of Suffering
5:12–14   Epistolary Closing

This carefully argued instruction to early Christians who were beginning to feel the pain from "being different" in society makes 1 Peter one of the literary and theological treasures of the NT.

The World in Front of 1 Peter

Unlike James, with its emerging but primitive Christology, 1 Peter has a distinctive and well-developed Christology. It is, as we have just remarked, an often unrecognized "jewel" in the New Testament. Martin Luther wrote of 1 Peter: "The one who understands this letter has without doubt enough so as not to need more . . . because the apostle did not forget anything in his letter that is necessary for a Christian to know." On another occasion, he described 1 Peter as "one of the noblest books in the New Testament." One of the most dominant interpretations of 1 Peter argued that it had its origins as a **baptismal homily**. More recent scholarship focuses more broadly upon the literary fact that it has the form of a letter and does not appear to be a "homily." However, baptismal teaching remains central. There can be no denying the central issue of persecution and resulting themes of suffering and hope as essential components of the Christian life. The author provides a perspective on life that enables the community to press on and survive persecution with its faith intact, and this all turns on hope. To instruct the world in front of 1 Peter on these fundamental truths can surely be seen as something that may lie behind the origins of this letter. An essential component of this is a look toward the future where suffering will be overcome. The key to reading the Christian life in this fashion is the figure of Christ, whose passion, death, and resurrection show the way that present suffering is related to future glory for all Christians. Christ is the model for faithful life in the midst of a hostile society, all based on the controlling metaphor of Christ as the fulfillment of God's promises to Israel and the church as its heir (1:10–12).

The Letter of Jude

The author, **Jude**, claims to be the servant of Jesus Christ, brother of James (Jude 1). This, according to tradition, would also make him a brother of Jesus Christ. If this identification is authentic, then the letter would have been composed ca. 65–80 CE. The author appears to be a Jewish Christian. In this brief letter (only twenty-five verses), he shows great familiarity with Jewish apocalyptic literature: the Assumption of Moses (see v. 11), the book of Enoch (v. 14), and other Jewish legends (see vv. 9, 11). We will deal with this important literature in more detail in the following chapter (chapter eight). Yet his argument presupposes a later development of the early church's traditions, and his language is cultivated Greek. It appears that the document comes from a later stage in the life of the early church. This would push its authorship to the end of the first century CE. Remarkably, however, the use of the letter in the early church is quite widespread. It seems to have been readily accepted early but then waned in authority as time passed. It is regarded by the Muratorian Fragment, Tertullian, and Clement of Alexandria as canonical. Origen is more circumspect about its place in the canon, and both Eusebius and Jerome place it among the "contested" documents. The problem the later tradition had with Jude, however, was not so much its antiquity or authority, but its use of Jewish extracanonical documents. As time passed, this was regarded as offensive. Nevertheless, despite its waning importance in the tradition, it is included in the canon of Athanasius and was never doubted.

The World behind Jude

Two factors, already mentioned above, point to the world behind the Letter of Jude. The first is his use of Jewish apocalyptic literature. As we will see, this literature, which had its birth in the pre-Christian era, developed further in the first century in light of the loss of the First Jewish Revolt (65–70 CE) and the subsequent anxiety about God's designs for Israel. Had God abandoned his

Saint Jude
by José de Ribera

people? Jude writes in this troubled era, and the question of God's design for humankind, present in the apocalyptic literature, appears also in these verses. The second factor is his fierce attack upon the dangers facing Christian communities (for which language from apocalyptic literature was helpful), most likely at the beginning of the second Christian century. He urges the Christians to remain loyal in the face of attacks from false believers. Once the first blush of exciting innocence of the Christian tradition was developed further in the Greco-Roman world, the danger that it would not only be used, but also misused, emerged. Jude argues passionately against all such misuse.

The World in Jude

Jude can properly be regarded as a "general" or "catholic" letter, following the discussion of these terms above. In his opening formula, Jude does not address any specific community, but "those who are called, who are beloved in God the Father and kept safe for Jesus Christ" (v. 1). The letter is written because of the urgent need for those who receive it to "contend for the faith" in the face of dangerous perversions (vv. 3–4). His attack on those perversions insists that the inevitable judgment of God will fall upon what the tradition would eventually call "heretics," those who are taking the Christian faith in the wrong direction (vv. 5–16). The ideal members of the community, according to Jude, are to be regarded as "saints": holy and kept in the love of God. The letter concludes abruptly, with a traditional "Amen." This summary leads to the following structure:

vv. 1–2   Address and Greeting
vv. 3–23   Body of the Letter
    vv. 3–4   Occasion for Writing
    vv. 5–16   Teaching: Avoiding False Teachers and Appealing to Guarding the Truth through Prophecy and Scripture
    vv. 17–23   Exhortations: Remember the Gospel through Building Up the Community in Fellowship
vv. 24–25   Doxology and Farewell

The brevity and the sharpness of the attack, associated with the holiness of the true believers, generate a powerful statement, issued in challenging times.

The World in Front of Jude

Despite its brevity, the Letter of Jude is written in very elegant Greek, while still showing a deep awareness of the Jewish world that produced the Christian church. Most significantly, Jude shows a sharp awareness of the dangers that necessarily face a system of belief, based upon God and his Son, Jesus Christ (v. 1). The need to carry on a "tradition" that is loyal to the origins of Christianity is central. We are unable to reconstruct the world that received this brief document, as Jude offers little or no information. But time is passing, and Christian origins must be preserved. The audience was most likely Christians in the Greco-Roman world who needed to be warned against the beginnings of a speculative understanding of the Christian tradition that would betray the authentic tradition and rob them of their holiness. The powerful closing doxology (vv. 24–25) is a prayer that belief in God and Jesus Christ, their "glory, majesty, power, and authority," endure forever. In this letter, we see the beginnings of a desire to keep safe the Christian tradition that can be falsely interpreted, to the detriment of all believers.

The Second Letter of Peter

Second Peter is notoriously challenging for Christians and has been from its earliest reception. Debates about its place in the canon in the first Christian centuries reflect concerns about both authorship and content. The earliest extant writer to mention 2 Peter directly is Origen (ca. 185–254 CE), who presents its authorship as doubtful. Eusebius (writing ca. 324 CE) follows this lead and questions its canonical status. Although the letter ultimately became part of the NT, these sorts of concerns have only grown over the centuries. The task for interpreters, therefore, is to find the practical method in the madness.

The World behind 2 Peter

The author of 2 Peter is most likely a second or third generation Christian writing at the end of the first century CE (90–110) in Rome and using the pseudonym of Peter in order to exercise both authority and pastoral responsibility over his intended recipients, likely Christians in Asia Minor. Second Peter is a letter in form, but it is addressed generally to those whose "faith is as precious as ours . . ." (1:1) and is, thus, a catholic epistle. It contains ethical advice and revelation of the future, which are basic elements of a genre known as the farewell address, such that it reminds audiences of tradition in light of the impending death of the author to exhort them to stand firm. Therefore, we can understand 2 Peter as a farewell speech preserved in letter form.

If the purpose of the letter is to give testament to the author's life and urge particular ethical action in the face of revelations about the future, then the style will present a strong rhetorical flair meant to affirm and persuade the audience. The numerous unusual words found in 2 Peter would keep an audience on its toes as members try to keep up with the speech. Complex sentences and a bit of poetic rhythm further indicate that the author was shooting for weighty effect. The Greco-Roman style associated with these characteristics is called **Asianism**, which is described as "bombastic," meaning it is verbose and leaning toward the bizarre. Suggesting that the author adopts this pompous rhetoric helps make sense of the impulsive tone and images, like "dog vomit" and "pig wallowing" (2:22), alongside otherwise refined wording. These features also give hints to the social location of the audience, since the Asiatic style was so named for its development and popularity in Asia. The author possesses a level of learning and vocabulary and expects his audience to understand both his words and the larger message embedded in his powerful rhetoric. Throughout all the mudslinging and elaborate calls to faith, the author remains intent on his mission in writing to defray rising conflicts and encourage unity in the developing tradition. In a farewell letter, testamentary features are geared toward reminding recipients of the author's life, teachings, and relationship with them, while also preparing them for his impending death. If the letter originates in Rome and is intended for the faithful in Asia Minor, purportedly from the hand of Peter, then the further purpose would be to extend the authority of Rome into the empire to warn against a growing conflict while urging unity. Therefore, although 2 Peter is brief and difficult for interpreters, its aim is true for Christian life in the church of any age.

The World in 2 Peter

Second Peter opens with the standard Hellenistic salutation. The author identifies himself as both "servant" and "apostle," and the recipients are known by their shared faith, which is equally honorable (1:1). Rhetorically, this designation draws them into the apostolic fold, while setting up a distinction between the honorable faith and teaching of the apostles and the false teaching of those who are a threat to the community in the body of the letter, which is structured in three broad strokes (1:3–3:16). The author readies his audience for the challenges to come through an introductory appeal around what God has accomplished in and through Jesus Christ (1:3–15). His central assertions focus the thesis on participation in the true teaching of God through the ages (1:16–2:22). This allows him to make a final appeal to stand fast and look forward to participation in what God will accomplish in the future (3:1–16) and to close with a final summons and doxology (3:17–18). The following structure attends to this chosen literary form, while also guiding audiences through his message:

1:1–2   Address and Greeting
1:3–3:16   Body of the Letter
    1:3–15   Introductory Appeal: Participation in What God Has Accomplished
        1:3–11   Initial Encouragement for the Christian Life
        1:12–15   Testamentary Purpose Statement
    1:16–2:22   Central Assertions: The Challenge of Participation in True Teaching
        1:16–21   God's Call and True Teaching
        2:1–16   False Teaching and God's Response
        2:17–22   Consequences for False Teachers
    3:1–16   Final Appeal: Participation in What God Will Accomplish
        3:1–10   The Promise of the Second Coming
        3:11–16   Final Encouragement for the Christian Life
3:17–18   Farewell Doxology

Themes of honorable faith expressed through just action are fully articulated in the first appeal. The author is positive and uses paranaesis to prepare his recipients for the challenges both the letter and their future will hold. These early verses teach a careful balance between faith and ethical action. Faith is the foundation and a gift from God, but it is realized in daily living through the practice of virtue in community. This is both the essence of 2 Peter's positive teaching and the ongoing challenge of Christian life. The author then turns to the core of his challenge to his recipients (1:16–2:22). The central assertions are the most intense and vitriolic and therefore most difficult portions of the letter. Second Peter 2 is also where the author draws from Jude, cleverly refashioning his source for his own purposes. He then pulls back from his intense rhetoric to return to a more paraenetic approach as he makes a final appeal for recipients to resist the enticement of false teaching and stand fast in participation in what God accomplishes now and in the future (3:1–10). He then offers a final encouragement for those who are striving to participate in the divine nature of God. Indeed, the final wish of this farewell address is for audiences rising to the challenge of **theosis** in this world to continue to "grow in the grace and knowledge of our Lord and Savior Jesus Christ" (3:11–18).

> **Theosis**
>
> Already in the NT (see, e.g., Rom 8:12–17; Gal 4:1–7; John 17:24–26), the idea arose that Jesus Christ's taking on the human condition made it possible for human beings to enter into an experience with the divine even as we live our everyday lives in the world. The imitation of the lifestyle of Jesus Christ renders the believer open to the gift of intimate closeness to Christ's human-divine status and condition. This idea became a major theological theme in early Christian writing, especially in the East, and remains important in contemporary theological anthropology. Every human being has the potential to be drawn into the divine life shared by the Father, his Son, and the Spirit. The expression *theosis* means "deification."

The World in Front of 2 Peter

The bombastic rhetoric of 2 Peter challenges any effort to draw out constructive theology and teaching. Faithful readers and scholars alike often focus on the strong denunciations and find little that is positive for Christian life in relationship with God. Beneath the grandiloquence and obsessive warnings, however, there is a powerful call to theosis, or participation in God's divine nature. In the early verses, the author makes an appeal that illustrates the essence of theosis: "His divine power has given us everything needed for life and godliness through the knowledge of him who called us," so that we "may become participants of the divine nature" (1:3–4). That he moves directly into a purpose statement by way of a testament to his own participation furthers this notion (1:12–15). He then asserts his central concern regarding the challenge of participation in true teaching (1:16–2:22). As the language of invective reaches its peak, he ironically characterizes his opponents' teaching as "bombastic nonsense" (2:18), using their rhetorical style both to present the seductiveness of their teaching and to expose the ultimate emptiness of its swollen rhetoric. The author can then provide an alternative to the false teaching by urging participation in what God will accomplish in the future (3:1–16). He urges self-reflection by asking the recipients, "what sort of persons ought you to be . . . ?" (3:11). This then becomes a final appeal to participation in God through the apostolic teaching memorialized in this address. The theology of 2 Peter is, therefore, based on an understanding of God the Father, who is Creator (3:5) and the one who inspires the prophets (1:21) and affirms his Son in majestic glory (1:16–17). For his part, Jesus is Christ, Lord, and Savior (1:1, 2, 8, 11, 14; 2:1, 20; 3:2, 18). The positive summons encapsulated by the letter is for the recipients and, by extension, all humankind to embrace the relationship between Father and Son by participating in their divine nature as manifest in the life of Christ and the teachings of the apostolic tradition. The possibility that 2 Peter borrows from Jude is an indication of an increasing awareness of the importance of "the apostolic tradition," that is, a "handing on" of the authentic message about God and Jesus Christ from one generation to the next.

The Johannine Epistles

The **Letters of John** are sometimes called, more formally, the **Johannine Epistles**. The two terms are synonyms, and either may be used to refer to these three texts. A determining factor for interpreting the Letters of John is their historical relationship to the Gospel of John and the community that produced it. Scholars take various positions in terms of whether the letters come from the same hand as the Gospel and whether they were written before or after the work of the Fourth Evangelist. The Gospel itself likely underwent several drafts and refinements over the years until it reached its final form that has been preserved in the New Testament. It is truly the product of a community's experience of God's activity in the world. Therefore, even if the letters did not come from the same first hand as the Gospel, they certainly arose from the same community of believers and reflect the ongoing life of that community as it sought to come to terms with its particular understanding of the good news of Christ and God's new covenant in a larger sociocultural environment. Further, they reflect a slightly different and somewhat later theological context where the author(s) thought that the message of the Gospel needed further clarification and adaptation. Indeed, the content of the letters is best understood as arising from the community after the crisis with postwar Judaism (after 70 CE), which lies behind the Gospel, has faded as it transitions to a focus upon the life and belief of the community itself. As we discussed in chapter five, the Gospel was likely written around 90–100 CE in a community that is defining itself over against the rest of the world, including the mainstream Judaism of its past. The letters, then, were likely written in the following decade, at the beginning of the second century, ca. 100–110 CE, in a community of churches that now found it necessary to define itself against schisms *from within*. The ideals of the new Christian community were proving difficult to live out in the larger Greco-Roman world with a variety of beliefs and ideals. The author writes from a position of authority to stem the tide of discord and dissolution in possibly a last-ditch effort to strengthen and unify his people into a community.

The World behind the Johannine Epistles

Several documents in the New Testament have been regarded by the Christian tradition as originating in a single person named "**John**." In addition to the Gospel of John, the three letters of John and the book of Revelation are an important part of that tradition. Only the book of Revelation refers to its author by the name "John," and he identifies himself as an **elder** or "presbyter" (***presbyteros***) writing from the island of Patmos (Rev 1:9). No historically verifiable evidence links John the Elder at Patmos with any of the disciples, but a long tradition associates all five of these documents with the disciple of Jesus, John the son of Zebedee. Similar to the anonymity of the Gospel, there is no address or salutation at all in 1 John. The author of 2 and 3 John describes himself as "the elder" (v. 1 in each), but this expression was widely used in the early church and can be found in many Christian documents. Thus, on the basis of the documents alone, it is not clear that "the elder" of Revelation and "the elder" of 2 and 3 John are the same or that one person named "John" was the "elder" John of Revelation, the "elder" of 2 and 3 John, the author of 1 John, and the Beloved Disciple of the Gospel. But the second-century church made such associations, and the link between "John the elder" of Revelation and "the elder" of 2 and 3 John was quickly made. Once that was in place, "John" was identified as the author of all three letters, and the same "John" was associated with the Gospel.

Gnosticism

In the second century CE, a speculative form of Christianity emerged, influenced by Eastern religions and Greek philosophy. It was called "Gnosticism" because of its belief that the physical reality of the human Jesus and the bloody event of Jesus's death, followed by God's action in the resurrection, were not "salvific." People were saved by "knowledge" (Greek: *gnōsis*) that came by enlightenment from above, not by Jesus's life, teaching, death, and resurrection. The author of the Letters of John insists on the humanity of Jesus as the Christ, throughout all the letters but especially in 1 John. It is as the human Jesus Christ that Jesus is the Son of God, and his self-giving death in love saves. As these letters may have been written early in the second century to help early Christians overcome false opinions about Jesus Christ as Son of God and the saving act of his death and resurrection, they may be very early indications of emerging gnostic tendencies in the early Christian church.

John the Evangelist in Silence. Wood panel by Nectarius Kulyuksin (1679)

As early as 180 CE, the church leader Irenaeus became a vital advocate of this literature and made the link between John the son of Zebedee and the Beloved Disciple. A large number of Christians had been attracted to a form of Christianity called **Gnosticism**, which was strongly influenced by speculative Greco-Roman religions. One of Gnosticism's many features was the way it minimized the importance of the physical life and death of Jesus—even denying that there ever was a real human life or a real experience of death. The Gnostics were very fond of John's Gospel, which provided them with a story of Jesus that was more spiritual and less down to earth than that of Matthew, Mark, and Luke.

Irenaeus fought hard against Gnosticism and strove to show that John's Gospel was deeply embedded in the life and death of the man Jesus of Nazareth, and not just an extraordinary speculation. One of the major elements that enabled Irenaeus to rescue the Gospel of John for the Christian community and its canon of Scripture was the identification of the author of the letter we now call 1 John with the author of the Fourth Gospel. In this letter, so many of the same theological, christological, and ethical issues found in the Gospel were stated in a more grounded, "orthodox" fashion. Irenaeus went on to be the first to identify the Beloved Disciple, and thus the author of both works, as John the son of Zebedee, one of the founding apostles of the Christian church. This position has been held down to our own time. There are good scholars who claim that Irenaeus was correct: John the apostle, the son of Zebedee, was the Beloved Disciple. But this once universally held position is not widely held today. Nonetheless, no contemporary scholar denies the close relationship between 1 John and the Fourth Gospel.

If the Gospel and 1 John were established very early as coming from the same author and this assured the place of both in the canon, what of 2 and 3 John? The history of their reception is complex, as one would imagine. It is not surprising that, during the second century CE, 1 John became well known as "the letter of John." It is equally unsurprising, given the brevity of the two other letters attached to the name "John," that they are not used by the church in the second century or even into the third century. Finally, 2 John and then eventually 3 John did begin to circulate more widely, and a connection began to be made between 1 and 2 John. Once 2 John began to gain acceptance, however, it brought into play the possibility that 3 John should be accepted as part of the canon of Scripture as well. The similarity of the message and the repetition of the title "elder" in both letters led the early church leaders eventually to regard 1, 2, and 3 John as Johannine Letters alongside the Gospel, and all four texts as part of the NT Canon.

The World in the Johannine Epistles

We will briefly address the literary characteristics and structures of the three Johannine Epistles to get a sense of their overall flow and content. First John shares much in common with the Gospel, including language, themes, and style. The second two letters are far briefer and, although they share some similarities with the Gospel, show more commonality with each other. We nonetheless discuss them together.

The formal, treatise-like tone of 1 John is evident even in a first encounter with it. We can see why early church leaders referred to it as a catholic epistle, because there is no personal address or distinctive audience. It seems to be written to a general group. Further, the relationship between 1 John and the Gospel of John becomes evident even across the first verses of the letter. Indeed, the celebrated interpreter of the Johannine literature, Raymond Brown, sees a link between the literary structure of 1 John and the structure of the Gospel, with its prologue, book of signs in which Jesus publicly reveals light and life, book of glory, where love is a major theme, and a conclusion. The author uses the same language and imagery in this more grounded and direct plea for the community. The evangelist's language of love, knowledge, and the gift of truth for the children of God continues to permeate these pages. Further exploration of the epistle's structure reveals a prologue that mirrors the prologue of the Gospel (1:1–4); while the final verses likewise echo the concluding sounds of the Gospel (5:13–21). Within this theological frame, the author makes three resounding appeals to the new community, in terms of the characteristics of God that form the heart and soul of God's children: light (1:5–2:27), justice (2:28–4:6), and love (4:7–5:12). The content of these appeals warns the community of the dangers of the world, while instructing it on the power of faith to conquer all for those who abide in Christ and thus remain in the new covenant community.

The brevity of the final two epistles diminishes neither their power nor the insight they give into the challenges faced by this early Christian community, which would have appealed to accept all humankind into their family. By this stage the faithful are struggling, and the community is falling prey to the contentiousness of human nature and the pressures of the larger world. The two letters offer direct appeals that address the real-life situations of early Christian communities. Second John counsels a particular church within the larger Johannine community to remain in the Gospel commandment of love and to guard against deceivers. Third John offers specific praise for the fidelity of Gaius and Demetrius, while warning against the betrayal of Diotrephes. The elder thus makes his final pleas for fellowship in truth.

The letters can, therefore, be outlined as follows.

Greco-Roman Letters and 2–3 John

Even as today we use a certain "style" when we write a letter (greeting, news, sharing, questions, sign-off), Greco-Roman letters also had a very fixed literary form. Surprisingly, while most letters of Paul, the other letters in the NT, and even the book of Revelation show an awareness of the literary form of a Greco-Roman letter, in the NT only 2 John and 3 John are exact representatives of that form. They both have an opening formula, containing the name of the sender, the person to whom they are sent, and a greeting (2 John 1–3; 3 John 1–2). The body of the letter follows (2 John 4–12; 3 John 3–14), opening with an expression of joy and transitioning into the main message of the letter (2 John 3; 3 John 3–4). After the message of the letter is delivered, the body of the letter closes with the promise of a visit (2 John 12; 3 John 13–14). The letter then ends with a traditional concluding formula (2 John 13; 3 John 15).

The First Letter of John

1:1–4   Prologue: The Word of Life for the Community
1:5–2:27   Opening Appeal to the New Community: God Is Light
    1:5–2:2   The Experience of the Light: The Word of God in Jesus
    2:3–11   The Message of the Light: Knowledge of God is Fellowship in God
    2:12–27   The Crisis of the Light: The Dangers of the World
2:28–4:6   Central Appeal to the New Community: God Is Just
    2:28–3:10   The Mark of the True Children of God
    3:11–24   The New Covenant Commandment
    4:1–6   Discernment and the Testing of Spirits
4:7–5:12   Closing Appeal to the New Community: God Is Love
    4:7–21   The Presence of God in Relationship: Love for God and One Another
    5:1–12   The Foundation of Love: Faith That Conquers the World
5:13–21   Epilogue: Prayer for the Faithful Community

The Second Letter of John

vv. 1–3   The Elder's Address to the Church: Life Lived Walking in the Truth
    vv. 4–6   Love is the Fulfillment of the Gospel Commandment
    vv. 7–11   Believers Are to Guard against Deceivers of the Gospel
vv. 12–13   Farewell: Joy Is the Mark of Fellowship

The Third Letter of John

vv. 1–4   The Elder's Address to Gaius: Encouragement in Love and Truth
    vv. 5–8   Praise for Hospitality—Gaius
    vv. 9–10   The Politics of Ecclesial Power—Diotrephes
    vv. 11–12   Faithfulness to the Community—Demetrius
vv. 13–15   Farewell: Desire for Fellowship and Appeal to Friendship

Initially the conflict that emerges in the Letters of John and seems to be dividing the community is the developing Gnostic Christianity in the early second century CE. First John indicates that some "went out from us," and the question is denial of Jesus as Christ and Son of the Father (2:18–25). The schisms fragmenting the community are made more explicit in 2 John as those "deceivers" who "have gone out in the world" are characterized as "those who do not confess that Jesus Christ has come in the flesh" (vv. 7–11). By 3 John, however, the conflicts and divisions have become personal as the community deteriorates further and the Elder's pleas for unity in their tradition have gone largely unheeded (vv. 9–11). Nonetheless, he unfailingly summons all Christians to fellowship in the love of God and for one another.

The World in Front of the Johannine Epistles

The three letters of John are direct appeals to the community at large and individuals within the community to stand fast in the Gospel traditions. The author is offering (possibly final) pleas for unity in faith and love in the manner of the Beloved Disciple, in the hopes of responses in action on the part of his recipients. The collective summons of the three letters of John revolves around theology, Christology, and ethics. They punctuate the Gospel's teaching on believing in God as revealed through Jesus, the human Christ who is also God incarnate, and on loving one another as the ethic that naturally follows from living as authentic children of God. One's vertical relationship with God through believing in Jesus Christ empowers, enlivens, and sets parameters for the ensuing horizontal relationship with other people who are likewise struggling to live in an often difficult world. These letters give testament both to the powerful self-giving love of God through Christ in relationship with humankind, as well as to the profound frailty of the nature of that same humankind. The open call for a community to live in equal fellowship through believing in Jesus as the Christ and Son of God and to live in the love of both God and one another is a vocation that every Christian can agree upon. This summons to relationship is never in question. What is in question is the ability of humankind to live in this ideal, if unstructured, relationship in an imperfect world. This is the ongoing challenge of living in community as children of God.

The preservation of these letters alongside the Gospel of John in the sacred Scripture of Christianity gives voice to the beauty of God's love and the fire of conviction that love sparks in humankind. Jesus and disciples of every sort, including the elder, speak to that truth. But these four books also reveal the journeys of faith and sometimes failures that human beings are destined to experience in this world. The letters indicate the beginnings of the tragic collapse of the Johannine community, but this is not the end of their story. This literature also teaches that God and God's plan succeed even when humans fail. These Christians are eventually integrated into the larger developing faith tradition of the church, and their writings live on and continue to give witness to the new life in Christ to which all human beings are called.

What Have We Learned So Far? The Final Texts of the New Testament

The books of the New Testament that this chapter has situated in the unfolding historical, literary, and theological life of the church do not play a major role in

The House of Simon
the Tanner, from
*Christian Herald and
Signs of Our Times* (1896)

the faith experience of many practicing Christians. They are primarily in touch with the Jesus of the Gospels and with the message of Saint Paul. Yet there is much to learn from what we have traced here. From the significant theological tract, the Letter to the Hebrews, to the pastorally oriented letters associated with the authority of the founding apostles, the process of "writing" continued over the second half of the first and into the earliest decades of the second Christian century. The reason for the existence of this literature was to address the life of the church in order to **continue the tradition**. The Letter to the Hebrews, although sparsely used in the contemporary liturgical life of the churches, continues to proclaim, in sometimes unforgettable ways (see, e.g., Heb 4:14–5:10), the uniqueness, superiority, and centrality of Jesus Christ. It summons hearers and readers to face the many challenges associated with the vocation to live within the community of Jesus Christ and the promise of a final "rest."

The other so-called "Catholic Epistles" may not feature largely in the liturgical life of the contemporary Christian churches, but they retain their importance when read in and with the church. Some of them (e.g., James, 1 Peter, and 1 John) are remarkably rich witnesses to the development of the Christian tradition's understanding of itself and how it was to be made relevant in the Greco-Roman world of the expanding church. The briefer letters (Jude, 2 Peter, 2–3 John) also make their contribution. They show the importance of a continual reading and rereading of the Gospels and the paraenesis of the founding traditions as Christianity moved further and further, east and west, away from its origins and into the larger world. The central message, however, is always one of faithfulness to the earliest traditions.

Key Terms and Concepts

Asianism	heresies
baptismal homily	James
Catholic Epistles	John
community conflicts	Jude
continue the tradition	Letters of John/Johannine Epistles
elder/*presbyteros*	paraenesis
epitomē	Peter
General Letters	pseudepigraphy/pseudonymity
Gnosticism	theological treatise
Hebrews	theosis

Questions for Review

1. What is the role of Hebrews in the New Testament canon? What sort of document is it, and what does it teach about Jesus Christ?
2. What does it mean to call a group of letters in the New Testament the Catholic Epistles? How are they addressed, and how are they identified in the Bible?
3. Who is James? What does his epistle add to the New Testament canon?
4. What is the relationship between the Epistles of Peter and Jude? What is their contribution to the New Testament canon?
5. How do the Johannine Epistles relate to the Gospel of John and to the Catholic Epistles? What conflict in early Christianity do they seem to be addressing and battling against?

Bibliography and Further Reading

Brown, Raymond E. *An Introduction to the New Testament*. Anchor Yale Bible Reference Library. New Haven: Yale University Press, 1997.

Brown, Sherri. "The Challenge of 2 Peter and the Call to Theosis." *Expository Times* 128 (2017): 583–92.

Davids, Peter H. *The Letters of 2 Peter and Jude*. The Pillar New Testament Commentary. Grand Rapids: Eerdmans, 2006.

Eusebius. *The Church History*. Translated by Paul L. Maier. Grand Rapids: Kregel Academic, 2007.

Johnson, Luke Timothy. *Hebrews: A Commentary*. The New Testament Library. Louisville: Westminster John Knox, 2006.

———. *The Letter of James: A New Translation with Introduction and Commentary*. Anchor Bible 37A. New Haven: Yale University Press, 2005.

Lieu, Judith M. *I, II, and III John: A Commentary*. The New Testament Library. Louisville: Westminster John Knox, 2008.

Lincoln, Andrew T. *Hebrews: A Guide*. London: T&T Clark, 2006.

Lockett, Darian. *An Introduction to the Catholic Epistles*. T&T Clark Approaches to Biblical Studies. London: T&T Clark, 2012.

———. *Letters from the Pillar Apostles: The Formation of the Catholic Epistles as a Canonical Collection*. Eugene, OR: Pickwick, 2016.

Moloney, Francis J., SDB. *James to Jude: The People's Bible Commentary*. A Bible Commentary for Every Day. Oxford: The Bible Reading Fellowship, 1999.

———. *Letters to the Johannine Circle: 1–3 John*. Biblical Studies from the Catholic Biblical Association of America. New York: Paulist, 2020.

———. *Reading the New Testament in the Church: A Primer for Pastors, Religious Educators, and Believers*. Grand Rapids: Baker Academic, 2015.

Powell, Mark Allan. *Introducing the New Testament: A Historical, Literary, and Theological Survey*. Grand Rapids: Baker Academic, 2009.

Vanhoye, Albert. *Structure and Message of the Epistle to the Hebrews*. Rome: Pontifical Biblical Institute, 1989.

Apocalyptic Literature and the Book of Revelation

PURPOSE Chapter eight discusses the genre of literature found in the book that closes the New Testament, the book of Revelation, also known by its Greek name, the Apocalypse. The purpose is to provide exegetical insight into the worlds of apocalyptic literature to enable students better to understand Revelation and other texts of this genre.

In this final chapter, we will again take a different approach by not only discussing the worlds of apocalyptic literature to prepare our readers for more in-depth study, but also providing an overview of the book of Revelation. We do this for two reasons. First, Revelation is the only complete example of this genre in the NT, so there is opportunity for deeper interaction with it. Second, and more significantly, this genre is the most foreign and fantastic to modern eyes and ears, so it needs further explication. There are many contemporary readings of the book of Revelation. We will present one of them but also respectfully refer to other suggested interpretations. We will begin by introducing the genre and the worlds of its exegesis and then turn to Revelation itself.

Apocalyptic Literature

The term "apocalypse" comes from the Greek word *apokalypsis*, which, contrary to popular conceptions of "the final battle" or "the end of the world" (thanks to Hollywood and centuries of pulp fiction), literally means "revelation" or "unveiling." When this English noun is used as an adjective, **apocalyptic**, it can be applied to several phenomena that emerged in Judaism in the second century BCE in response to crisis and suffering. Biblical scholar Mitchell Reddish identifies **apocalyptic eschatology** as an understanding of the "end times" or "last things" that expresses the expectation that God will *reveal* Godself and intervene so that the adverse conditions of the present world would end in judgment for the oppressors and justification for the faithful, thereby ushering in a new era of peace. Notice that this does not necessarily mean the end of the world, but rather the end of the world as we know it, to make way for a new time or a new world order. In this same vein, **apocalyptic discourse** refers to the assortment of apocalyptic topics and characteristics as they function in the interaction of larger societies and literary works. It is, therefore, a flexible set of resources for persuasive speaking and writing that includes **innovation** (displays of remarkable mystical imagination, the likes of which had not yet been seen) and **authority** (appeals to the authority of revelation by God to well-known sages/authoritative figures of the past). As a mode of apocalyptic discourse, then, **apocalyptic literature** is a genre of revelatory literature of various forms, but often with a narrative framework, in which a revelation is given that shares these transcendent realities and messages about God's plan. The idea is that God reveals to select faithful people truths that transcend the immediate experience of suffering and hardship and tell of God's ultimate victory over evil. These chosen **sages**, or wise ones, then share this information in literary form—that is, they write about it. Again, this literature first arose in Judaism.

The World behind Apocalyptic Literature

Apocalypticism thus describes the worldview of a given group in which apocalyptic eschatology is dominant. During the Hellenization program of the Greek Empire from the fourth to the second century BCE, a core of those faithful to Jewish tradition began to respond to what they saw as an erosion of values from within (Jewish leaders who were advocating syncretism) and an attack on those values from without (Greek ideologues like Antiochus IV Epiphanes in the second century). Apocalyptic literature is, therefore, essentially crisis literature often written in fictional narrative form to provide commentaries on what is going on in real life. They are stories that combine fiction, history, and current reality. This new genre

---

Key Ancient Apocalyptic Texts

Proto-Apocalyptic Biblical Texts
  Ezekiel
  Isaiah 24–27
  Zechariah
  Joel
Classical Biblical Apocalypses
  Daniel (OT)
  Revelation (NT)
Other Jewish Apocalyptic Discourse
  1 Enoch
  The Testament of Moses
  Jubilees
  4 Ezra
  Testaments of the Twelve Patriarchs
  The Testament of Abraham
  2 Baruch
  3 Baruch
  Portions of the Dead Sea Scrolls (The Community Rule; The War Scroll; The New Jerusalem)
Other Christian Apocalyptic Discourse
  5 Ezra
  6 Ezra
  The Proto-Apocalypse of James
  The Apocalypse of Paul
  The Apocalypse of Peter
  The Ascension of Isaiah 6–11
  The Sibylline Oracles
  The Apocalypse of Thomas
  The Shepherd of Hermas (Visions 4–5; Similitudes 3, 4, 6)

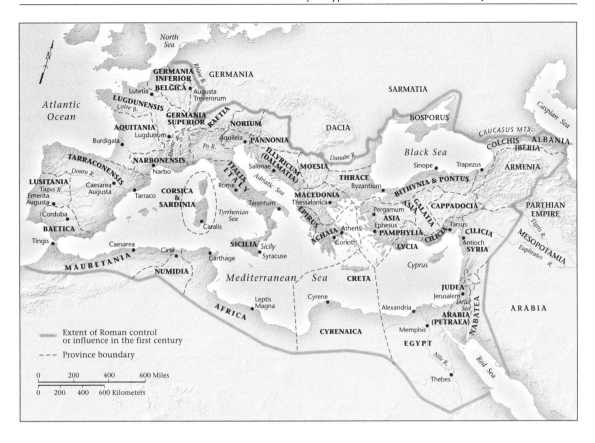

THE MEDITERRANEAN WORLD IN THE SECOND CENTURY BCE

found its classic expression in the Jewish Scriptures in the book of Daniel, written during the Maccabean period ca. 165 BCE. That said, characteristics of apocalyptic literature began to appear in prophetic books such as Ezekiel and Zechariah as early as the sixth century BCE as a result of Jewish interaction with the Eastern sensibilities of the Babylonian Empire. This aspect of these prophetic books is thus called **proto-apocalyptic**, indicating that they are prior to or predictive of the development of the new genre. Over the last two thousand years or so, apocalyptic literature has continuously appeared across societies of all kinds in times of persecution, rejection, and severe hardship, both real and perceived.

The historical context of apocalyptic discourse begins as far back as the eighth century BCE and the **prophetic literature**. As we discussed in chapter three, prophecy arose in Judaism in response to perceived apostasy within the monarchy. The prophet is the spokesperson for God who shares God's message and intentions. Much later in Judaism, **wisdom literature** arose in the fifth-century BCE post-exilic age. This genre of literature was oriented toward both theological and practical applications of living the good life. The search for wisdom is the quest for the meaning of life, and the sages pass onto and through the family the collective wisdom of the ancients. **Mysticism** and literature from the surrounding Babylonian, Persian, and Greek cultures then began to influence the social, political, and religious life of Judaism in the late post-exilic eras (ca. third century BCE) and allowed for an integration of literary conventions to grapple with emerging theological concerns.

Jewish apocalyptic literature, therefore, arose from both prophetic and wisdom literature to take on and grapple with new experiences of reality in the post-exilic Hellenistic age. Biblical scholar Luke Timothy Johnson identifies the imperatives of this literature that the current world order demanded. To those who were wavering in their convictions, it counseled, even demanded, fidelity. To those already holding fast in obedience to God, it encouraged endurance. To those who might lose their lives through martyrdom, it promised reward. To those persecuting the faithful, it promised judgment and punishment. In the end, this literature provides comfort in times of crisis by interpreting and reinterpreting history. A writer in a particular time of crisis would set his book in an ancient time period and use the authority of that antiquity to analyze his current situation and show that all is working toward God's plan in history. For example, the author of the book of Daniel, who is responding to the crisis of Antiochus IV's severe hellenizing program ca. 165 BCE, set the court tales of the first half of the book during the Babylonian exile and early post-exilic period of the sixth century BCE. This storytelling tactic allowed authors to fly under the radar of those who persecuted them in their own time, since they wrote what were seemingly fantastical narratives of a minority group's distant past. It also reminded intended audiences that, just as God has revealed Godself and redeemed the people in various ways in the past, they can expect God to act in just that way now, in their own time.

> **Luke Timothy Johnson on Revelation**
>
> "Few writings in all of literature have been so obsessively read with such generally disastrous results as the Book of Revelation (= The Apocalypse). Its history of interpretation is largely a story of tragic misinterpretation, resulting from a fundamental misapprehension of the work's literary form and purpose. Insofar as its arcane symbols have fed the treasury of prayer and poetry, its influence has been benign. More often, these same symbols have nurtured delusionary systems, both private and public, to the destruction of their fashioners and to the discredit of the writing" (Luke Timothy Johnson, *The Writings of the New Testament*, 573).

The World in Apocalyptic Literature

Apocalyptic discourse can thus manifest in both oral tradition and a variety of genres of literature. Our focus in this chapter will be on the particular genre wrought by apocalypticism that has been so influential across the last two millennia. An **apocalypse** is a narrative form of apocalyptic literature that almost always includes: (a) a revelation, (b) by a supernatural being, (c) to a human recipient (d) concerning cosmic mysteries of the present or God's plan for the future. The typical construct of an apocalypse is that a contemporary writer would put on the cloak of prophecy and the authority of antiquity to analyze his or her current situation. This history is always understood on two levels. The crises occurring in the present in this world are depicted as having a heavenly counterpart. In fact, all that happens in this realm is a reflection of the state of the conflict in the heavenly realm. Each nation is understood to have its own representative on the heavenly level, a guardian angel, who goes to battle on its behalf in the heavenly sphere.

Thus, apocalyptic literature is essentially revelatory, and it plays out in a conventional fashion. Chosen sages ascend to heaven in spirit or have dreams so that they can see the transcendental reality and its future realization in history. They are then typically charged to communicate this vision to others. Apocalyptic literature uses a wide range of fanciful symbols, with a heavy emphasis on numerology, cosmic catastrophes, and outrageous beasts. Scholars often note that, after considerable effort, these images may, possibly, be sorted into some coherent picture, but such an exercise would be

Michael as Israel's Archangel/Guardian Angel

Already in Jewish tradition, Michael, whose name means "who is like unto God?," was regarded as the angel who protects both heaven and earth. He was the leader in the angelic realm, the member of the heavenly court who stood for righteousness, mercy, and justice. He is thus the heavenly model of how things should be in Israel. His role in defending the heavenly realms from Satan, defeating him in battle, and casting him down to earth in Revelation 12 fits this Jewish understanding of the Archangel Michael.

Symbolism in Numbers

The use of numbers is particularly interesting because it combines an aura of precision within the mystery. The number three is perfection. The number seven is prominent as the number of fullness or completion. The number three and a half also becomes important as half of seven and thereby a symbol of incompleteness, instability, and even evil. The number twelve and multiples of it gain significance through their connection with the twelve tribes of Israel and then the twelve disciples in Christian writings. Very often these numbers come from biblical traditions (the seven from Dan 9, and the twelve from the tradition of Israel and the Gospels). The most famous number in the Apocalypse is found in 13:18, where the number of the beast, whose actions are described in 13:11–18, is 666. Most use a Jewish practice of adding the numerical value of letters of the alphabet (called gematria) to identify the emperor Nero as 666. The other widely supported opinion is that 666 is three (i.e., perfection) times the number six, which is one short of seven (i.e., completion), indicating perennial frustration and imperfection.

largely beside the point. No particular symbol is significant in and of itself; rather, it is the cumulative effect that creates the sense of mystery and transcendence essential for the full impact of the revelation.

The World in Front of Apocalyptic Literature

The language and symbolism of apocalypticism is so foreign and yet so vibrant and mesmerizing to contemporary readers that apocalyptic literature practically begs for abuse and misuse. Scholars notice that this seems to have been the case from the beginnings of the Christian tradition. We can use the book of Revelation as an example here before we go into greater detail below. The text opens with the self-description of "the revelation of Jesus Christ, which God gave to him to show his servants what must take place quickly" (1:1 AT [= authors' translation]), and it speaks of "the words of its prophecy" (1:3). At the end of the body of the work, the final vision describes a thousand-year reign of Christ on earth, along with his resurrected holy ones (20:4–6), and then closes with a series of imperatives about what to do with the "prophecy" of this work

---

Common Literary Characteristics of Apocalyptic Discourse

Alternative worlds in space (earthly/heavenly realms) and time (this world/the world to come)

Visions and audible messages addressed to the visionary by God, which provide the authority and source for the message shared

Heavenly intermediaries, usually angels and occasionally the deity, serve as guides and interpreters for the visions and auditions

Intense symbolism that is obscure and fantastical, drawing on earlier traditions and cultural conventions known to the first readers

Pseudonymity, which means attributing the literary work to a fictitious author from the revered cultural traditions of the community; the heroes of antiquity lend to the overall purpose of the apocalypse

Cosmic catastrophe always precedes the ultimate deliverance in the historical apocalypses

Dualism in the sense of either/or ideology (people are either righteous or wicked; reality is earthly or heavenly; the present evil age is against the righteous age to come; etc.)

Determinism in the expectation that the course of history has been set by God, or at least is known by God as his plan

Judgment and the afterlife are key concerns that provide for justice in the historical apocalypses

Ex eventu **prophecy** translates to "prophecy after the fact," which serves to provide authority/authenticity to God's work in the past, as well as the visionary's message for the present and future

Cosmic speculation is provided in some apocalypses to explain natural phenomena, the calendar, and other remarkable events

(22:7–21). These statements led the church father Papias to be the first of many **millenarians** to look forward to the imminent fulfillment of this "prophecy." People in every age, including our own, have continued to turn to Revelation as a guide to the future of our world. They always manage to find in their own time the person of the beast who rises against the faithful and who is eventually defeated by Christ and the heavenly cohort. On the contrary, many contemporary biblical scholars suggest that the clue to the right path of interpretation of all this literature is in the first word of that famous NT book, Revelation.

The original Greek term, as we identified in the opening of this chapter, is *apokalypsis*, and it is from this word that the genre of literature gets its name. This is the major point of contention in Christian eschatology today. Some of the contents *are* prophetic, but we must get to a proper definition of that word before we go back and consider the impact of apocalyptic literature. In the Jewish milieu, as evidenced by the OT, a "prophet" is one who is the mouthpiece of God. He or she is God's spokesperson on earth (Exod 7:1–2). God tells the prophet what to say, and he or she says it to other people who may eventually record the message in written form. In the NT, that definition expanded to include any inspired preaching about God and the good news of Jesus Christ. In neither case is "prediction of events in the future" a fundamental aspect of the definition of a prophet or prophecy. Although it is sometimes part and parcel of it, prophecy is not, strictly speaking, future prediction. This notion of prediction has a more modern sense that is a distortion of the ancient concept. Thus, conflict about how to interpret Revelation and other such literature lies between those who understand the development of a new genre of apocalyptic literature in the second century BCE (which we have outlined thus far in this chapter) and those who do not—that is, those who espouse the idea that this literature is in the strictest sense a prediction of the future, something claimed by neither the texts nor their genre.

> **Exodus 7:1–2: Identity of a True Prophet**
>
> The Lord said to Moses, "See I have made you like God to Pharaoh, and your brother Aaron shall be your prophet. You shall speak all that I command you, and your brother Aaron shall tell Pharaoh to let the Israelites go out of his land."

According to Mitchell Reddish, several models may be helpful for interpreting apocalyptic discourse once we accept that these texts were not intended to predict the future in the mundane sense. One such model is **constructive theology**. The idea is that theological reflection requires imagination and the invention of new models and the reassessment of traditional ones to grapple with the world and our place in it over time. Thus, interpreters emphasize the creative and artistic dimension of this work. Another model is **poetry**. Apocalyptic discourse employs the sort of dense language typical of poetic art, including evocative symbols, images, complex webs of literary allusions, and idealized descriptions. Therefore, interpreters can utilize similar methods employed to study poetry, particularly that of the ancients. A final suggested model is **rhetoric**. Apocalyptic literature aims to persuade its audiences to adopt certain dispositions, believe particular things, and behave in specific ways. Thus, it uses every imaginative resource at hand to do just that. All these models can assist exegetes in understanding the genre and interpreting its various texts.

Despite its elaborate symbolism, however, apocalyptic literature typically presents a rather straightforward interpretation and resulting picture of history. Even when all appearances are to the contrary, God is in control of the world God created. Therefore, even if God's people suffer trials and tribulation, God will ultimately intervene decisively on behalf of the faithful and the oppressed to bring history to its final goal: the communion of God with humankind and all God's creation. Further, the consoling power of these messages lies in the convention that all that is to happen is promised to be coming *quickly*. Thus, the function and emphasis are always exhortatory, focused on encouragement and comfort. The outcome is certain, so those suffering are given hope and encouraged to hold on to the end. Regardless of the plot and details, then, the main objective of apocalyptic literature is to give suffering people of any and all times in any and all places hope in times of affliction. These general principles must be applied to the reading of the NT book of Revelation. However, care must be taken with the reconstruction of the "suffering" of the world behind the text of the NT book.

Mark Allan Powell on Revelation

"Revelation is a book to excite the senses. . . . There is hardly a moment's peace. No, wait— there are a thousand years of peace, but that's just three verses (20:4–6), and then all hell breaks loose (literally). The imagery is fantastic: buildings and furniture made of gems, and a menagerie of creatures like something Dr. Seuss might have thought up after a sleepless night reading Stephen King: the locusts wear armor like horses (9:7–9), and the horses have serpents for tails (9:19). And what's this thing that's part leopard, part bear, and part lion but lives in the sea (13:1–2)?

"In a sense, to 'interpret' this book is to misinterpret it, for often the appeal is to the imagination; it's a book to be experienced, not explained" (Mark Allan Powell, *Introducing the New Testament*, 519).

The Book of Revelation

Our presentation of apocalyptic literature in general clears the ground to approach the NT book of Revelation. The literary form of Revelation is clearly derived from the widespread phenomenon of apocalyptic writing of the era. It reaches back to the prophets and emerged more insistently in the Maccabean period and in the period that followed the destruction of Israel's Temple and land after the First Jewish Revolt of 65–70 CE. As we have seen, at the heart of apocalyptic literature is a message about the faithfulness of God. No matter how difficult the situation might be for God's people, no matter how much suffering and death they are experiencing at the hands of their enemies, those powers are also enemies of God. God will ultimately be victorious over the evil powers.

Revelation is especially dependent upon Ezekiel and Daniel, even though **John of Patmos** (the book's stated author; 1:9) never explicitly cites any OT passage.

Because it uses an apocalyptic literary form, Revelation looks to the future action of God to establish his rule over all evil power. At this point, we encounter the source of major conflicts between contemporary interpreters of Revelation and the popular use of the document. Many popular readers and preachers identify specific events and people as "coded" in the numbers and symbols of the book. This approach is the source of much fantastic speculation about the figure of **the beast** named 666 (Rev 13:18). Further, precise indications of how and when God will return are identified. The idea of a "rapture" of the holy ones to heaven is based in John's words on the "thousand-year reign" in

Anastasis fresco, Church
of St. Savior in Chora,
Istanbul (fourteenth
century) © Joseph Kranak

20:4–6 (coupled with 1 Thess 4:13–18). Revelation is then used as an authoritative "biblical word" about situations and people from the past and present and
makes firm prophecies about the future. In the sixteenth century, at the time
of the Reformation, major figures from the various sides hurled abuse at other
Christians, using the language and imagery of Revelation. These sentiments
are still passionately argued today but are now often also aimed at those who
practice other religions. All of this is an abuse of the biblical document. They
have also harmed the Christian tradition and reflect a negative and punishing
understanding of the God of Jesus Christ.

Revelation must be interpreted in the light of the world behind the text:
the difficulties faced by late first-century Christian communities. In order to
address these Christians, the world in front of the text, John adopted and modified the apocalyptic literary form, which tells us a great deal about the world
in the text. As we have seen, the use of an apocalyptic literary form necessarily
indicates that the message of Revelation points to an "end." However, we insisted
that this end may not necessarily be the "end of the world," but the "end of the
world as we know it." Contemporary interpreters differ on this question, and
these differences lead to contrasting interpretations. All interpreters agree on
the importance of its apocalyptic eschatology, but detailed analyses of the often
spectacular and highly imaginative scenarios used to arrive at that eschatology,
and the nature of the eschatology itself, necessarily produce contrasting readings of the book. Our reflection on the world in front of the text will describe
three of these, including the reading adopted for this chapter.

Directed to Christians challenged to live their resurrection faith in a
Greco-Roman world, Revelation is not primarily about a conflict between

Roman authority and emperor worship and the church in Asia Minor (the location of the churches addressed in the text). The Roman Empire was certainly the context that produced Revelation, but the message of the book reaches beyond that immediate situation. Heavily dependent upon the prophet Ezekiel and the apocalyptic book of Daniel, John of Patmos is concerned to describe the perennial presence of evil and human sinfulness. He points to Jerusalem's collusion with that evil, producing the historical event of the death of Jesus. The situation of conflict between God and evil, between the holy ones and evil-inspired powers, reaches back to the beginnings of history. But so do the saving effects of the death and resurrection of Jesus Christ: "the Lamb who was slaughtered from the foundation of the world" (13:8). The eschatological promise of Revelation is not an "other world" experience, but the lived experience, in history, of the Christian church, the bride of the Lamb. In that place, all ambiguity has been overcome by God's perennial victory in and through the death and resurrection of Jesus Christ. Sinfulness will continue (see 22:11, 15), but the faithful "will have the right to the tree of life and may enter the city by the gates" (22:14).

The World behind the Book of Revelation

The above introduction to Revelation agrees with mainstream interpretation on a number of important issues. In the first place, it is the work of an otherwise unknown "John," identified in the work itself (see 1:1, 4, 9; 22:8). The name is quite common, and he would have been a zealous Christian prophet and witness to Jesus Christ in Asia. He should not be identified with the name "John," traditionally taken as the author of the Fourth Gospel.

He was most likely a Jewish Christian, and by this we mean that he was an ethnically Jewish man who believed that Jesus was the Christ and began to order his life and work accordingly. He is extremely familiar with the Jewish Scriptures, writes in a Greek style that is heavily influenced by Hebrew, and alludes to Jewish apocalyptic literature easily. He never actually cites any of the Scriptures that he uses. Revelation must have taken its final shape in the last years of **the emperor Domitian** (81–96 CE), as we are told by early witnesses (e.g., Irenaeus [130–202 CE]). Finally, we should accept

---

"John" as the Author

As the communities of the early church pondered and discussed which books belonged to Christianity's sacred Scriptures, known to us as the New Testament, one of the criteria was the antiquity of the document and its possible apostolic origins. Late in the second century, Irenaeus linked the Beloved Disciple of the Gospel of John with "John" the son of Zebedee. The similarity of thought and language that exists between the four Gospels and the letters we now know as 1–3 John followed logically. It was also Irenaeus who taught that the "John" who is named in Revelation was also John the son of Zebedee. Thus, the so-called Johannine literature is made up of the Gospel, the Letters of John, and Revelation. Only in Revelation is the name "John" mentioned. He was not the son of Zebedee.

PATMOS AND THE SEVEN CHURCHES OF REVELATION 2:1–3:22

the author's witness: it was written in Patmos, an island close to the coast of Asia Minor (today's western Turkey; see 1:9).

Contemporary Greek and Roman historians question many current presuppositions about the world behind the text of Revelation. For most interpreters, it is a Christian form of late Jewish apocalyptic literature, directed to Christian communities, most likely the seven churches of 2:1–3:22, to exhort them to patience. In their suffering, they are encouraged that God will destroy the evil powers of Rome, its cult, and its pagan ways. Those suffering will eventually be victorious. It is now clear that there was no systematic persecution of Christians at the time of the emperor Domitian. Similarly, although **emperor worship** was certainly part of the Roman policy to engender loyalty and unity across its empire, there is no proof that, at the end of the first century CE, Christians were being executed because they refused to worship the emperor. Equally significant is the total lack of evidence that Patmos was ever a prison colony. By contrast, John was most likely on Patmos as part of his prophetic-missionary experience, "because of the word of God and witness to Jesus" (1:9 AT).

Once these widespread presuppositions about the "world behind the text" have been removed, the interpreter can look more broadly to the lived experience of the Christian church in the Greco-Roman world. Like other apocalypses, Revelation is written to encourage its recipients, but they are not suffering under Roman

---

Craig R. Koester on Patmos

"John is the only person known to have been sent there" (Craig R. Koester, *Revelation*, 243).

imperialism, as is generally claimed. In fact, the opposite may have been the case: the danger that Christians are facing was a loss of intense focus upon the death and resurrection of Jesus Christ, as they settled into the well-governed and economically stable empire. In that situation, John looked back to those who have suffered for the word of God (Torah) and the witness of the prophets to Jesus Christ in the past (including the martyrs under Antiochus IV). In the light of that glorious past, he exhorts Christians who are wavering in the ambiguity of the Greco-Roman world, described in the letters to the churches in 2:1–3:22. John states and restates that God's victory has been achieved from all time, through the death and resurrection of Jesus Christ. The victory has been won, but Christians are still wavering, living a lukewarm form of Christianity in the attractive dominant Greco-Roman society. These are the tumultuous times

---

Leonard L. Thompson on Revelation

"The seer and his audience did not live in a world of conflict, tension, and crisis. Christians lived quiet lives, not much different from other provincials. The economy, as always, had its ups and downs; and the government kept the peace and demanded taxes. . . .

"It would be at best hazardous to assume an empire-wide political crisis during Domitian's reign. . . . Domitian was no more or less demanding an emperor than those who came before or after him. It would be a mistake to interpret the book of Revelation as a response to Domitian's supposed excessive claims to divinity or to a reign of terror at the end of Domitian's rule. Domitian provided economic and political stability for the whole empire at least as well as other emperors did at the end of the first century and the beginning of the second" (Leonard L. Thompson, *The Book of Revelation: Apocalypse and Empire*, 95, 116).

The "Bending" of the Apocalyptic Genre

In his article "Genre Bending in the Fourth Gospel," Harold Attridge made a significant contribution to the interpretation of the Fourth Gospel by suggesting that the focus of the Fourth Evangelist on the incarnation led to what Attridge called "genre bending." This means that the author of the Gospel often appears to be using literary forms (genres) that are traditional (e.g., miracle stories, pronouncements of Jesus), but he uses them in a way that "bends" them to address the newness of his teaching on the incarna-tion. Similar "bending" takes place in Revelation. Here the genre is traditional Jewish apocalyptic. However, John "bends" the literary form of apocalyptic, which usually focuses upon the future interventions of God, because of an event that has already happened: the death and resurrection of Jesus. The literary form is apocalyptic, but John surprises his audience by using it to tell of the effects of the death and resurrection of Jesus Christ across all time.

and circumstances (so powerfully caught by the widespread use of apocalyptic language and imagery across the narrative) that have been overcome by the death and resurrection of Jesus. Believing Christians are called to be transformed into **the new Jerusalem**, the gift of God from heaven.

The World in the Book of Revelation

The above understanding of the world behind the text does not take away from the apocalyptic nature of the world in the text of Revelation. As we have already indicated, the uniqueness of Revelation is John's focus upon the victory that has already been won by the death and resurrection of Jesus (see 1:4–8, 17–18; 5:9–10, 12–14; 7:15–8:1; 12:10–12; 14:4–5; 16:17, etc.). Nevertheless, the world in the text must also be interpreted in the light of the genre and message of both the biblical and non-biblical apocalyptic literature that we surveyed earlier in this chapter. That said, the central Christian belief of God's saving action in and through the death and resurrection of Jesus "bends" the genre.

John argues passionately for the end of the world as the recipients of Revelation knew it, but not for the end of the world as such. The "new Jerusalem" of Rev 21–22 belongs to this world. What makes Revelation different from any other apocalypse is its celebration of something that has already taken place: the death and resurrection of Jesus Christ. Revelation should not be understood as a document written to Christians undergoing the physical suffering of Roman persecution, promising them that God will intervene at the end, destroying all evil and rewarding the faithful with an otherworldly "new Jerusalem." Perhaps the most determining image of Revelation is **the Lamb**, whose first appearance in the narrative is "the Lamb standing as if it had been slaughtered" (Rev 5:6). Indeed, the saving power of the slain and risen Lamb has been present "from the foundation of the world" (13:8). All Christian interpreters recognize the importance of the death and resurrection in Revelation, but most argue that John bases his exhortation to faithfulness upon a victory yet to be won, as the audience awaits God's final intervention at the end of all time.

Interpreting Revelation should be guided by its literary structure. All agree that the book opens with a prologue (1:1–8) and closes with an epilogue (22:6–21). The key to the narrative is John's fourfold use of **sevens**: seven letters to churches (2:1–3:22), the opening of seven seals (6:1–8:1), the blowing of seven trumpets (8:7–11:19), and the pouring out of seven bowls (16:1–21). Each of these "sevens" is prefaced by a heavenly encounter (1:9–20; 4:1–5:14; 8:2–6; 15:1–8) and leads to fulfillment (seven!). Each one of them closes with a proclamation of the effects of

---

Craig R. Koester on Revelation

"The redeemed have no independent dominion. They reign by sharing fully in the life brought about through the reign of God and the Lamb" (Craig R. Koester, *Revelation*, 836).

the death and resurrection of Jesus (3:20; 6:12–8:1; 11:15–19; 16:17–21). A problem for many interpreters is the relative brevity of the section on the pouring out of the seven bowls (16:1–11). As the final and most intense of the four "sevens," the pouring out of the bowls claims to bring everything to an end. The promise that the mystery of God is fulfilled, made at the blowing of the seventh trumpet (10:7), is resolved as the final bowl is poured out: "It is done" (16:17).

Precisely because of the definitive nature of the proclamation of the judgment and salvation wrought by the death and resurrection of Jesus in the pouring out of the seven bowls (15:1–8 [heavenly encounter]; 16:1–21 [pouring out of the bowls]), it is *prefaced* by *three* descriptions: the ambiguity of "**the woman**" fallen and pursued by Satan (12:1–18), the pervasive presence of political and religious corruption (13:1–18), and **the one like a Son of Man** exercising God's judgment (14:1–20). The presentation of Jesus Christ as "one like a Son of Man" appears only twice in Revelation. The expression was used by Jesus in the Gospels to speak of his authoritative presence, his suffering, and his return as judge. The origins of

---

John's Use of "the Woman"

One of the most striking literary techniques John uses in his presentation of God's final victory in the pouring out of the bowls is his use of the symbol of "the woman." She is the potential perfection of humankind who falls into ambiguity in Revelation 12:1–18; a prostitute who has made a decision for wickedness, mounted on the beast in 17:1–6; and a symbol of those who united with the Lamb as his bride in 21:2, 9–14, to form the new Jerusalem. John's use of "the woman" as a character in his narrative guides the audience to see all possibilities for humankind.

The One Like a Son of Man

In the Gospels, Jesus regularly uses the expression "the Son of Man" to speak of himself as an authoritative figure (see Mark 2:10, 28) who will suffer death and be raised by God (see Mark 8:31; 9:31; 10:32–34), to return in glory as judge (see Mark 13:24–27; 14:62). John develops these themes in Revelation 1:13 and 14:14. The inspiration for this understanding of Jesus Christ comes from the book of Daniel: "And as I watched, thrones were set in place, and an ancient one took his throne; his clothing was white as snow, and the hair of his head like pure wool; his throne was fiery flames, and its wheels were burning fire. A stream of fire issued and flowed out from his presence. . . . The courts sat in judgment, and the books were opened. I watched then because

of the noise of the arrogant words that the horn was speaking. And as I watched, the beast was put to death, and its body destroyed and given over to be destroyed, to be burned with fire. As for the rest of the beasts, their dominion was taken away, but their lives were prolonged for a season and a time. As I watched in the night visions, I saw one like a son of man coming with the clouds of heaven. And he came to the ancient one and was presented before him. To him was given dominion, glory, and kingship that all peoples, nations, and languages should serve him. His dominion is an everlasting dominion that shall not pass away, and his kingship shall be one that shall never be destroyed" (Dan 7:9–14 AT).

Steven J. Friesen on Revelation

"John understood the churches to represent God's kingdom, chosen from among the people of the earth. The citizens of the kingdom faced hostility and death threats but were not to respond with violence. Their task was to maintain the testimony of Jesus even at the cost of their lives, for they knew that the Lamb had already defeated their enemies and that the second death would not harm them" (Steven J. Friesen, *Imperial Cults and the Apocalypse of John*, 193).

Richard Bauckham on Revelation

"John's apocalypse, however, is exclusively concerned with eschatology: with eschatological judgment and salvation, and the impact of these upon the present situation in which he writes" (Richard Bauckham, *The Theology of Revelation*, 6).

the expression are found in Daniel 7. In Daniel, suffering Israel is promised vindication at the court of God, who gives all authority to the one like a son of man (see Dan 7:9–14). In Rev 1:13, in order to indicate the glory and the divine status of the crucified and risen Jesus, the description of God in Dan 7:9 is applied to the "one like a Son of Man." But the role of judge, also central to the action of God in Dan 7, is assumed by "the one like a Son of Man" in 14:14. Poised between two sets of three angels who execute judgment (vv. 6–7, 8, 9–13 and vv. 15–16, 17, 18–20) sits "the one like a Son of Man," crowned as a king and bearing the sword of judgment (v. 14). What is said of God in Daniel 7 is applied to Jesus as "the one like a Son of Man," an authoritative divine figure (1:13), who exercises judgment (14:14).

After the pouring out of the bowls (15:1–16:21), *three consequences* of God's victory in the death and resurrection of Jesus Christ are spelled out: the destruction of Jerusalem (identified as Babylon in the text), presented as an unholy union with the woman now mounted upon the beast (17:1–19:10), **the final battle** and its results (19:11–21:8), and the new Jerusalem, where the woman is now the bride of the Lamb (21:9–22:5). The new Jerusalem is the Christian church as it should be, leaving behind the ambiguities of 2:1–3:22, despite the ongoing presence of sin and evil (see 22:11, 15). In the new Jerusalem, God has transformed the human situation. Its ambiguous situation, cast down from heaven into the wilderness, pursued by Satan but protected by God, was described in 12:1–18. At its worst, humankind has mounted the beast in unholy alliance (17:1–6). But through the action of God and the gift of the new Jerusalem, humankind has become "the bride of the Lamb" with access to living water and an undying light (21–22). This is a world alternative to the one the audience of John's Revelation inhabit in their day-to-day lives.

The World in Front of the Book of Revelation

As we have mentioned, for some, the signs, the numbers, warnings, threats, and blessings are to be applied to the world or to the Christian community wherever and whenever it is read. This is not only unhelpful but also a dangerous approach to a document of the New Testament, eventually accepted into the

Christian canon because it addressed Christian communities in the earliest times of the church. Rather, sound Christian readings rightly interpret Revelation within its own historical, social, and religious context. The book is a Christian version of traditional Jewish apocalyptic literature, condemning the present situation of evil and suffering, normally associated with Roman persecution and the presence of the emperor cult.

For some important interpreters (e.g., Richard Bauckham and Edmondo Lupieri), victory lies in the final intervention of God, which will generate an alternative world where all such evil will be conquered and God will be the only God. Others (e.g., Adela Yarbro Collins, Craig Koester, and James Resseguie) also look to Roman background, persecution, and the problem of emperor worship but claim that the narrative leads to God's final intervention that will not be outside time and human experience. The indication that sin and evil continue outside the new Jerusalem (see 22:11, 15) suggests that God's eschatological intervention will be in history, normally understood as the promise of the Christian community's victory over suffering and persecution, the definitive establishment of God's kingdom.

We have adopted a third possible interpretation, based upon contemporary scholarly agreement that there was no systematic persecution under the emperor Domitian and that emperor worship had not yet become the measure of a citizen's faithfulness to the emperor and Roman religious traditions. Living under Roman authority, the most recent experience of corrupt religious and political authority, the first audience of the book of Revelation was told, by means of language and visions that come from apocalyptic literature, and especially from Ezekiel and Daniel, that satanic evil has been conquered by the death and resurrection of Jesus. Faithful Christians are urged to look back to the sufferings of others who have identified with the crucified Christ as they live their Christian faith in the ambiguity of a Greco-Roman world with its religious and cultural traditions. In the new Jerusalem, God's gift of the Christian church, they wait for the final coming of Jesus Christ (Eugenio Corsini and Francis Moloney).

The cosmic presence of evil is forcefully told by means of narrative imagery that comes to John from an apocalyptically oriented world. But the world in the text is a world that faces evil confident that the victory has already been won

---

Craig R. Koester on Revelation

"Revelation departs from the usual pattern. The eschatological struggle had already begun with the Messiah's exaltation and would culminate in his return. Those events define the present time" (Craig R. Koester, *Revelation*, 22).

Wes Howard-Brook and Anthony Gwyther on Revelation

"[The Roman Empire] was simply the latest manifestation of a false imperial reality that had plagued the people of God since the days of slavery in Egypt. . . . New Jerusalem is a territory carved out of empire that embodies an alternative social reality. . . . *Babylon exists wherever sociopolitical power coalesces into an entity that stands against the worship of YHWH alone.* . . . *New Jerusalem is found wherever the human community rejects the lies and violence of empire and places God at the center of its shared life*" (Wes Howard-Brook and Anthony Gwyther, *Unveiling Empire*, 121, 129, 156–57; emphasis in original).

The Harrowing of
Hell (Hosios Loukas,
tenth century)

from the beginning of time (5:6; 13:8). This message communicates to Christians in front of the text that they are blessed with the gift of the new Jerusalem, coming down from heaven, where all sin and evil is eliminated. As with all apocalyptic literature, the new Jerusalem is a gift of God "from heaven": 21:1–2). However, unlike much apocalyptic material, the new Jerusalem does not belong to a post-temporal existence. It is God's gift to those who, like all those before them who suffered for their beliefs, resisted the allure of the Greco-Roman world and its religions to become the ideal Christian community. However, John maintains traditional Christian eschatological hope. A victory has been won in this world, which enables God's gift of the new Jerusalem. Nevertheless, Christians still wait for the final coming of Jesus Christ (22:20). Like the Gospel of John, the letters of Paul, and other Christian documents, present in Revelation is a traditional apocalyptic vision of the Christian vocation to live in the tension between, on the one hand, the **"now"** made possible by the death and resurrection of Christ and, on the other, the **"not yet"** associated with Jesus's final advent.

What follows is a synthesis of the background and argument of Revelation in a single schema. We must remember, however, that apocalyptic literature in general and the book of Revelation in particular evoke strong positions and passions from scholars and more casual readers alike. Responsible exegetes can draw out different structures and intentions. What we offer is one such guide, based upon contemporary research, to suggest a "key" to the structure and message of the document. It lays no claim to having resolved the many enigmas that will forever surround the interpretation of this surprising New Testament book.

The Worlds of Revelation

The World behind the Text

Who: John, the servant of Christ (1:1). There is no use of pseudonymity. Traditionally, John is identified with John the son of Zebedee and disciple of Jesus who is also author of the Gospel and three letters of John. This identification is most unlikely.

What: An apocalypse (1:1) that has been "bent" by John's intense focus upon the saving action of Jesus's death and resurrection (see p. 226, "The 'Bending' of the Apocalyptic Genre"). Seven letters from the risen Christ to Christian communities point to strengths and weaknesses of the church as a whole. The narrative of the rest of the book proceeds from the letters through John's visions, shaped by the Jewish apocalyptic literary form to tell of God's plan for humankind.

Where: On the island of Patmos (1:9), off the coast of Ephesus in Asia (modern Turkey). He is there as a prophetic missionary, preaching God's word and giving witness to Christ.

When: Likely during the latter years of the Roman emperor Domitian (81–96 CE).

Why: For the hope and encouragement of late first-century Christians, attracted by the glitter of the Greco-Roman world, including gods and emperor worship. The crucified and risen Lamb promises establishment of the church as it should be: the new Jerusalem.

How: Apocalyptic visions presented in a narrative framework highlight the perennial presence of satanically inspired evil and the victory of God and the Lamb over all such evil.

The World in the Text

Suggested Structure:

1:1–8   Prologue: The Revelation of God and Christ
   1:9–3:22   Heavenly Encounters and the Letters of the Risen Christ to Churches
   4:1–8:1   Heavenly Encounters and the Opening of the Seven Seals
   8:2–11:19   Heavenly Encounters and the Blowing of the Seven Trumpets
   12:1–14:20   Preparation for the Bowls: (1) The Human Situation, (2) Political and Religious Corruption, (3) Judgment
   15:1–16:21   Heavenly Encounters and the Pouring out of the Seven Bowls
   17:1–22:5   Consequences of the Bowls: (1) The Destruction of Babylon (Jerusalem), (2) the Final Battle, (3) the Gift of the New Jerusalem
22:6–21   Epilogue: Worship God, Come Lord Jesus

Key Apocalyptic Characteristics:

- Alternative worlds temporally (present vs. future); spatially (earth vs. heaven realms);
- Visions given the sage directly from the risen Christ or by a heavenly intermediary;
- Intense symbolism, notably fantastic creatures and numerology;
- Determinism: God not only has a plan, but that plan is already in motion;
- Cosmic catastrophe that integrates with the judgment of good and evil;
- End-time eschatology, but no description of when or what it will be like.

The World in Front of the Text

The conviction that Jesus has risen from the dead "bends" apocalyptic symbols. Hope is based on the present power of God, manifest in the Christian experience of the resurrected, living Jesus, encapsulating Christian theology, Christology, theodicy, soteriology, and eschatology.

What Have We Learned So Far? The Good News and the Book of Revelation

The interpretation we have presented is only one of several possible, given the enigmatic nature of apocalyptic literature and the book of Revelation, which makes rich use of that literature and its themes. We have used this interpretative paradigm as it is based firmly on the centrality of the death and resurrection of Jesus Christ in the Christian tradition and on a more contemporary evaluation of the situation of the world behind the text in the last decade of the first Christian century. We are also attracted to this interpretation because, despite the often fantastic use of apocalyptic language and dramas, it brings a message to Christians of all times: God has conquered all evil in the death and resurrection of Jesus Christ. Christians are to persevere in faith in the crucified and risen Lamb so that God might grant the heavenly Jerusalem, a church, "a kingdom of priests serving his God and Father" (1:6; see 5:10; 20:6). In the meantime, Christians of all times wait for God's final intervention in the second coming of Jesus Christ. But evildoers still do evil, the filthy are still filthy, the righteous still do what is right, and the holy are still holy (see 22:11).

Key Terms and Concepts

apocalypse	the Lamb
apocalyptic	millenarians
apocalyptic discourse	mysticism
apocalyptic eschatology	the new Jerusalem
apocalypticism	"now"/"not yet"
apocalyptic literature	the one like a Son of Man
authority	poetry
the beast	prophetic literature
constructive theology	proto-apocalyptic literature
the emperor Domitian	rhetoric
emperor worship	sages
the final battle	sevens
innovation	wisdom literature
John of Patmos	the woman

Questions for Review

1. What does the term "apocalypse" mean, and how might that affect how books from such a genre are interpreted?
2. What is the general premise of narratives called apocalypses?

3. Discuss the genre of apocalyptic literature and how understanding this ancient genre as such sets the stage for its interpretation and the interpretation of Revelation.
4. What makes the book of Revelation different from other forms of apocalyptic literature?
5. What are the "sevens" in Revelation? Why are they important?
6. What is the role of the Lamb in Revelation?
7. What is the significance of the new Jerusalem?
8. How important is the ongoing presence of evil outside the new Jerusalem for an understanding of when and how God will resolve the ambiguity of the Christian situation?
9. Is there a link between the charges of lukewarmness made against the "seven churches" in 2:1–3:22 and the description of the new Jerusalem in 21:9–22:5?

Bibliography and Further Reading

Bauckham, Richard. *The Theology of the Book of Revelation.* New Testament Theology. Cambridge: Cambridge University Press, 1993.

Brodd, Jeffrey, and Jonathan L. Reed, eds. *Rome and Religion: A Cross-Disciplinary Dialogue on the Imperial Cult.* Writings from the Greco-Roman World Supplement Series. Atlanta: Society of Biblical Literature, 2011.

Carey, Greg. *Ultimate Things: An Introduction to Jewish and Christian Apocalyptic Literature.* St. Louis: Chalice, 2005.

Collins, Adela Yarbro. *The Apocalypse.* New Testament Message 22. Wilmington, DE: Michael Glazier, 1979.

———. *Crisis and Catharsis. The Power of the Apocalypse.* Philadelphia: Westminster, 1984.

Collins, John J. *The Apocalyptic Imagination: An Introduction to Jewish Apocalyptic Literature.* Rev. ed. Grand Rapids: Eerdmans, 1998.

Corsini, Eugenio. *The Apocalypse: The Perennial Revelation of Jesus Christ.* Translated and edited by Francis J. Moloney. Wilmington, DE: Michael Glazier, 1983. Repr., Eugene, OR: Wipf & Stock, 2019.

Friesen, Steven J. *Imperial Cults and the Apocalypse of John: Reading Revelation in the Ruins.* New York: Oxford University Press, 2001.

Hill, Craig C. *In God's Time: The Bible and the Future.* Grand Rapids: Eerdmans, 2002.

Howard-Brook, Wes, and Anthony Gwyther. *Unveiling Empire: Reading Revelation Then and Now.* Maryknoll, NY: Orbis, 1999.

Johnson, Luke Timothy. *The Writings of the New Testament.* 3rd ed. Minneapolis: Fortress, 2010.

Koester, Craig R. *Revelation.* The Anchor Yale Bible Commentary 38A. New Haven: Yale University Press, 2014.

———. *Revelation and the End of All Things*. 2nd ed. Grand Rapids: Eerdmans, 2018.

Moloney, Francis J. *The Apocalypse of John: An Alternative Commentary*. Grand Rapids: Baker, 2020.

Powell, Mark Allan. *Introducing the New Testament: A Historical, Literary, and Theological Survey*. Grand Rapids: Baker Academic, 2009.

Reddish, Mitchell G., ed. *Apocalyptic Literature: A Reader*. Peabody, MA: Hendrickson, 1995.

Resseguie, James L. *The Revelation of John: A Narrative Commentary*. Grand Rapids: Baker Academic, 2009.

Thompson, Leonard L. *The Book of Revelation: Apocalypse and Empire*. New York: Oxford University Press, 1993.

CHAPTER NINE

Conclusion: The Good News of the New Testament

PURPOSE This brief conclusion draws together the themes of the texts and the textbook by discussing the challenge of the New Testament to our present world.

We have come to the end of a long journey through several worlds. In the first place, we have had the opportunity to travel through the historical world that produced the Bible, what we often call the Old and New Testaments. We have insisted, however, that there would be no New Testament without the chronologically prior collection of the sacred Scriptures of Israel. In that sense, Israel's Scriptures are older than the more recent collection of books we have interpreted and introduced. We called this "the world behind the text." We then looked at the many literary techniques that can be found in the New Testament, made up of narratives, letters, theological tracts, and an apocalypse. We called that "the world in the text." We also decided on the approach that we wanted to adopt in introducing and reading through all the books of the New Testament. We did not ignore the historical and literary questions, but we must not decide why something was said in a certain way in the first Christian century and leave it there. For many people, the books of the New Testament are a guide, indeed a word of life. Thus, we have continually asked the question of the ongoing meaning of these texts, sacred to many, for those who read it, hear it, or see it performed. We called this "the world in front of the text."

Once we had our "worlds" in place, we have attempted to trace the structure and message of each document. Given the nature of this book, aware that many students commit themselves to a study of the whole of the New Testament, we have consistently attempted to produce an overview that provides answers to the questions of where, when, and why a document was written, followed by a summary of the argument of the book under consideration. The crucially important encounter that must take place between you—our reader—and the New Testament is, however, your responsibility! Some would differ from our proposals, but you can be sure that what you have read in this book is mainstream opinion. Only in our presentation of the book of Revelation have we differed slightly from that criterion. We do so because we suspect that Revelation may be a more Christian book than is often suggested. It is a major affirmation of the timeless presence of the saving effects of the Lamb, slain before the foundation of the world (Rev 13:8).

We are very aware that a textbook like *Interpreting the New Testament: An Introduction* will find its place in the classrooms and the studies of students who do not regard the Bible, and thus the New Testament, as sacred Scripture. Nevertheless, if the Christian tradition is not your "home," we trust that this introduction to the books of the Christian Bible has shown how one should approach the New Testament from its first to its final book, and we hope that your experience of these texts from Christianity's formative years has been helpful. Hopefully, you have discovered some credible answers to the question of why Christians live and celebrate the way they do.

The New Testament is one of the most treasured pieces of literature in Western society. The book that we are now bringing to a close follows an earlier, very similar, book in which we introduced the Gospel and the Letters of John: *Interpreting the Gospel and Letters of John: An Introduction* (Grand Rapids: Eerdmans, 2017). One of the many reasons we have turned our minds and given our time to the writing of *Interpreting the New Testament: An Introduction* has been the warm reception of the first book that we have written together. We can now say for a second time that we have been honored to lead our readers through the various books that form the New Testament, and we congratulate you for coming to these final words. Returning to the Gospel of John, we recall, as we did in closing our earlier book, what an ancient Christian author wrote in John 21:25: "the world itself could not contain the books" that could be written about Jesus and the earliest church's attempts to articulate, by writing gospels, what he meant for them.

The library becomes even larger when we incorporate books that deal with Jesus's impact upon the women and men who belonged to the earliest Christian communities and shared their experiences. As we have seen, they shared many of them in the remaining books that form the New Testament: an acts, the letters, the theological tracts, and an apocalypse. You have now made a solid start on those "books" by working your way through all we have shared with you. May it stand you in good stead, no matter what your faith background and the future you will create.

The Christian traditions that generated the books of the New Testament, and also the Christian communities that are bearers of those traditions, ask you, however, to create that future *with others*, in contexts of genuine love and care, in a world that is becoming dangerously self-centered and self-sufficient. May this book create a certain restlessness in us, authors and readers, generating a desire to look beyond ourselves and our immediate needs. More and more of our fellow human beings are in need and yet are increasingly abandoned. This is not the way of Jesus Christ, nor the way of those who claim to be his followers: "For the Son of Man came not to be served, but to serve, and to give his life a ransom for many" (Mark 10:45).

Bibliography and Further Reading

Commentaries

What follows is a list of commentaries for readers who wish to pursue their interest in a single New Testament book, or several of them. We have generally not provided commentaries in our bibliographies of further reading at the end of each chapter. Most of the following publications are listed here for the first time. For the purposes of this book, we provide here only established single-volume commentaries published in English. These lists, however, are by no means exhaustive.

Commentaries are the fundamental building blocks for any serious study of the New Testament. Although we provide only a selection of the many commentaries available for each of the NT books, they are reliable guides for anyone who wishes to become familiar with the text of a whole book. They work through each chapter and verse and offer a general introduction to its time and place of writing, the author, and why he or she wrote it. Commentaries are especially important. Other studies focus upon one or another issue in the Gospel, calling for further investigation.

Several most helpful large, single-volume commentaries upon the whole Bible are available. As well as a succinct commentary on every book of the Bible (both OT and NT), they contain general articles that deal with history and principles and methods of interpretation. We especially recommend: José Enrique Aguilar Chiu, Richard Clifford, Carol J. Dempsey, Eileen M. Schuller, Thomas D. Stegman, and Donald Witherup, eds. *The Paulist Biblical Commentary*. New York: Paulist, 2018. The authors of the present book wrote the commentary on the Gospel of John (Francis J. Moloney) and the commentary on 2 Peter (Sherri Brown).

The Gospel of Mark

Byrne, Brendan. *A Costly Freedom: A Theological Reading of Mark's Gospel.* Collegeville, MN: Liturgical, 2008.

Culpepper, R. Alan. *Mark.* Smyth & Helwys Bible Commentary. Macon, GA: Smyth & Helwys, 2007.

Donahue, John, and Daniel J. Harrington. *The Gospel of Mark.* Sacra Pagina 2. Collegeville, MN: Liturgical, 2003.

Dowd, Sharon. *Reading Mark: A Literary and Theological Commentary on the Second Gospel.* Reading the New Testament. Macon, GA: Smyth & Helwys, 2000.

Hooker, Morna D. *The Gospel according to St Mark.* Black's New Testament Commentary. London: A. & C. Black, 1991.

Moloney, Francis J. *The Gospel of Mark: A Commentary.* Grand Rapids: Baker Academic, 2012.

Schweizer, Eduard. *The Good News according to Mark.* Translated by Donald H. Madvig. London: SPCK, 1971.

The Gospel of Matthew

Byrne, Brendan. *Lifting the Burden: Reading Matthew's Gospel in the Church Today.* Collegeville, MN: Liturgical, 2004.

Garland, David E. *Reading Matthew: A Literary and Theological Commentary.* Macon, GA: Smyth & Helwys, 2001.

Meier, John P. *Matthew.* New Testament Message 3. Wilmington, DE: Michael Glazier, 1980.

Nolland, John. *The Gospel of Matthew.* New International Greek Testament Commentary. Grand Rapids: Eerdmans, 2005.

Schweizer, Eduard. *The Good News according to Matthew.* Translated by David Green. London: SPCK, 1976.

Senior, Donald. *Matthew.* Abingdon New Testament Commentaries. Nashville: Abingdon, 1998.

The Gospel of Luke

Byrne, Brendan. *The Hospitality of God: A Reading of Luke's Gospel.* Collegeville, MN: Liturgical, 2000.

Carroll, John T. *Luke: A Commentary.* The New Testament Library. Louisville: Westminster John Knox, 2012.

Evans, Christopher F. *Saint Luke.* Trinity Press International New Testament Commentaries. London: SCM, 1990.

Johnson, Luke Timothy. *The Gospel of Luke*. Sacra Pagina 3. Collegeville, MN: Liturgical, 1991.

Schweizer, Eduard. *The Good News according to Luke*. Translated by David Green. London: SPCK, 1984.

Talbert, Charles H. *Reading Luke: A Literary and Theological Commentary on the Third Gospel*. New York: Crossroad, 1982.

Tannehill, Robert C. *Luke*. Abingdon New Testament Commentaries. Nashville: Abingdon, 1996.

———. *The Narrative Unity of Luke-Acts: A Literary Interpretation*. Volume 1: *The Gospel according to Luke*. Foundation & Facets: New Testament. Philadelphia: Fortress, 1986.

The Gospel of John

Beasley-Murray, George R. *John*. Word Biblical Commentary 36. Waco, TX: Word, 1986.

Byrne, Brendan. *Life Abounding: A Reading of John's Gospel*. Collegeville, MN: Liturgical Press, 2014.

Culpepper, R. Alan. *The Gospel and Letters of John*. Interpreting Biblical Texts. Nashville: Abingdon, 1998.

Hoskyns, Edwyn C. *The Fourth Gospel*. Edited by Francis N. Davey. London: Faber & Faber, 1947.

Lincoln, Andrew T. *The Gospel according to Saint John*. Black's New Testament Commentary. London: Crossroad, 2005.

Lindars, Barnabas. *The Gospel of John*. New Century Bible. London: Oliphants, 1972.

Moloney, Francis J. *The Gospel of John*. Sacra Pagina 4. Collegeville, MN: Liturgical, 1998.

Stibbe, Mark W. G. *John*. Readings: A New Biblical Commentary. Sheffield: JSOT Press, 1993.

Special Gospel Commentaries

Brown, Raymond E. *The Birth of the Messiah: A Commentary on the Infancy Narratives in Matthew and Luke*. Garden City, NY: Doubleday, 1977.

———. *The Death of the Messiah: From Gethsemane to the Grave. A Commentary on the Passion Narratives in the Four Gospels*. 2 vols. Anchor Bible Reference Library. New York: Doubleday, 1993.

Moloney, Francis J. *The Resurrection of the Messiah: A Narrative Commentary on the Resurrection Accounts in the Four Gospels*. New York: Paulist, 2013.

The Acts of the Apostles

Gaventa, Beverly R. *Acts*. Abingdon New Testament Commentaries. Nashville: Abingdon, 2003.

Johnson, Luke Timothy. *The Acts of the Apostles*. Sacra Pagina 5. Collegeville, MN: Liturgical, 2006.

Parsons, Mikeal C. *Acts*. Paideia Commentaries on the New Testament. Grand Rapids: Baker Academic, 2008.

Tannehill, Robert C. *The Narrative Unity of Luke-Acts: A Literary Interpretation*. Volume 2: *The Acts of the Apostles*. Minneapolis: Fortress, 1990.

The Letters of Paul

Barrett, C. Kingsley. *The First Epistle to the Corinthians*. 2nd ed. Black's New Testament Commentary. London: A. & C. Black, 1971.

———. *The Second Epistle to the Corinthians*. Black's New Testament Commentary. London: A. & C. Black, 1973.

Byrne, Brendan. *Galatians and Romans*. Collegeville, MN: Liturgical, 2010.

———. *Romans*. Sacra Pagina 6. Collegeville, MN: Liturgical, 1996.

Collange, Jean-François. *The Epistle of Saint Paul to the Philippians*. Translated by A. W. Heathcote. London: Epworth, 1979.

Furnish, Victor P. *1 Thessalonians, 2 Thessalonians*. Abingdon New Testament Commentaries. Nashville: Abingdon, 2004.

Holloway, Paul A. *Philippians*. Hermeneia. Minneapolis: Fortress, 2017.

Lambrecht, Jan. *Second Corinthians*. Sacra Pagina 8. Collegeville, MN: Liturgical, 1999.

Matera, Frank. *Galatians*. Sacra Pagina 9. Collegeville, MN: Liturgical, 1992.

———. *Romans*. Paideia Commentaries on the New Testament. Grand Rapids: Baker Academic, 2010.

Perkins, Pheme. *First Corinthians*. Paideia Commentaries on the New Testament. Grand Rapids: Baker Academic, 2012.

Thurston, Bonnie, and Judith Ryan. *Philippians and Philemon*. Sacra Pagina 10. Collegeville, MN: Liturgical, 2005.

Ephesians and Colossians

MacDonald, Margaret Y. *Colossians and Ephesians*. Sacra Pagina 17. Collegeville, MN: Liturgical, 2008.

Talbert, Charles H. *Ephesians and Colossians*. Paideia Commentaries on the New Testament. Grand Rapids: Baker Academic, 2007.

The Pastoral Epistles

Bassler, Judith M. *1 Timothy, 2 Timothy, Titus*. Abingdon New Testament Commentaries. Nashville: Abingdon, 1996.

Collins, Raymond F. *I and II Timothy and Titus*. The New Testament Library. Louisville: Westminster John Knox, 2002.

Hebrews

Johnson, Luke Timothy. *Hebrews: A Commentary*. The New Testament Library. Louisville: Westminster John Knox, 2006.

Lincoln, Andrew T. *Hebrews: A Guide*. London: T&T Clark, 2006.

The Catholic Epistles

Achtemeier, Paul J. *1 Peter: A Commentary on the First Epistle of Peter*. Hermeneia. Minneapolis: Fortress, 1996.

Bauckham, Richard J. *Jude, 2 Peter*. Word Biblical Commentary 50. Waco, TX: Word, 1983.

Davids, Peter H. *The Letters of 2 Peter and Jude*. The Pillar New Testament Commentary. Grand Rapids: Eerdmans, 2006.

Feldmeier, Richard. *The First Letter of Peter*. Translated by Peter H. Davids. Waco, TX: Baylor University Press, 2008.

Hartin, Patrick. *James*. Sacra Pagina 14. Collegeville, MN: Liturgical, 2009.

Johnson, Luke Timothy. *The Letter to James*. Anchor Bible 37A. New York: Doubleday, 1995.

Lieu, Judith M. *I, II, and III John: A Commentary*. The New Testament Library. Louisville: Westminster John Knox, 2008.

Moloney, Francis J. *From James to Jude: A Bible Commentary for Every Day*. Abingdon, UK: Bible Reading Fellowship, 1999.

Neyrey, Jerome H. *2 Peter, Jude*. Anchor Bible 37C. New York: Doubleday, 1993.

Painter, John. *1, 2, and 3 John*. Sacra Pagina 18. Collegeville, MN: Liturgical, 2002.

Rensberger, David. *1 John, 2 John, 3 John*. Abingdon New Testament Commentaries. Louisville: Abingdon, 1997.

The Apocalypse

Boring, Eugene. *Revelation*. Louisville: John Knox, 1989.

Boxall, Ian. *The Revelation of Saint John*. Black's New Testament Commentary. London: A. & C. Black, 2006.

Collins, Adela Yarbro. *The Apocalypse*. New Testament Message 22. Wilmington, DE: Michael Glazier, 1979.

Corsini, Eugenio. *The Apocalypse: The Perennial Revelation of Jesus Christ*. Translated by Francis J. Moloney. Wilmington, DE: Michael Glazier, 1983. Repr., Eugene, OR: Wipf & Stock, 2019.

Harrington, Wilfred J. *Revelation*. Sacra Pagina 16. Collegeville, MN: Liturgical, 1993.

Koester, Craig R. *Revelation*. Anchor Yale Bible Commentary 38A. New Haven: Yale University Press, 2014.

Moloney, Francis J. *The Apocalypse of John: An Alternative Commentary*. Grand Rapids: Baker, 2020.

Resseguie, James L. *The Revelation of John: A Narrative Commentary*. Grand Rapids: Baker Academic, 2009.

General Books and Articles

The books and articles mentioned at the conclusion of each chapter are listed below. This is by no means a complete bibliography for the study of the New Testament. Such a list would require a book of its own! In some cases, the books and articles have been listed because they have guided our interpretations, and in others because they can serve an advanced student for reading beyond what is provided in this book. Students who are interested in further study are encouraged to consult their libraries for these authors, as well as authors mentioned in the bibliographies of their works.

Adam, A. K. M. *What Is Post-Modern Biblical Criticism?* Edited by Dan O. Via Jr. Guides to Biblical Scholarship. New Testament Series. Minneapolis: Fortress, 1995.

Aland, Kurt. *Synopsis of the Four Gospels: Greek-English Edition of the Synopsis Quattuor Evangeliorum*. 10th ed. Swindon: United Bible Societies, 1993.

Alter, Robert, and Frank Kermode, eds. *The Literary Guide to the Bible*. Cambridge: Harvard University Press, 1987.

Anderson, Bernhard W., Steven Bishop, and Judith H. Newman. *Understanding the Old Testament*. 5th ed. Upper Saddle River, NJ: Pearson, 2007.

Ashton, John. *Understanding the Fourth Gospel*. Oxford: Clarendon, 1991.

Attridge, Harold. "Genre Bending in the Fourth Gospel." *Journal of Biblical Literature* 121 (2002): 1–21.

Bauckham, Richard. *The Theology of the Book of Revelation*. New Testament Theology. Cambridge: Cambridge University Press, 1993.

Beker, J. Christiaan. *Paul's Apocalyptic Gospel: The Coming Triumph of God*. Philadelphia: Fortress, 1982.

Brodd, Jeffrey, and Jonathan L. Reed, eds. *Rome and Religion: A Cross-Disciplinary*

Dialogue on the Imperial Cult. Writings from the Greco-Roman World Supplement Series. Atlanta: Society of Biblical Literature, 2011.

Brown, Raymond E. *An Introduction to New Testament Christology.* Mahwah, NJ: Paulist, 1994.

———. *An Introduction to the New Testament.* Anchor Yale Bible Reference Library. New Haven: Yale University Press, 1997.

Brown, Sherri. "The Challenge of 2 Peter and the Call to Theosis." *Expository Times* 128 (2017): 583–92.

———. "Faith, Christ, and Paul's Theology of Salvation History." In *Unity and Diversity in the Gospels and Paul: Essays in Honor of Frank J. Matera,* edited by Christopher W. Skinner and Kelly R. Iverson, 249–71. Early Christianity and Its Literature 7. Atlanta: Society of Biblical Literature Press, 2012.

———. *God's Promise: Covenant in John.* New York: Paulist, 2014.

Brown, Sherri, and Francis J. Moloney. *Interpreting the Gospel of John: An Introduction.* Grand Rapids: Eerdmans, 2017.

Burridge, Richard. *What Are the Gospels? A Comparison with Graeco-Roman Biography.* The Biblical Resource Series. 2nd ed. Grand Rapids: Eerdmans, 2004.

Carey, Greg. *Ultimate Things: An Introduction to Jewish and Christian Apocalyptic Literature.* St. Louis: Chalice, 2005.

Carvalho, Corrine. *Encountering Ancient Voices: A Guide to Reading the Old Testament.* Winona, MN: Anselm Academic, 2006.

———. *Primer on Biblical Methods.* Winona, MN: Anselm Academic, 2009.

Collins, Adela Yarbro. *Crisis and Catharsis: The Power of the Apocalypse.* Philadelphia: Westminster, 1984.

Collins, John J. *The Apocalyptic Imagination: An Introduction to Jewish Apocalyptic Literature.* Rev. ed. Grand Rapids: Eerdmans, 1998.

Collins, Raymond F. *Letters That Paul Did Not Write: The Epistle to the Hebrews and the Pauline Pseudepigrapha.* Eugene, OR: Wipf & Stock, 1988.

Cone, James. *God of the Oppressed.* Maryknoll, NY: Orbis Books, 1997.

Dawes, Gregory. *Introduction to the Bible.* New Collegeville Bible Commentary: Old Testament, vol. 1. Collegeville, MN: Liturgical, 2007.

Eusebius. *The Church History.* Translated by Paul L. Maier. Grand Rapids: Kregel Academic & Professional, 2007.

Fitzmyer, Joseph A. *Paul and His Theology: A Brief Sketch.* 2nd ed. Englewood Cliffs, NJ: Prentice Hall, 1989.

———. *Scripture, the Soul of Theology.* New York: Paulist, 1994.

Friesen, Steven J. *Imperial Cults and the Apocalypse of John: Reading Revelation in the Ruins.* New York: Oxford University Press, 2001.

Frigge, Marielle. *Beginning Biblical Studies.* Rev. ed. Winona: Anselm Academic, 2013.

Goodacre, Mark. *The Synoptic Problem: A Way through the Maze.* Understanding the Bible and Its World. New York: T&T Clark, 2004.

Gorman, Michael J. *The Apostle of the Crucified Lord: A Theological Introduction to Paul and His Letters.* 2nd ed. Grand Rapids: Eerdmans, 2016.

———. *Reading Paul.* Eugene, OR: Cascade, 2008.

Green, Barbara. *From Earth's Creation to John's Revelation: The INTERFACES Biblical Storyline Companion.* Collegeville, MN: Liturgical, 2003.

Gutiérrez, Gustavo. *A Theology of Liberation: History, Politics, and Salvation.* 15th Anniversary Edition with new introduction by the author. Maryknoll, NY: Orbis Books, 1988.

Hays, Richard. *The Faith of Jesus Christ: The Narrative Substructure of Galatians 3:1–4:11.* 2nd ed. Grand Rapids: Eerdmans, 2002.

Hill, Craig C. *In God's Time: The Bible and the Future.* Grand Rapids: Eerdmans, 2002.

Hillers, D. R. *Covenant: The History of a Biblical Idea.* Seminars in the History of Ideas. Baltimore: Johns Hopkins Press, 1969.

Horrell, David G. *An Introduction to the Study of Paul.* 2nd ed. T&T Clark Approaches to Biblical Studies. London: T&T Clark, 2006.

Howard-Brook, Wes, and Anthony Gwyther. *Unveiling Empire: Reading Revelation Then and Now.* Maryknoll, NY: Orbis, 1999.

Hurtado, Larry. *How on Earth Did Jesus Become a God? Historical Questions about Earliest Devotion to Jesus.* Grand Rapids: Eerdmans, 2005.

Iverson, Kelly, ed. *From Text to Performance: Narrative and Performance Criticisms in Dialogue and Debate.* Biblical Performance Criticism 10. Eugene, OR: Wipf & Stock, 2014.

Johnson, Luke Timothy. *The Writings of the New Testament: An Interpretation.* 3rd ed. Minneapolis: Fortress, 2010.

Junior, Nyasha. *An Introduction to Womanist Biblical Interpretation.* Louisville: Westminster John Knox, 2015.

Kloppenborg, John S. *Q, the Earliest Gospel: An Introduction to the Original Stories and Sayings of Jesus.* Louisville: Westminster John Knox, 2008.

Knight, Douglas A., and Amy-Jill Levine. *The Meaning of the Bible: What the Jewish Scriptures and Christian Old Testament Can Teach Us.* New York: HarperOne, 2011.

Koester, Craig R. *Revelation and the End of All Things.* 2nd ed. Grand Rapids: Eerdmans, 2018.

Law, Timothy M. *When God Spoke Greek: The Septuagint and the Making of the Christian Bible.* New York: Oxford University Press, 2013.

Lennan, Richard. *An Introduction to Catholic Theology.* New York: Paulist, 1998.

Lockett, Darian. *An Introduction to the Catholic Epistles.* T&T Clark Approaches to Biblical Studies. London: T&T Clark, 2012.

———. *Letters from the Pillar Apostles: The Formation of the Catholic Epistles as a Canonical Collection.* Eugene, OR: Pickwick, 2016.

Martyn, J. Louis. "Apocalyptic Antinomies in Paul's Letter to the Galatians." *New Testament Studies* 31 (1985): 410–24.

Matera, Frank J. *God's Saving Grace: A Pauline Theology*. Grand Rapids: Eerdmans, 2012.

———. *New Testament Christology*. Louisville: Westminster John Knox, 1999.

Miller, John W. *How the Bible Came to Be: Exploring the Narrative and Message*. New York: Paulist, 2004.

Moloney, Francis J. *Letters to the Johannine Circle: 1–3 John*. Biblical Studies from the Catholic Biblical Association of America. New York: Paulist Press, 2020.

———. *The Living Voice of the Gospels: The Gospels Today*. Grand Rapids: Baker Academic, 2007.

———. *Reading the New Testament in the Church: A Primer for Pastors, Religious Educators, and Believers*. Grand Rapids: Baker Academic, 2015.

Nickle, Keith F. *The Synoptic Gospels: An Introduction*. Rev. and exp. ed. Louisville: Westminster John Knox, 2001.

Perry, Peter S. *Insights from Performance Criticism*. Reading the Bible in the Twenty-First Century: Insights. Minneapolis: Fortress, 2016.

Powell, Mark A. *Fortress Introduction to the Gospels*. Minneapolis: Fortress, 1998.

———. *Introducing the New Testament: A Historical, Literary, and Theological Survey*. Grand Rapids: Baker Academic, 2009.

———. *What Is Narrative Criticism?* Guides to Biblical Scholarship: New Testament Series. Minneapolis: Fortress, 1990.

Reddish, Mitchell G., ed. *Apocalyptic Literature: A Reader*. Peabody, MA: Hendrickson, 1995.

Reid, Barbara E. *Wisdom's Feast: An Invitation to Feminist Interpretation of the Scriptures*. Grand Rapids: Eerdmans, 2016.

Resseguie, James L. *The Revelation of John: A Narrative Commentary*. Grand Rapids: Baker Academic, 2009.

Rhoads, David. "Performance Criticism: An Emerging Methodology in Second Testament Studies." *Biblical Theological Bulletin* 36 (2006): 118–40, 164–88.

Sanders, E. P., and Margaret Davies. *Studying the Synoptic Gospels*. Salem, OR: Trinity Press International, 1990.

Schneiders, Sandra M. *Written That You May Believe: Encountering Jesus in the Fourth Gospel*. New York: Crossroad, 1999.

Skinner, Christopher W. *Reading John*. Eugene, OR: Cascade, 2015.

Skinner, Matthew L. *Intrusive God, Disruptive Gospel: Encountering the Divine in the Book of Acts*. Grand Rapids: Brazos, 2015.

Steggemann, Ekkehard W., and Wolfgang Steggemann. *The Jesus Movement: A Social History of Its First Century*. Translated by O. C. Dean. Minneapolis: Fortress, 1999.

Tatum, Gregory, OP. *New Chapters in the Life of Paul: The Relative Chronology of His Career*. Catholic Biblical Quarterly Monograph Series 41. Washington, DC: Catholic Biblical Association of America, 2006.

Thompson, Leonard L. *The Book of Revelation: Apocalypse and Empire*. New York: Oxford University Press, 1993.

Throckmorton, Burton H., Jr. *Gospel Parallels, NRSV Edition: A Comparison of the Synoptic Gospels.* 5th ed. Nashville: Thomas Nelson, 1992.

Vanhoye, Albert. *Structure and Message of the Epistle to the Hebrews.* Rome: Pontifical Biblical Institute, 1989.

Wasserman, Tommy, and Peter J. Gurry. *A New Approach to Textual Criticism: An Introduction to the Coherence-based Genealogical Method.* Atlanta: SBL Press; Stuttgart: Deutsche Bibelgesellschaft, 2017.

White, L. Michael. *From Jesus to Christianity: How Four Generations of Visionaries and Storytellers Created the New Testament and Christian Faith.* New York: HarperCollins, 2004.

Wright, Nicholas T. *Paul: A Biography.* San Francisco: HarperOne, 2018.

Index of Authors

Index of Subjects

Index of Scripture